Steinerian Economics

A Compendium

Steinerian Economics

A Compendium

From the works of

Rudolf Steiner

Compiled and annotated by

Gary Lamb and Sarah Hearn

Editors

Adonis Press

ISBN: 978-0-932776-47-1

Published by Adonis Press
321 Rodman Road
Hillsdale, New York 12529
adonispress.org
socialself.org

Adonis Press is a branch of the Hawthorne Valley Association.

Cover design by Ella Lapointe
Typesetting by Michael R. Lapointe

The Illustrations were developed through a collaboration between Ella Lapointe, Gary Lamb and Sarah Hearn.

"It is only the whole earth

that, as an economic body,

can truly be compared with

a living organism . . .

As economists, what we really need

is an understanding

of the social organism

in its totality."

–

Rudolf Steiner

Rethinking Economics, pp. 13-14, 1922

Contents

Rudolf Steiner: Social Reformer and Economist xi

Foreword xiii

Editors' Introduction xix

Whom is this Economics Compendium for . . . and not for? xix
The Path We Traveled xx
Ways to Use This Compendium xxi
The Compendium as a Thought Organism xxii
Clarification of Some Important Terms xxii
Repetition of Some of the Quotations xxii
Editing of Quotations xxiii
Acknowledgements xxiii

1. Social and Antisocial Forces in the Human Being and Social Life 1

The Need for Inner and Outer Change 2
Rising Individualism and Antisocial Forces 4
The Interplay of Sleeping and Waking in Human Encounter 5
Taking Greater Interest in Others: The Foundation of Social Life 8
Creating Social Forces by Consciously Fostering Interest in Others 9
Interest in Others and Economic Life 16
From Personal Opinion to Collective Wisdom 19

2. The Fundamental Social Law 23

Egoism and Self Interest in Social Life 25
Egoism and Altruism 29
Spiritual Worldview 35
Community Spirit and Spiritual Mission 36
The Influence of an Independent Cultural Life 37
Rights Life and the Will to Work 38
Labor as a Rights or Equity Issue Rather Than an Economic One 40
Fostering Altruism by Overcoming Labor as a Commodity 43
Ways to Overcome Paid Labor 48

3. **The Threefold Social Organism** ... 53
Healthy Social Life is Threefold ... 57
National and International Relations ... 61
Transgressing Boundaries as a Main Cause of Social Problems ... 64
Cultural Freedom Begins with Educational Freedom ... 70
The Economy and the Political State ... 73
Implementing Social Threefolding ... 76
The Relation of the Physiological and Social Organisms ... 80
True Social Renewal Requires a Change in Thinking ... 87

4. **Economic Science** ... 89
The Evolution of Economic Life ... 93
From World Trade to World Economy ... 97
Constant Fluctuations within the World Economy ... 102
Picture-Thinking ... 105
Economics and the Color Spectrum ... 108
Viewing the Economic Process from the Inside ... 109
Elements of a New Method for Economic Science ... 111

5. **Economic Associations** ... 117
Characteristic Features and Dynamics ... 118
Evolution of the Role of the Individual and the Need for Associations Today . 120
Informed, Transparent, and Freely-Formed Agreements ... 124
Economic Judgments Via Living Associations ... 126
Insight, Collective Consciousness, and Group-Born Intelligence ... 127
Balancing Egoism and Love in Economic Life ... 129
Answering the Need for Constant Price Corrections ... 131
From Profit Motive to Satisfaction of Human Needs ... 135
A New Relation of Management and Investors to Workers ... 138
Associations in Relation to Gift Money and Cultural Life ... 140
Implementing Economic Associations ... 141

6. **Economic Values** ... 145
The Economic Process as Context for Economic Value ... 146
Origin of Economic Values: Labor Transforming Nature ... 147
Diagram 1: Value Creation ... 147
Value Creation through the Human Spirit, or Intelligence Transforming Labor ... 149
Fluctuating Character of Economic Values ... 151

Consumer Needs and Value Creation 152
Socially Correct Value 153
Consumption, Elimination of Value, and Value-Creating Tension 154
Values and Spiritual-Cultural Work 157
Machines and Cultural Productivity 166

7. **Capital** 169
Capital Creation 170
The Social Necessity and Benefit of Free Access to Capital 171
Capital and Property Rights 173
Administration and Transference of Capital 176
Profit Motive and Capital Increase 188
Land and Capital 191
Diagram 2: Economic Cycle: Nature, Labor, Capital 191
Surplus Capital 196
Redefining Ground-Rent and Calculating Subsistence Income 200
Land Rent as Capital and the Support of Cultural Life 202

8. **Credit** 203
Motivation 204
Capability 208
Mutuality and the Service of Lending 210
Personal and Real Credit 213
The Role of Associations in the Giving and Receiving of Credit 216
The Coming Day (Der Kommende Tag) Experiment 217

9. **Money** 221
Money as a Measure of Economic Value 222
The Illusory Nature of Money as a Commodity 223
Money as Power 224
Money as Rights and Cultural Capacities Realized 226
Money as Spirit Realized 227
Money as Bookkeeping and Medium of Exchange 230
A New Basis for Determining the Value of Money (Currency) 231
The Relation of Money to Value of Cultural and Political-Legal Work 233
Impersonal Nature of Modern Banking and Finance 235
Taxation 239
Aging Money 241
Purchase, Loan, and Gift Money 253
Diagram 3: Money Cycle: Payment, Loan, Gift 257

Issuing Currency 262
Inflation 265
Money as a Means to Exercise Social Responsibility 266

10. Price Formation 269
Price in the Context of Perpetual Circulation 270
True Price 274
Falsification of Prices 280
Price Fluctuation 283
Associations and Price Regulation 284
Fundamentals of Pricing 287

11. The Interplay of Spiritual-Cultural and Economic Life 289
Constructive Forces of Spiritual-Cultural Life 290
Capacities and Capital 292
Financial Support of Cultural Life 294
Freedom and Funding in Education 295
Value of Spiritual Work for the Economy as a Whole 300

Resources 305
A Selection of Publishers of Rudolf Steiner's Social and Economic Writings and Lectures in English 305
Basic Texts by Rudolf Steiner on the Threefold Social Organism, Associative Economics, and the Fundamental Social Law 306
Texts by Other Authors 306
Businesses, Organizations, & Initiatives Directly Inspired by Rudolf Steiner's Social & Economic Ideas 308
Organizations and Initiatives Working to Some Degree in Harmony with Rudolf Steiner's Ideas 313

Bibliography 322

Rudolf Steiner:

Social Reformer and Economist

*"First of all, get a broom and out with everything that negates the spirit in economic life! On that depends the future welfare of [humanity]."**

Rudolf Steiner (1861-1925) is most widely known as a European philosopher, educator, social reformer, and the founder of anthroposophy (wisdom of the human being), a modern form of spiritual science. He initiated various practical endeavors based on anthroposophy, including Biodynamic agriculture, Waldorf education, and impulses toward the renewal of art, science, and religion.

His interest and activities in social renewal extended throughout his adult life, beginning with his philosophical treatise, *Intuitive Thinking as Spiritual Path: A Philosophy of Freedom*, published in 1893. It provides a philosophical foundation for ethical individualism: an individualism that retains, and even generates, moral and social capacities which flow into all aspects of life: cultural, political, and economic.

After decades of studying and contemplating the human organism, Steiner came to the realization that the human being consists of three distinct, yet interrelated and interdependent systems: nerve sense, rhythmic, and metabolic-limb. This led him to recognize that the social organism also has three inherent, yet distinct systems that are interrelated and interdependent – economic, political, and cultural – which are in themselves equally important and have their own function and purpose.

From 1917 to 1922 he wrote and lectured widely on the threefold nature of social life as a foundation for peace, equity, and prosperity. His book on a threefold social organism, *Towards Social Renewal,* published in 1917, was a bestseller in Germany and was

* Quotation from *Spiritual Science as a Foundation for Social Forms*, 1920, SSFSF.

heralded in England and the United States as one of the most original social works to come out of Europe following WWI.

Within the context of a threefold social organism, Steiner developed a unique and bold approach to economics often referred to as *associative economics.* Bold in that it challenges some of the cherished ideals of both capitalism and socialism concerning land, labor, and capital, as well as providing social ideas that recognize the spiritual aspect of the human being, nature, and society. For example, he makes the case for freely circulating capital being made available to capable entrepreneurs who are meeting recognized needs in society rather than it being privately owned or state controlled. His economic perspectives culminated in a series of lectures and seminars in 1922 now published as *Rethinking Economics: Lectures and Seminars on World Economics.**

Many of the economic and social ideas that Steiner advanced at the turn of the 19th and 20th centuries can now be found within cutting-edge economic thoughts and initiatives that contribute to a more spiritual, humane, and sustainable approach to economic life. The Resources chapter in this book provides examples of people and initiatives that are working in harmony with or directly out of Steiner's economic and social ideas.

* Published by SteinerBooks, www.steinerbooks.org.

Foreword

Rudolf Steiner: Towards an Architecture of Social Transformation

by John Bloom

In introducing any aspect of Rudolf Steiner's work, it is important to be clear from the outset that through his insights he not only pushed the boundaries of *what* we know, but also *how* we know. He offered guidance for both through his lectures, writings, and leadership during his lifetime. His spiritual worldview was cosmological in scope, yet much of his work focused on practical ways to be in the world with awareness of how spiritual forces are at work in and through it. He urged his audiences to be interested in current affairs and popular thought, as he was, even while he often pointed out their limitations. In particular, self-development as a basis for knowing the world and the capacity for imaginative or intuitive thinking were at the heart of his hopes for anyone interested in grasping the spiritual foundation of knowledge. This approach is as relevant to understanding the nature of the human being as it is to re-enlivening the fields of agriculture, education, natural science, the arts, or in the case of this publication, economics, money, and how best to organize our societies.

Through lectures in his own time, and in the transcriptions and writings that remain for us, Steiner asked repeatedly to be understood rather than believed. I think he also knew that the path of understanding would be the more difficult of the two, especially because it requires discipline and a continual openness to self-development. Such inner work can lead to a transformation of consciousness informed by multiple modalities of knowing – observation, practice, and reflection – and a fluid sense of time and space measured by the reality of experience rather than by clocks and rulers.

He encouraged all students of his work to follow scientific methodology, despite the fact that the phenomenon being studied might not fit the conventional definition of research material. The key to all science, and therefore all knowing, is observation. But Steiner, deeply inspired by the scientific work of Johann Wolfgang von Goethe, understood observation as a process of engagement, of seeing the physical reality as nothing more than a particular moment in a metamorphic process which itself can be "seen" in a context of time and space. This capacity for cognitive imagination, what Goethe described as "seeing his ideas," plays an important part in working toward understanding Rudolf Steiner's work, and it is a capacity patiently acquired.

At the core of Steiner's work stands the human being. Each person is on a path of evolution unique to his or her individuality, a path that evolves across numerous incarnations. Each of us comes, according to William Wordsworth, "trailing clouds of glory." This would be complicated enough to understand by itself, if only we did not need others in order to come into this world, into this body, at this time. But we do need others. We find ourselves on earth where we need to work with, live with, and love others, each of whom has a unique pre-history and a destiny path to map and follow that is different from our own. Thus we struggle to find commonality, to find ways to get along, and to support each other along our paths. No wonder social life, whether in a relationship of two or across a whole community, is complex. No wonder that conflicts and confluences in human relationships occur given the diversity and disjuncture of human beings and societies in different stages of cultural evolution.

The invention and intervention of political boundaries and bodies of law, and the organic or competitive creation of economies simply to meet the needs of material existence add further layers of complication. Each of these domains – culture, polity, and economy – has its own logic, its own origins, and its own practices that have supported the evolution of individuals and humanity. At the same time, each of these domains has an equally powerful shadow side that, wrongly applied, has denied and oppressed human beings and the growth of human consciousness. If we are sensitive to currents at work in the contemporary world, we can sense that the shadows are quite present and active. Yet we lack clarity about each of the domains, and how they best function separately and together.

In the face of the catastrophe of World War I, Steiner articulated his vision of a threefold commonwealth as a way to bring peace and reorganize society based upon principles deeply rooted in human nature. He linked *freedom* to the domain of culture, *equality* to the domain of rights and agreements, and *compassionate interdependence* ("brotherhood" in Steiner's language) to the domain of economics. In doing so, he bridged his profound understanding of the threefold human being with an imagination of human beings organizing their public lives in a way that would be congruent with their inner nature. By effecting this harmony between the inner integrity of each individual and a trifurcated high-functioning social organism, Steiner was putting in place an architecture of social transformation. Such architecture requires each individual to move past an ego-centric, self-interested view of the world to one motivated by interest in others and trust in the forces of reciprocity. He offered tools for each person to do the inner work needed for this self-transformation and created an education that would support the development of such capacities for future generations. Steiner's threefold principles provide a framework and tools with which to approach social life in a way that is regenerative, and inspired by an affirmation of the values of being human and being in community, albeit global in scale.

Within the threefold commonwealth, compassionate interdependence in the economic domain is probably least understood. Nothing in our current free market economic system speaks to an altruistic perspective, one which holds that we work to meet others' needs as our needs are met through others' work. Enlightened self-interest, the notion that acting as if others mattered is in one's best self-interest, has given way in current time to raw competitive self-interest. And, this self-interest has proven to be a failed, flawed, destructive concept. As a guiding principle, self-interest may have worked at a time when moral and ethical boundaries – whether driven by church, community, or family – were operative in systems of self-governance. But, the fragmentation of such social forms and the atomization of individuals through the hyper-presence of technology have contributed to the atrophy of moral foundations in societies. As remedy, Steiner posited that all economic activity operates on the principle of brotherhood and sisterhood, and further, arises out of the interaction of land (or all natural resources), labor, and capital. The key point here is their interaction, particularly the production of commodities and services that emerge through those interactions. Contrary to how economics is typically conceived, what Steiner established was that these three basic elements are fundamentally not commodities in and of themselves. Imagine how different the world would be with the decommodification of land, labor, and capital. This is hard to grasp in an age when real estate and land are treated as investment rather than a means of production, labor is purchased on an hourly basis with workers regarded as replaceable parts in a production schema, and capital is used for nothing more than making more capital and is thus devoid of real economic value.

As part of this shift of economic paradigm, Steiner indicated that the management of interdependent practices was best done through freely formed associations. These associations would bring together producers, distributors, and consumers to determine how to steward natural resources, labor, and capital to assure that everyone's material needs were met. As a result, setting prices was a key association function. Associative economics was Steiner's antidote to what he perceived as the overreaching power of corporations and the state in managing economic affairs, which rightly belonged to the stakeholders most directly engaged in the economy, who would reap the benefits and bear the consequences of their choices.

Steiner also understood money not as a thing but rather as a multifunctional servant – through purchase, loan, and gift – to the circulation of value and economic activity. Much of what he had to say recasts these forms of money in order to serve their original purposes in support of the creation of real value. He also gives some powerful indications for how to work with money in a corrective healing way in our current distorted inequitable system. One could look at money as a postmodern threshold experience, a mirror and magnifier of who we are as human beings. Money tends toward being antisocial in how we attach to it and it to us, even though each dollar is, as Steiner states, connected to all the division of human labor in the economy.

In movement, in circulation, it reflects the pulse of material life. Money is both mystery and monster, misunderstood and misanthropic, a bearer of light and good intention, and evocator of rapacious desire. Money is as much a symptom of our inability to connect to the world as it is a symbol of just how deeply interdependent we are. Knowing money is a path to knowing oneself in relation to the economic world and its intersections with the political and wider cultural worlds. Money is social technology that pits self against the other and the world in the process of getting, and celebrates relationship in the world in the process of gifting and letting go. To see that we can live in multiple worlds and a multitude of transactions, maintain our integrity and recognize our interdependence through all of them, and still account for every penny, requires a new consciousness and a significant level of personal transformation.

Such transformation requires an architecture that acknowledges present reality with all its flaws, greed, corruption, and extreme inequity, and yet stands as a new structural system in which we can find aid and comfort, challenge and guidance, and above all, a way to live out of love and forgiveness rather than power and violence.

The task for our time is to bring practice and visibility to the social architecture that Rudolf Steiner described. What he articulated was that this structure is already there and further that we operate within it, but unconsciously. Through inner discipline, we can develop a social consciousness of the threefold nature of social life. Then, through that work we can more fully inhabit the architecture of self and world in a way that brings about social harmony and supports a resilient structure – not unlike the ancient cathedrals, temples, and mosques – that is home to, honors, and inspires that which is spiritual in the human being and connects the individual with the wisdom of the cosmos.

This compendium of Rudolf Steiner's writings and transcribed lectures begins with a focused journey into how the human being relates to a social world organized on threefold principles. Following those sections, we are taken deeper into the domain of economic science, economic life, associations, and a new understanding of how money works. Steiner takes us into the depths of economic processes in the hope that what we see will be understood as being in constant formation; we are as much actors in that formation as we are shaped by what is formed. It is this foundational level of interdependence and reciprocity that Steiner is calling on us to recognize and reckon with. He is challenging us to develop new capacities that can grasp not only the physical forces at work, but also the less visible and measurable, so that we can proceed in a way that honors the spiritual reality of which each of us is a part – whether we perceive it that way or not.

What Gary Lamb and Sarah Hearn have accomplished with this compendium is nothing short of extraordinary in its breadth and focus. And it is clearly a labor of love, inquiry, and service. They have left no text in English unturned in their effort to illuminate the gifts and insights that Rudolf Steiner brought forth on the topics of threefold social life, economics, and money as expressions of human aspiration. This guide provides a basis for study, understanding, and transformation. The beauty of freedom is that it can lead to all three of these depending upon what we make of it, as individuals or through group effort. My hope for this introduction is to have set enough context in the larger framework of Steiner's thinking so that any student engaging with this material will develop a sense for the social value of personal transformation, and how important working with the threefold imagination is as a regenerative impulse for our time and the future.

John Bloom
©2014
San Francisco, CA

John Bloom is the Senior Director of Organizational Culture for RSF Social Finance in San Francisco, CA.

Editors' Introduction

The purpose of this Compendium is to provide a concise single-source document on Rudolf Steiner's main thoughts and perspectives regarding money, economics, and the basic principles of a threefold social organism.

Whom is this Economics Compendium for . . . and not for?

> *The friends I seek are seeking me;*
> *No wind can drive my bark astray,*
> *Nor change the tide of destiny.*
>
> *"Waiting," John Burroughs (1837-1921)*

In general, the Compendium can be of use to anyone who has a genuine concern for the many social problems we are facing today and who is looking for a holistic approach to addressing them that honors the spiritual dimension of the human being and of the world in which we live.

This Compendium is intended especially for the following audiences:

- Farmers, business people, social activists, economists, regardless of whether they are familiar with Steiner's social ideas or not;
- Students and advocates of Steiner's social ideas who want to deepen and broaden their understanding of particular aspects of his social theory;
- Individuals who may have an outer connection to one or more of the many social initiatives arising from Steiner's thinking and who want a deeper understanding of his social ideas – Biodynamic agriculture, Waldorf education, Anthroposophical medicine and natural and social scientific research endeavors, communities for individuals with special needs and the elderly, the Christian Community, the visual, performing, and literary arts, and various youth initiatives.

As a collection of quotations taken out of context, this Compendium was not intended to be a persuasive literary work that could change the minds of people who are either deeply embedded in an extreme left- or right-wing political mentality, or who view the state or the free market as the ultimate arbiter of social problems. While we do not rule out the possibility that there are people who may experience the equivalent of the conversion of St. Paul upon reading this work, they are not our "target audience." Rather, the Compendium is intended more for those who already are predisposed toward or looking for the ideas and perspectives represented in this document, even if only in the deepest recesses of their soul, as expressed in John Burroughs' poem, "Waiting."

The Path We Traveled

The initial idea for this Compendium arose through a series of conversations that we had on the subject of local or complementary currencies. Given that both of us were conversant with and inspired by Rudolf Steiner's economic ideas, we felt it would be helpful to use his ideas to formulate metrics that would aid us in evaluating such alternative currencies.

What started out as a rather casual effort to collect various comments by Steiner on money and finance ended up being an extensive multi-year effort to create a comprehensive compendium that embraces the breadth of his main economic ideas. In so doing, we found that his radical ideas on money and economics, which are contrary to much of what is considered economic science today, are intimately connected to and derive their ultimate meaning from:

- the interplay of *social and antisocial forces* within and between human beings;
- his broader views of society encompassed by the principles of a *threefold social organism*;
- the *fundamental social law*, an ancient spiritual tenet applicable to economic life;
- the concept of *true price* that eliminates human exploitation; and
- trans-sector *producer, distributor, consumer associations* that would coordinate the overall economy.

We researched all the available sources in English on Steiner's social ideas and drew material from about 35 of his works. We sorted the material into hundreds of index terms, and arranged them by theme into eleven chapters. While this sourcing and organizing was time consuming and tedious, the real inner work came when we began arranging Steiner's complex, far ranging ideas into a coherent flow.

Once we had completed an initial draft, we had eight people review it *[See Acknowledgements, pg. xxiii.]* and provide us with suggestions on how to improve the document. This proved to be an exceedingly important and helpful process. The reviewers made suggestions regarding improving the annotations and how to arrange the flow of quotations in each chapter. They also suggested additional quotations that were not included in the original draft and additional resources for our resource chapter.

We incorporated all appropriate suggestions and then proceeded with detailed copyediting, illustrations, and graphic design.

Ways to Use This Compendium

This Compendium can be used in a variety of ways, some of which are:

An Efficient Resource for Gaining an Overview of Rudolf Steiner's Economic Insights: Steiner is known for his multiple, even paradoxical perspectives on social issues, which are scattered throughout his work. One otherwise would have to spend considerable time sorting through and reading his vast work to gain an overview of his perspective.

Group Study Material: The various thematic chapters or the whole Compendium can be used as material for study groups.

Meditation Material: The spiritually-based social ideas in this Compendium provide abundant material for personal contemplation and meditation when considering social issues and problems.

Resource Guide for Initiatives: A chapter in the Compendium is dedicated to individuals and groups who are working directly out of Steiner's perspectives, or who are working in harmony with them, even though they may not be conversant with his ideas.

The Compendium as a Thought Organism

While the Compendium can be useful to people who are interested in a single subject such as money or pricing, we did arrange the chapters and the flow of thought within the chapters in such a way as to take the reader on a specific path of thought and inner experience. In general, the Compendium starts with broad contextual issues and becomes increasingly specific as the reader progresses through the chapters.

Clarification of Some Important Terms

Spirit: While Steiner took the spiritual nature of the human being and of the world in all of its possible manifestations as a given, in economics he uses the word spirit (Geist) to indicate particular qualities or capacities, such as intelligence or human creativity. An example of such use can be found in the phrase "spirit transforms labor," by which he means that creative human intelligence is able to arrange labor in an efficient and effective manner.

Cultural Life, Spiritual Life, Spiritual-Cultural Life: These all refer to one of the three main spheres of social life, and often can be used interchangeably. It is the realm that embraces everything that has to do with education and all of its subsets: art, science, religion; health care, esthetic tastes, languages, and so on. While a cultural life devoid of spiritual values is possible, for Steiner it is essential for individual and social development.

Social and Antisocial Forces: These are viewed as polarities in the human soul that need to be brought into balance in modern life primarily by nurturing the social forces. This view is in contrast to a view that considers these concepts as good (social) and bad (antisocial) with the goal of eliminating the anti-social and preserving the social.

Repetition of Some of the Quotations

Some quotations appear in more than one chapter. When cross-referencing quotations, we found that they sometimes take on varying connotations, and support different ideas depending on the context in which they are being presented. Moreover, not all readers will have the whole work in mind when engaged in any particular chapter, either because of long delay between reading sessions, or simply because a reader may read selective chapters rather than the whole work.

Editing of Quotations

We relied on translated texts of written works and transcribed lectures by Rudolf Steiner, from both American and British publishers, that span several decades. The reader should be aware that the text taken from lectures that have been referenced here are different than from books he wrote. The majority of his lectures were recorded in the original German by skilled stenographers and many were translated into English. Steiner gave over 6,000 lectures during his lifetime. For the most part the transcriptions were not meant for publishing and distributing to the public, but a demand for them did occur, which led to their being published into books and pamphlets. With such a volume of lectures, relatively few were reviewed and revised for publication by Steiner. Because of this, the editors of this Compendium made the effort to watch out for possible errors in transcription or translation. Consequently, we have made slight changes in the text on occasion, where the English translation appears awkward, infelicitous, or inaccurate. In some cases, where there were multiple translations available we selected the most accurate one.

Acknowledgements

Many people helped us along the way to create this Compendium. On the ground level, the Rudolf Steiner Library staff members, Judith Ellis Sweningsen and Judith Keily, were instrumental in enabling us to access hard-to-find documents (see www.rslibrary.elib.com).

We are deeply indebted to a group of nine people who read through the first draft of the Compendium and gave us extensive comments and advice from multiple perspectives on how to improve the document. They were, in the associative sense outlined in this book, our representatives of the future users/consumers of this production. They are John Bloom, Christopher Budd, Arthur Edwards, Megan Durney, Travis Henry, Rosemary McMullen, John Mugge, Jeffrey Stamler, and Nathaniel Williams.

We extend our appreciation to our proof readers – Brigitte Choura, Jade Lamb, Jennifer Zimberg and John Barnes – who spent many hours reviewing the manuscripts. Special thanks go to Claire Brannon for her copyediting and her willingness and capacity to enter into the heart and essence of each chapter, to Ella Lapointe for her chapter illustrations, and to Michael Lapointe for his work on the graphic layout.

We would like to especially thank the various publishers whose works we drew upon. These include SteinerBooks, Rudolf Steiner Press, and Mercury Press. Contact information for each one can be found in the Resources chapter.

Research of any kind, including materials research, cannot take place without "gift money" – in Steiner's terms, money that is given to free up individuals to engage in some type of educational activity, whether it be education per se, or one of its aspects, such as scientific research, artistic development, or religious transformation. We gratefully acknowledge the financial assistance from the following individuals and organizations that enabled us to create this Economics Compendium: Gordon Edwards, the Foundation for Rudolf Steiner Books, the Mahle-Stiftung, RSF Social Finance, the Triodos Foundation, and James Willets.

Gary Lamb and Sarah Hearn, Editors

Gary Lamb is Co-Director of the Hawthorne Valley Center for Social Research and the author of Associative Economics: Spiritual Activity for the Common Good, *published by AWSNA Publications. He taught high school economics for 11 years at Hawthorne Valley Waldorf School and was the managing editor of The Threefold Review, a magazine based on Rudolf Steiner's social ideas and their application in modern life.*

Sarah Hearn and her partner manage a diverse biodynamic Community Supported Agriculture (CSA) farm in New York State. She is co-founder of Think OutWord, a peer-led training in social threefolding, and previously worked at the Schumacher Center for New Economics where she managed the BerkShares local currency program.

ONE

Social and Antisocial Forces

in the Human Being and Social Life

[Human interchange] consists of one person trying to put the other to sleep [in thinking], while the other tries to resist and stay awake. This is the archetypal phenomenon of social science . . . All thinking about social forms can bear no fruit if we do not make the effort to take these things into account. SASF 18

ONE

Social and Antisocial Forces
in the Human Being and Social Life

Rudolf Steiner identifies what is for many – and particularly for an economist – an unusual starting point for understanding and addressing social problems. As the modern world tends to look to outer causes and solutions, Steiner directs us inward. Specifically, he indicates the necessity of understanding the soul nature of the human being, which is comprised of social and antisocial forces. Social forces are the result of taking an interest in the thoughts and situations of others. Antisocial forces arise through self-interest and a disregard for the thoughts and feelings of others. These forces flow through and between us in our relationships with each other and guide our thinking and feeling, which ultimately shape our institutions. Steiner describes the soul's oscillation between these forces as "the archetypal social phenomenon." This phenomenon is an omnipresent, concrete reality, which we must work to perceive and understand if we are to work toward greater social health.

The Need for Inner and Outer Change

We have reached a stage in human evolution in which the transformation of social life cannot be achieved simply by changing our outer structures and institutions. There is a reciprocal interplay between outer forms and the thoughts, feelings, and intentions of the people connected to them. Each works upon and influences the other towards health or illness. Ultimately, our structures and institutions embody and reflect the inner life and relations of the human beings who have created them. Thus the thinking – especially the habitual thoughts – of the people working in organizations and communities must change and evolve if true and systemic social transformation is to occur.

No matter how cleverly we arrange our outer forms, antisocial people, if their power and numbers are sufficient, can find a way to use those forms for their own benefit. While our institutions may often appear appropriate and efficient in a technical sense, they will only function in a socially healthy way if the individuals within them serve the community rather than themselves, and do so with loving devotion to the work at hand and a sincere interest in the work of others.

> *In the present social movement there is a great deal of talk about social institutions, but very little talk about social and antisocial human beings. Very little regard is paid to the "social question" that arises when one considers that institutions in a community take their social or antisocial stamp from the people who run them. Socialist thinkers expect to see in the community's control of the means of production something that will satisfy the demands of a wide range of people. They take for granted that, under communal control of the economy, human relations will necessarily assume a social form as well. They have seen that the economic system along the lines of private capitalism has led to antisocial conditions. They believe that when this industrial system has disappeared, the antisocial tendencies at work within it will also necessarily come to an end.* RSO 24

> *External institutions . . . are . . . the creations of human souls, who embody in these institutions their sentiments, their habits of mind, their thoughts.* ASQ 22

> *There is no form one can give to external institutions by which these institutions can, of themselves, enable us to lead a socially satisfying life. Such institutions will be good in a technical sense if they enable commodities to be produced and conveyed to human use in the most efficient manner possible. However, they will be good in a social sense only if socially-minded people administer the commodities produced in the service of the community. No matter what the institutions may be, there is always some conceivable way human individuals or groups can operate them antisocially.*

People expect better conditions through the implementation of external measures... It is believed that improvements in the social sphere depend on the creation of institutions. And, yet these are the least significant factors in social development. You can set up any institutions you like, be they monarchist or republican, democratic or socialistic; the decisive factor will always be the kind of people who live and work under any of these systems. For those who spread a socializing influence, the two things that matter are a loving devotion toward what they are doing, and an understanding interest in what others are doing...

Think about what can flow from just these two attributes; at least people can work together again in the social sphere. *CCC 142*

Just as we cannot claim to do arithmetic if we have never learned our multiplication tables, so too we cannot claim to discuss social reforms and the like when we have never learned those things which I have just explained: namely, that socialism and antisocialism exist quite concretely in the way described. *SASF 8*

Now, a matter-of-fact and positive admission that humans are at the same time social and antisocial beings is a fundamental requirement for a social knowledge of humanity. *CT 121-122*

One should not give oneself over to the illusion that any kind of satisfying social life can be created without "socially-minded" human beings; such illusions are a hindrance to really practical social ideas. *RSO 99*

Rising Individualism and Antisocial Forces

As humanity moves through an evolutionary process of ever greater individuality and self-expression, we are becoming increasingly self-assertive and self-centered. Though these developments are necessary aspects of our evolution toward greater inner freedom and individuality, they bring corresponding challenges for social life. In order for human beings to increasingly develop individual consciousness, antisocial forces also need to develop. These forces and the tendency to turn our interest away from our fellow human beings will grow stronger as modern life evolves.

> *We live in [an age] in which human beings must become independent. But on what does this depend? It depends on people's ability . . . to become self-assertive, to not allow themselves to be put to sleep. It is the antisocial forces which require development in this time, for consciousness to be present. It would not be possible for humanity in the present to accomplish its task if just these antisocial forces did not become ever more powerful; they are indeed the pillars on which personal independence rests. At present humanity has no idea how much more powerful antisocial impulses must become.* *SASF 6-7*

The Interplay of Sleeping and Waking in Human Encounter

Whenever we meet another human being, an experience of connection begins to flow between us and a bond is formed. If we look more closely, we see that a constant interplay of social and antisocial forces takes place in every human encounter.

If we look at how these forces function when we interact with others, we see that when social forces are active, we are asleep to our own thoughts, and when antisocial forces are at work, we are active and focused on our own thinking, to the exclusion of the other. When we listen to someone communicate their thoughts to us, we are 'asleep' to our own thoughts, and awake, engaged and receptive to the thoughts of the speaker. However, we then naturally resist this experience of falling asleep to ourselves by waking up and consciously reasserting our own thoughts. In this way, we separate ourselves from the other, allowing antisocial forces to take hold and work in us.

By our very nature as human beings, we are thinkers, active and awake in our own thoughts. At the same time, we are social beings. Thus, in each social encounter a perpetual struggle takes place in the realm of thinking. We yield to the thoughts of the other person, allowing our own thoughts to fall asleep, and then wake up to our own thoughts and displace the thoughts of the other. Since modern-day humanity tends to be self-assertive and, in doing so, antisocial, we must consciously educate ourselves to become more social.

> *What really happens then, not merely in that which presents itself to the senses, but in the total situation, when one person stands opposite another, when one person meets another? Nothing less than that a certain force works from one person to the other. The meeting of one with another leads to the working of a certain force between them. We cannot confront another person in life with indifference, not even in mere thoughts and feelings, even though we may be separated from them by distance. If we have any kind of relation to other people, or any communication with them, then a force flows between us creating a bond. It is this fact which lies at the basis of social life and which, when broadened, is really the foundation for the social structure of humanity.* SASF 4

> *When you stand as a conceiving, thinking human being in the presence of another person, it is a strange fact that the reciprocal relationship that comes about between you and the other brings into existence in your sub-consciousness the tendency to be put to sleep by the other person . . . When you come together, the one strives – and, naturally, the relationship is reciprocal – to put to sleep the subconscious of the other . . . Thus, when you come into the presence of a person, he puts you to sleep; that is, he puts your thinking to sleep, not your feeling and willing. Now, if you wish to continue to be a thinking human being, you must defend yourself inwardly against this. You must activate your thinking . . .*
>
> *This requires that we are in great measure antisocial beings as regards our conceptual life, our thinking, and can become social beings only by educating ourselves.* CT 124-125

> *A perpetual struggle and opposition to falling asleep in social relationships is also present. If you meet a person, you are continuously standing in a conflict situation in the following way: Because you meet him, the tendency to sleep always*

develops in you so that you may experience your relationship to him in sleep. But, at the same time, there is aroused in you the counter-force to keep yourself awake. This always happens in the meeting between people – a tendency to fall asleep, a tendency to keep awake. In this situation a tendency to keep awake has an antisocial character, the assertion of one's individuality, of one's personality, in opposition to the social structure of society. Simply because we are human beings, our soul-life swings to and fro between the social and the antisocial. SASF 6

If you meet another person, the following occurs: For a short period you perceive the person, and he or she makes an impression upon you. That impression disturbs you inwardly; you feel that the person, a being comparable to yourself, makes an impression upon you like an attack. The result is that you defend yourself inwardly, you resist this attack and become inwardly aggressive toward the person. In this aggression you become crippled, and the aggression ceases. Then the other person can again make an impression upon you, and after you thus have time to regain your aggressive strength, you carry out another act of aggression. Again, you become numb, and the other person again makes an impression upon you, and so forth. This is the relationship that exists when one person meets another and perceives the other "I": an alternation of devotion to the other – inner resistance; sympathy – antipathy. I am not speaking now of feeling, but just the perception of meeting. The soul vibrates; it vibrates sympathy – antipathy, sympathy – antipathy, sympathy – antipathy. You can read about this in the new edition of Intuitive Thinking as a Spiritual Path. *There is still something else. As sympathy develops, you go to sleep in the other person; as antipathy develops, you wake up, and so forth. In the vibrations of meeting another person, there is a rapid alternation between waking and sleeping.* FHE 140-141.

This oscillation between opening up to the thoughts of others and reasserting our own thoughts often happens so rapidly that we typically are not aware of it.

Just as my daytime consciousness is shut out in dreamless sleep, so is the content of my own consciousness when I perceive another person's. The illusion that this is not so persists because, first, when perceiving another person, what replaces my own content of consciousness is not unconsciousness (as in sleep) but rather the content of the other person's consciousness; and, second, the oscillations between the extinction and re-illumination of my consciousness of myself follow one another too rapidly to be normally noticed. *IT 246*

Of what does human interchange in fact consist? As we have seen, it consists of one person trying to put the other to sleep, while the other tries to resist and stay awake. This is the archetypal phenomenon of social science in Goethe's sense. This archetypal phenomenon points to something which mere material thinking cannot grasp; it points to that which can only be understood when one knows that in human life one is not only asleep during sleep – when we slumber along for hours, oblivious to the world – but the same applies to daily waking life, where the same forces which lead to sleep and wakefulness also play into our social and antisocial forces. All thinking about social forms can bear no fruit if we do not make the effort to take these things into account.* *SASF 17-18*

Taking Greater Interest in Others: The Foundation of Social Life

Because antisocial forces necessarily arise in every human encounter, rather than trying to eradicate these forces, we need to consciously foster and strengthen a counterbalance of social forces. For the individual, the primary way to accomplish this is to develop ever greater interest in our fellow human beings. This process is the foundation or backbone of all social life and social renewal now and in the future.

---

* Johann Wolfgang von Goethe (1749-1832), German writer, artist, and natural scientist, who formulated a theory of plant metamorphosis in which all existing plant forms can be derived (in thought) from an archetypal plant that exists as a dynamic potential that manifests differently in each plant. Steiner is suggesting here that the archetypal phenomenon of every human encounter consists in sleeping and waking in thought life due to the interplay of social and antisocial forces.

This antisocial spirit can only be held in balance by the social. But the social must be nursed, must be consciously cared for. And in our day this becomes truly more and more difficult because the antisocial forces are really in accord with our natural development. The social element is essential; it must be cherished. We shall see that in this . . . [age] there is a tendency to take no notice of the social in merely acting naturally. Rather it must be acquired consciously in working with one's soul forces, while formerly it was felt instinctively. What is necessary and must be actively acquired is the interest of [one person in another]. This is indeed the backbone of all social life. SASF

A favorable change in [a] social movement cannot come about in any other way than through an increase in the interest that a person feels in another human being. CT 45

Creating Social Forces by Consciously Fostering Interest in Others

Rudolf Steiner suggests three ways to foster the development of greater interest in other people, which is essential in order to enliven the social forces that are needed to serve as a counterbalance to the antisocial forces that naturally occur in the human being.

i. Imaginative Concepts in Education

We need to make the development of pictorial or imaginative thinking an essential aspect of the education of children. The abstract concepts of natural scientific thinking form the basis for most modern approaches to education. However, we can encourage the development of imaginative thinking by teaching imaginative concepts, that is, by teaching in pictures.

. . . this ability to develop an imaginative faculty for the other is something that must enter into pedagogy and the education of children. SASF 14

The future requires that we base general education upon concepts that can serve as a foundation for imaginative

> *thoughts, not just upon ideas taken from science or industry. As improbable as this may seem now, in the future we will be unable to properly interact socially if we do not teach people imaginative concepts. That is, if we do not teach concepts that affect human feeling much differently than the abstract natural scientific concepts of cause and effect, force and matter, and so forth. In the future, we will be unable to begin anything social with those scientific concepts that influence everything today, even art. In the future we must understand the world in pictures.* *EFSC 45*

In the hope of ensuring that the development of imagination would become an essential task of the education of children, Rudolf Steiner envisioned and founded what came to be known as Waldorf education. When he spoke to educators, he emphasized the importance of teaching every subject in living concepts that can breathe, expand, and be transformed as the children live with them. This kind of education speaks to the feeling life of the child, out of which arise both a capacity for imaginative thinking and a sound moral basis for life.

> *It is really appalling when a teacher's ideas and concepts have been worked out to the degree that they are no longer adaptable or flexible. They would have an effect similar to the effect of iron gloves forced onto a child's little hands, preventing them from growing naturally. We must not chain children's minds to finished concepts, but give them living concepts that can grow and expand further. We must give them concepts that can be transformed. But this can be achieved only through an imaginative approach in every subject, certainly until the twelfth year.* *CCC 109*

> *When children have reached age nine or ten, we may begin to present pictures that primarily stimulate the imagination . . . We should approach children through aesthetics and imagination. We should awaken pleasure or displeasure in good and bad things, in just and unjust things, in high ideals, in moral action, and in things that occur in the world*

to balance incorrect action . . . Before puberty, children should receive morality as a feeling [not moral commandments; cultivated inner judgement in feeling is the guide]. WEA2 12

ii. Inner Exercises for Imaginative Thinking

We can practice certain inner exercises that help develop pictorial or imaginative thinking as distinct from abstract thinking. Thinking in pictures, and picturing oneself in the situation of the other, give us mobility of soul and help us to empathize with another person. In contrast, abstract thinking and isolated judgments leave our soul rigid and instill a tendency to distance ourselves from others.

How can we consciously establish social impulses to balance those antisocial forces which are developing naturally within us? How can we cultivate the social element, this interest of one person in another, so that it springs up in us – going ever further and deeper, and leaving us no rest? . . . The precise need of the future is that the social shall be brought to meet the antisocial in a systematic way. For this there are various inner soul methods. SASF 12-13

Imaginations will be required by human beings, for only through them will the antisocial impulses, so rampant today, develop into social impulses. Thus, through imaginations, human beings will acquire the faculty to put themselves in the place of other persons . . . You cannot put yourself in the place of others merely through abstract thinking. Abstract thinking makes you stubborn, abstract thinking causes you to be attentive only to your own opinion. Above all, abstract thinking generally leads us to close ourselves off more or less from the mobility that is needed for us to live with the spiritual world. T-S 3

Only when the effort is made not to form any judgment regarding such relationships [social and human], but to form pictures – in other words, when we ascend to the imaginative life – shall we take the path that is approximately right. In our epoch it is of special importance to make the effort to form pictures, not really abstract, isolated judgments. It must be pictures too, that will open a path to socialization. CT 145

There are various exercises to develop pictorial thinking. One is to picture ourselves as reflections of all of the people who have influenced us in a positive way through the course of our lives. We can include even people whose impact on our lives we might not have noticed or appreciated at the time that we knew them. In our reflection, we develop a feeling of gratitude or indebtedness for their contribution to our lives. In time, we come to see how little we actually owe to ourselves and how much we owe to everything that has flowed into us from others. By developing an objective picture of our indebtedness to such people from the past, we diminish our egotism and awaken a capacity to form true and appropriate pictures of the people we meet in the present and in the future. Through this exercise, we thus cultivate social capacities.

If we try to develop a sense of the debt we owe to this or that person – if we try to see ourselves in the mirror of those who have influenced us in the course of time, and who have been associated with us – then we shall be able to experience the opening-up of a new sense in our souls, a sense which enables us to gain a picture of the people whom we meet even in the present, with whom we stand face to face today. This is because we have practiced developing an objective picture of our indebtedness to people in the past. It is tremendously important that the impulse should awaken in us, not merely to feel sympathy or antipathy towards the people we meet, not merely to hate or love something connected with a person, but to awaken a true picture of the other in us, free from love or hate. SASF 13-14

Now the question may arise in your minds as to how we shall gradually attain to the capacity of causing the picture of the other person to leap to meet us. It is in life that we must gain this capacity . . . It is most important of all that the instinct shall be implanted in people to look back more frequently during this life, but in the right way. What people develop at present as memories of earlier experience is marked as yet for the most part by a selfish character . . .

Look back into your life and pay less attention to what interests you in your own respectable person and much more to those figures that have come into contact with you, educating you, befriending you, assisting you, perhaps also injuring you – often injuring you in a helpful way . . . Let us immerse ourselves with real love in what has come into our life . . . It would be advantageous to people if they more frequently exercised such a survey of their lives.

. . . this has such a germinating power in us that we really acquire the imaginative forces necessary to confront contemporary human beings in such a way that something manifests in them that appears to us only after many years in our backward survey of those figures with whom we have lived together. We thus acquire such a capacity that pictures actually come to meet us from the individuals we confront.

The cultivation of social life, which in earlier times had its source only in the bonds of blood, does not depend so much upon any sort of socialistic programs, but upon our becoming spiritually social beings. We will become such beings by awakening within ourselves, in the manner I have described, the deeper forces that can bring to birth within us the capacity for conceiving the other human being pictorially. Otherwise, we shall always remain antisocial beings, capable of approaching others only according to our sympathies and antipathies, incapable of approaching them according to the picture that may stream forth from each person if we only develop the picture-forming forces in our intercourse with them. *CT 173-177*

We can turn our attention to the persons who have figured in our lives as parents, brothers and sisters, friends, teachers and so on, and we can summon before our soul the inner nature of each of these persons, in place of our own. After a time we shall find ourselves reflecting how little we really owe to ourselves, and how much to all that has flowed

> *into us from others. If we honestly build up this kind of self-scrutiny into an inner picture, we shall arrive at quite a new relationship to the outer world. From such a backward survey we retain certain feelings and impressions. And these are like fertile seeds planted in us – seeds for the growth of a true knowledge of what is human. When we undertake again and again this inward contemplation, so that we recognize the contribution which other persons, perhaps long dead or far distant, have made to our own life, then when we meet another person, and establish a personal relationship with him or her, an imagination of the other person's true being will rise before us.* IASQ 19

A complementary exercise to the aforementioned is one in which we reflect and picture our younger selves. We observe ourselves as if we were a stranger, forgetting that we were once that person we are observing. The goal here is to gain an objective experience of ourselves in the present by repeatedly disconnecting ourselves from our past experiences, thereby diminishing our egotism. Moreover, we cultivate the capacity for imagination that is needed for fruitful social encounters when we turn all our focus and attention to our experience in the present.

> *The other [inner exercise] is something that can be linked up with this review of our relations to others. It is when we try to become more and more objective about ourselves. Here we must also go back to our earlier years . . . "I will picture myself as another boy or girl of ten years old. I will try to forget that I was that child. I will really take pains to objectify myself." This objectifying of oneself, this freeing of oneself in the present from one's own past, this shelling-out of the Ego from its experiences, must be specially striven for in our present time.* SASF 14-15

> *. . . nothing can be done by comfortably remaining in one's position . . . nothing should depend on remembering, but on one's immediate experience in the present. It is therefore a question of training this faculty in ourselves . . . that we picture [ourselves at an earlier time in our lives as if we were*

strangers] . . . On the one hand, we cultivate the social instinct and impulses in us by looking back upon those who have been connected with us in the past and regarding our souls as the products of these persons. In this way we acquire the imagination for meeting people in the present. On the other hand, through objectifying ourselves, we gain possibilities of developing imagination directly . . . Egoism has tremendous power, but its power is lessened when you separate your earlier years from yourself and when you make them objective. SASF 15-16

iii. Conscious Design of Social Structures

We also need to consciously design our social structures, institutions, communities and other forms to facilitate social health, connection and relationships between individuals.

In our day, when people on their own account, for their individual selves, must evolve antisocial forces, which are evolving because humanity is now subjected to this evolution against which nothing will prevail, something must also come about with which we resist them: a social structure which will balance this antisocial evolutionary tendency. The antisocial forces must work inwardly so that human beings may reach the height of their development. Outwardly, in social life, structures must work so that people do not totally lose their outer connections in life. SASF 7

It is not a matter of finding prescriptions for resisting the antisocial forces, but of so shaping, of so arranging the social order, the structure, the organization of that which lies outside of the individual, that a counter-balance is present to that which works as antisocial force within human beings. Therefore it is vital for our time that the individual achieves independence, but that social forms provide a balance to this independence. Otherwise neither the individual nor society can develop properly. SASF 8

Anyone who lived entirely alone would never develop human speech – human speech arises only in a social community.

In the same way, those who live alone cannot form a social way of thinking; they will have no social perceptions and no social instincts. Only in a rightly formed community is it possible to build up social life in the face of the happenings of the present time. *IASQ 61*

When we meet social arrangements and structures in society . . . they are . . . a manifestation of this pendulum between social and antisocial forces. National economists may reflect upon what credit, capital and interest are. Yet even these things which make for regularity in social transactions are only outward swings of the pendulum between social and antisocial forces. Those who seek to find healing remedies for these times must intelligently and scientifically connect with these facts. *SASF 6*

Interest in Others and Economic Life

The development of interest in others is not meant to be merely an abstract ideal. It needs to enter into all aspects of our practical work together in social life, including how we relate to and use money. We must strive to understand and remember with every exchange that money is worth nothing in itself. Rather, we must develop an ever stronger consciousness of the fact that we are able to exist as human beings on account of what others provide for us through their work. When we truly understand that our lives depend on the work of others, we develop a sense of duty to give back to society. In this way, we strive to contribute our own labor in gratitude and recognition of the work of others.

What has been said regarding the necessity for individuals to acquire an interest in one another must not be regarded only in a manner harmonizing with the mood presented in the Sunday vesper sermon. It must be considered according to the profound indication it gives in regard to the social structure of the present age.

Consider a concrete example. How many people there are today who have an abstract and confused conception of their own personal lives! If they ask themselves, for example,

"What do I live on?" . . . they would say to themselves, "Why, on my money." . . . Money is not something on which we can live. . . . This question is intimately connected with the real interest that one individual has in another. Those who think they live on money . . . have no interest in their fellow human beings because they cannot live on . . . money they have acquired in any way whatever except by receiving money to pay for other people's work . . . We must eat, and what we eat has been produced by a human being. We must have clothing. What we wear must be made through the labor of people . . . They work for me. It is on this labor that I live, not on my money. My money has no value other than that of giving me the power to make use of the labor of others. Under the social conditions of the present time, we do not begin to have an interest in our fellow men until we answer that question in the proper way, until we hold the picture in our minds of a certain number of persons working for a certain number of hours in order that I may live within the social structure. It is of no importance to give ourselves a comfortable feeling by saying, "I love people." We do not love people if we suppose that we are living on our money and do not in the least conceive how people work for us in order to produce even the minimum necessary for our lives.

But the thought that a certain number of persons labor in order that we may possess the minimum necessities of life is inseparable from another. It is the thought that we must recompense society, not with money but with work in exchange for the work that has been done for us. We feel an interest in others only when we are led to feel obligated to recompense in some form of labor the amount of labor that has been performed for us . . .

Permit me to ask whether you cannot answer out of your experience the question: How many people realize that money is only a claim upon human strength employed in labor, that money is only a means for gaining power? How many persons really see clearly that they could not even exist in this physical world but for the labor of other persons upon which they depend for what they demand for their lives? The feeling of obligation to the society in which we live is the beginning of the interest that is required for a sound social order . . .

. . . During recent centuries, people have gradually formed the habit of developing a real interest in the matter of social impulses only with regard to their own respected persons. To a greater or lesser degree everything has borne in a round-about way only upon one's personality. A wholesome social life is possible only when interest in one's own respected personality is broadened into genuine social interest . . . *CT 54-58*

. . . enjoyment should really never be accepted without re-paying its equivalent to the whole of society . . . the necessary steps can be taken to make sure that whatever is enjoyed by one may also be enjoyed by others. *CT 58*

Imagine you have a $5 note in your pocket . . . and you spend the full $5 . . . The $5 note is really an illusion – it is worth nothing in reality . . . Money is namely only a 'go-between' . . . This $5 note . . . is nothing else than an equivalent for so many days of labor of so many people. A number of people must have completed so many days of work, so much human labor must have flowed into society – must have crystallized itself into merchandise – in order for the apparent worth of the bank note to have any real value, but only at the command of society. The bank note only gives you the power to call into your service so much labor, or to put it another way, to command its worth in work. You can picture it in your mind: Here I have a bank note, which assigns to me, according to my social position, the power over so many people. If you now see these people selling their labor hour by hour, as the equivalent value of that which you have in your purse as the $5 note, then you begin to get a picture of the real facts. *SASF 10-11*

You do not have sufficient interest [in the other] if you think that you can buy yourself something with a $5 note and do not remember the fact that this brings about a social relationship with certain other human beings and their labor-power. You only have an adequate interest when in your *picture you are able to substitute for each apparent transaction . . . the real transaction which is linked with it.* SASF 11

From Personal Opinion to Collective Wisdom

As we develop a greater interest in others, we also need to cultivate a tolerance for their opinions, even if those opinions are contrary to our own. In a group situation, everyone's viewpoint is 'right' from his or her own perspective, though it may be limited, inaccurate, or incorrect when all perspectives are taken into consideration. We should even take an interest in the fact that another person thinks about something in a way that is different from our own. When, out of love and understanding, we make an effort to forge a connection to a diversity of opinions, free of judgment, we are able to experience the collective wisdom of the whole group. Moreover, we are able to experience ourselves as part of a larger whole, a necessary step toward a healthy future for social life.

> *. . . we have to educate ourselves to understand the many-sidedness of people; we have to develop an inward tolerance. It should be of interest to us when we find that another person thinks about some subject or other in an entirely different way from ourselves; for we should have the feeling that thereby our own thoughts are rendered more complete. Let us be more and more ready to take the following point of view: Here are a number of individual human beings; let us say, there are ten, and I am one of them. I say to myself: I think in this way on a certain matter, the second thinks in that way, the third in still another other way, the fourth and fifth in still another, and so on, – all more or less differing from one another. We are all right, and [none of us are] right. When we begin to feel, more or less, the arithmetical mean of it, when we feel ourselves linked up with all the opinions and able to comprehend them all with equal love, regardless of whether we have expressed them or one of the others, when we learn to feel ourselves within the whole, then we are well on the way to finding together the kind of relationship that will*

> *hold good for people in the future. It is essential we should put all our effort to this end. We must do so, for only thus can we acquire a feeling for a true social life. We must learn to feel that we have our place in all that is encompassed by the genius of language, and in all that is encompassed by the life of common rights. We must learn also to feel that we stand within all that is encompassed by the genius of the common economic life. This living feeling of being within a whole has to be acquired consciously in the age of consciousness so that it may bear us onwards towards a right determination of the future life of humanity. And the first thing needed is to make our interests wider and wider. In no other way can we achieve this direction of life towards the future.* SQ, FSL 31-32

Only when we make a continual effort to broaden our interests does our individuality become meaningful and of interest for others and the world. When we contemplate merely what is in us, ignoring what is in the wide world around us, we lose interest in the world and the world loses interest in us. We eventually even lose interest in ourselves and become bored and discontented.

> *This means, in other words, we have to get more and more free of ourselves. If we are perfectly honest with ourselves, we shall ultimately come to see that what we are able to think and feel about our self in the narrow circle of our ego is in truth the most uninteresting thing in the whole world! And yet so many people in the present day spend a great deal of thought upon this little ego of theirs. That is why life is so tedious for them; that is why they are so discontented. We shall never become interesting as long as we go on revolving around this point. If, on the contrary, we look outwards and turn our eyes always upon what the external world shows to us, upon all the impressions it lets stream in upon us, if we widen our interests more and more, then our ego will become interesting for the reason that it affords a vantage point for the observation of the external world: Our ego will acquire significance for us, through the fact that we alone, and no other, are able to behold the world just from*

the particular standpoint it affords. Another person sees the world from another standpoint. But so long as we remain within ourselves and revolve around ourselves, we are really contemplating only that within us which we have in common with all other human beings; and at last it comes to this, that we lose interest in every other human being and in the whole world outside ourselves. A broadening of interests – that is what spiritual science above all tries to achieve.

This means, however, that we must educate our souls to become receptive and sensitive for all that comes to meet us from the world outside, we must educate our souls to be actually able to receive new things. *SQ, FSL 32*

TWO

The Fundamental Social Law

In a community of human beings working together, the well-being of the community will be the greater, the less individuals claim for themselves the proceeds of the work they themselves have done; i.e., the more of these proceeds they give over to their fellow-workers, and the more their own requirements are satisfied, not by the results of their own work, but by work done by others. ASQ 32

TWO

The Fundamental Social Law

Between 1905 and 1925, Rudolf Steiner gave several different articulations of what he called the Fundamental Social Law. This law concerns the effects of the social and antisocial forces at work in humanity on the health and wellbeing of society. Specifically, The Fundamental Social Law indicates that the wellbeing and prosperity of society will be greater, to the extent that we are able to overcome the antisocial forces of egoism (e.g. self-interest and greed in economic life) and instead work out of the social forces of altruism (e.g. care for one another and mutual support). Steiner maintained that the law is as valid as any law of physics or mathematics and, on the other hand, that it is an ancient spiritual truth recognized by many different cultures.

> *In a community of human beings working together, the well-being of the community will be the greater, the less individuals claim for themselves the proceeds of the work they themselves have done; i.e., the more of these proceeds they give over to their fellow-workers, and the more their own requirements are satisfied, not by the results of their own work, but by work done by others.* ASQ 32

> *Genuine social progress is possible only if I do my work in the service of all, and the totality of the community gives me what I need.* SSSQ, FSL 13

> *The work of the community must be so organized that the proceeds of labor belong to society, and so that the means of subsistence are created not as the reward for labor, but through the structure of society.* HBFJSQ Lecture 8

It is a fundamental law, which holds good for all social life with the same absoluteness and necessity as any law of nature within a particular field of causation. ASQ 33

[The Fundamental Social Law] is just as certain as mathematics . . . What I introduced to you as a social science derived from spiritual science [the Fundamental Social law] is much like the theorem of Pythagoras. CT 59

[The Fundamental Social Law] is an ancient theme of every esotericist and an ancient tenet of Spiritual Science. TEL, FSL 9 and SSSQ, FSL 13

Egoism and Self Interest in Social Life

The Fundamental Social Law is in direct contradiction to a generally accepted tenet of modern economic life, which contends that the overall prosperity of society will increase if individuals work out of self-interest, and personally reap the benefits of their work.

People are much more ready to go on the principle that a human community will, as a whole, be most prosperous, when it also allows individuals to reap and garner the full – or the largest possible – proceeds of their own labor. ASQ 31

How often has it been said that humanity would progress best if each person asserted and benefited himself, as much as he could. The word "individualism" has even become a catchword mostly in connection with material life, to be sure, but also, and not without validity, in connection with the inner, spiritual life.

It is the belief of many economists and social theorists that people can serve others best when they take as much as possible from life, because if they become economically strong they can better serve the community. BSE 2

Contemplation of the Fundamental Social Law leads to the conclusion that egoism and self-interest are not only unhelpful behaviors, in the economic sector and otherwise, but that they actually lie at the root of all social ills, including poverty and exploitation. Rudolf Steiner indicates that there is a lawfulness to social life that is as indisputable as a law of natural science, and as intertwined as cause and effect. The Law indicates that misery, suffering, and poverty are the inevitable consequences of humanity's egoism. And if we turn our focus toward institutional life we can perceive the same phenomenon at work. In institutions that are governed by self-interested behavior, it is the antisocial forces at work in the individuals within these organizations that shape and form their motivations and consequent actions. And although the social consequences may not be immediately visible, they will eventually appear, possibly in another country or as a burden to future generations.

> *Want, misery and suffering are nothing but a result of egoism. This statement is to be taken as a law of nature.*
> *TEL, FSL 10*

> *Human suffering is purely a consequence of egoism, and suffering, poverty, and want must of necessity arise in every human community at some time or other, if this community is founded in any way upon egoism.* *ASQ 31*

> *What is the basic fact, the fundamental phenomenon, as it were, to which all misery, all social suffering in the world can be attributed? . . . Life shows us that need, suffering, and destitution are not – and least of all if one gets to the bottom of it – dependent on outer conditions alone, but rather on a certain constitution of soul and its outer effects.*
>
> *Practical people who consider themselves very clever would find this ridiculous. But it is the most practical thing in life, something that can only be emphasized: . . . need, misery and suffering are nothing but a consequence of egoism. We are to take this as a law of nature, not as though with every person who is an egoist, need and suffering must appear, but rather that it may, even in some different context, still be connected with this egoism. Like cause and effect, egoism and suffering are intertwined. In human life, in the human social structure, egoism leads to the struggle for existence. The struggle for existence is the actual origin of need and*

> *suffering to the extent that they are social. Now, on the basis of our current mode of thinking, there is an attitude on the basis of which what we have been talking about seems downright absurd. Why? Because today one is convinced that a great part, far and away the greatest part, of human life must be built on egoism.* SSSQ, FSL 13

> *Those alone can form a right judgment of the external institutions of life who see that they are nothing but the creations of human souls, who embody in these institutions their sentiments, their habits of mind, their thoughts . . . That one is an exploiter of other people's labor power has nothing whatever to do with [class status], or at least not directly. It has . . . to do . . . with the fact that our institutions, or the conditions of our environment, are based on personal self-interest.* ASQ 22-24

It is important to note that egoism is not solely a characteristic of wealthy individuals. For example, in examining the economic process as a whole, we can perceive egoism as a motivating factor in producers as well as in consumers, regardless of their economic status. As consumers, we exploit others whenever we pay as little as possible for the goods we purchase without regard for externalized costs, such as the working conditions of those who produced the goods.

> *In terms of clear thinking, who is the exploiter and who the exploited? Let us look at the person who makes a garment, earning starvation wages. Who is his or her exploiter? One could talk about someone who buys the garment and pays a very meager price for it. Does, by chance, only a rich person buy this garment? Wouldn't this same worker who complains about exploitation buy this same cheap garment? And doesn't he or she require today, within our social order, that the garment be as cheap as possible? See how the manual laborer, who makes her fingers bleed during the week can wear her dress on Sunday for such a low price because the work power of another person like her has been exploited! For clear thinking this has nothing to do with wealth or poverty, but*

> *rather exclusively with whatever in the world our idea is of how people stand in relation to other people.* SSSQ, FSL 13

Individuality and autonomy have become two crowning features of humanity's development over the past centuries and millennia. Consequently, implementation of the Fundamental Social Law cannot be compelled or enforced en masse. Rather it must arise out of the free will of individuals, out of their own thoughts and feelings of responsibility for the world. In this way our motivation for work needs to evolve beyond monetary compensation. In fact, the healthy evolution of society depends on the degree to which we are able to work freely for the love of work itself.

> *The animals go and find their food by instinct, and if there isn't enough they starve. Human beings work to create food, and once they begin to work they begin to have thoughts. Only when thoughts begin does the social question arise. If human beings are to work, they must have a stimulus to work, but the stimulus that has existed hitherto will cease to be there in the future. There will have to be a new stimulus to work. What has to be said is that once people have thoughts that come from a feeling of responsibility for the world, thoughts that motivate their souls, then the forces that emerge from these thoughts will pass over into their hands and will, and work will arise. Everything depends on thoughts. And the thoughts depend on whether we open our hearts to the impulses of the spiritual world.* INE 37

> *The main point is that every single member is in a position of complete freedom to respect this principle and to practice it in life. The point is not to enforce this principle through overall compulsion. This principle of making what has been, and still is to be earned, independent of what one does for the community has to penetrate into every single human life. And how does it accomplish this?*
>
> *There is only one way of doing it, something that to so-called practical people will seem to be quite impractical. There must be reasons why people work, and work diligently*

and devotedly when self interest is no longer the motive for labor . . . The motive for working must lie in something other than compensation. And that is the solution to the Social Question: the separation of compensation from labor. SSSQ, FSL 13

Only when I follow my love for an object is it I myself who act. At this level of morality, I do not act because I acknowledge a lord over me or an external authority or a so-called inner voice. I acknowledge no outer principle for my action, because I have found within myself the basis of my acting – love for the action. I do not check rationally whether the action is good or evil; I do it because I love it . . . What directs me is not common usage, not general custom, not a universal human principle, and not an ethical norm, but my love for the deed. I feel no compulsion, neither the compulsion of nature, which guides me in my drives, nor the compulsion of ethical commandments. I simply want to carry out what lies within me. IT 151-152

To act out of freedom does not exclude moral laws, but rather includes them. Still, it stands on a higher level than action dictated by moral laws alone. Why should my action serve the welfare of the whole any less if I have acted out of love than if I acted only because I feel a duty to serve the welfare of the whole? The simple concept of duty excludes freedom, because duty does not recognize individuality but demands instead subjection of individuality to a general norm. Freedom of action is thinkable only from the standpoint of ethical individualism. IT 154

Egoism and Altruism

In modern times it is the division of labor that has introduced altruism into economic and social life. Practically speaking, the more the division of labor is applied to any process, the less it is possible to work for oneself. Today we provide few or none of the goods and services we require for ourselves. We have all become dependent on the work of others, just as others depend on the products we produce.

Therefore it is ultimately the outer form of modern economic life, specifically the division of labor, that actually 'demands' and necessitates the kind of altruism and mutual support in society that religious leaders and the science of ethics have historically encouraged.

> *In former times the division of labor had no particular significance because it too was embraced in the religious impulses. Everyone, so to speak, had an assigned place. It was very different when democratic striving united with the tendency toward the division of labor – a process which only began in the last few centuries and reached its climax in the nineteenth century. Then the division of labor gained very great significance.*
>
> *The division of labor entails a certain economic consequence. (We shall yet, of course, get to know its causes and the course of its development.) To begin with, if we think it abstractly to its conclusion, we must say that in the end it leads to this: none of us uses what we ourselves produce . . . no one any longer works for themselves at all. All that is produced by an individual's labor is passed on to others; and what one requires oneself must come, in turn, from the community.* RE 33-34

> *Meanwhile, it is absolutely true, and indeed self evident, that the more the division of labor advances, the more it will come about that one always works for others – for the community in general – and never for oneself . . . the more the division of labor advances, the more must I do everything for others.*
>
> *The summons to altruism has, in fact, come far more quickly through purely outward circumstances in the economic sphere than it has been answered on the ethical and religious side . . .*
>
> *The word "egotism," you will find, is a relatively old one, though not perhaps with the negativity that we attach to it today. Its opposite, however – the word "altruism," "to think of another" – is scarcely a hundred years old . . . human thought*

on ethics was far from having arrived at a full appreciation of altruism at a time when the division of labor had already brought about its appreciation in the economic life. Taking it, therefore, in its purely economic aspect, we see at once the further consequences of this demand for altruism. We must find our way into the process of modern economic life, wherein one does not have to provide for oneself, but only for others; and so each individual will, in fact, be provided for in the best possible way.

It is neither God, nor a moral law, nor an instinct that calls for altruism in modern economic life – altruism in work, altruism in the production of goods. It is the modern division of labor, a purely economic category, that requires it. RE 35-36

Even though mutual support is inherent in the very organization of the division of labor, there are countless other ways in which we fail to a achieve altruism in social life, and we often work in direct contradiction to it. For example, when we strive to maximize personal profits or work to obtain the highest possible wage for ourselves. In fact, when we work for a wage at all, fundamentally we are working for ourselves rather than responding to a social need.

In recent times our economic life has begun to require more of us than we are ethically, religiously, capable of achieving. This is the underlying fact of many a conflict . . .

Because of this discrepancy in the mentality of present-day humanity – the discrepancy between the demands of economic life and of ethical and religious ability – the following state of affairs is largely predominant in practice. To a large extent, in present-day economic life, people are providing for themselves. That is to say, our economic life is actually in contradiction to what, by virtue of the division of labor, is its own fundamental demand . . . Basically, all wage earners in the usual sense provide for themselves . . . In effect, to provide for oneself is to work for one's earnings, to work "for a living." To work for others is to work out of a sense of social necessity.

> *To the extent that the demand implicit in the division of labor has been fulfilled in our time, altruism is actually present – namely, working for others. But to the extent that the demand is unfulfilled, the old egotism persists.* RE 36-37

> *They will see that one actually cannot work for oneself within an economic organism based on the division of labor. One can only work for others, and let others work for oneself. Working for oneself in such circumstances is as impossible as eating oneself up. What is possible, however, is to work against all that division of labor implies. This occurs when production is solely geared to making private property of something which an individual can only produce thanks to his or her position within the social organism.* Division of labor puts pressure on the social organism to make individuals subject to conditions pertaining in the whole organism, and thus precludes economic egotism. If such egotism is nevertheless present in the form of class privilege, etc., a socially unsustainable condition arises which leads to upheavals of the social organism. Such a state of affairs holds sway at the present time. There may be many who think it would be a foolish idea to base legal relationships on the non-egotistic principles of the division of labor. But the truth is that without this the social movement will be unable to achieve anything at all. Nothing of any lasting value in the social sphere can be achieved without acknowledging reality. The thinking underlying this book aims to base human action within the social organism on the real, living laws of this organism.* TSR 97

All of economic life originates as a response to human wants and needs. Stated differently, we can say that an understandable egoism lies at the root of all human consumption. In order for altruism to serve this legitimate egoism, producers must take genuine interest in

* Editor's Note: This idea recognizes that the individual cannot produce things alone. Under the division of labor, an untold number of people help to produce goods. Therefore no individual should be able to claim private ownership of the proceeds from the goods that are produced collectively.

humanity and try lovingly to understand human needs. According to their capacities, they must then devote themselves to producing goods and services that meet those needs.

Consequently, while consumption is governed by egoism and production by altruism, the distribution of commodities holds the balance between these polarities. In a free market economy, the rise and fall of markets is guided unconsciously by supply and demand. In a new, healthy economic system, associations of producers, distributors and consumers will work to consciously perceive and understand consumer needs and will guide production accordingly.

> *Even if economic life were governed by its own conditions, and an attempt were made to understand it, it would still be necessary to point to the two impulses in the human soul just mentioned. What we have called the threefold human life element in these lectures leads us back to these two impulses in the human soul. Think of the economic system . . . consider how it pervades the whole national and international life of humanity. Let us examine this economic system. We are compelled to recognize its origin in human wants, in consumption. The satisfaction of these wants is really the whole task of economic life. Production and distribution of commodities, administration, human intercourse, and so on, are necessary to supply human requirements. Here again we may ask what element of human nature lies at the root of this requirement, of consumption. Egoism is at its root. It is important that this fact should be properly understood. If it is understood, no one will feel impelled to ask with regard to economic life, "How can we overcome egoism?", but rather, "How is it possible for altruism to meet the just demands of egoism?" Perhaps this question may sound less idealistic, but it is the true question.*
>
> *When we turn our attention to production, by which consumption is satisfied, we see at once that something else is necessary. Producers are of course at the same time consumers. Those whose business it is to produce must have an understanding not only of the process of production, but also of the lives of others, so that they can devote themselves*

to the work of production in a manner corresponding to their needs. Producers must be able, indirectly or directly through institutions of which we have spoken, to see what people need for their consumption. They must then devote themselves unselfishly and with understanding to some kind of production for which they have the capability. It is only necessary to describe this, and people will be forced to see that the real motivating power behind production is self-sacrificing love towards human society, even though the sphere in which it manifests may appear dry and uninteresting. And nothing constructive will ever be said regarding the actual solution of the social problem until it is understood that production can only be regulated in a social manner by the creation, through spiritual and equity organizations, of a source from which unselfish love for the various branches of production can flow into the human soul, because of the producers' interest in others and in life. [See Chapter Three on the Threefold Social Organism for more on spiritual and equity organizations.]

Between these two – consumption governed by egoism, and production, in which love is the ruling principle – there is the distribution of commodities, holding the balance between them. Today this is brought about through the rise and fall of the market, through supply and demand, but in future times an association of people will substitute intelligence for the fluctuation of the market. People will be there who will make it their task to regulate production in conformity with their observation of the needs of consumers. So that the market will consist of commodities that the associations . . . will be able to produce, these associations having first studied and observed intelligently the needs of consumption. [See Chapter Five on Economic Associations for more on associations.] All catchwords in this department of life will be discarded, and attention will be given wholly to realities. Who has not seen that in modern times something has arisen that was bound to appear as a result of the continual widening of people's horizons all over the world?

Instead of the national economies of the past, limited to small territories, we have a world economy. It is true that so far this world economy is only at the stage of a sort of demand, though it has developed to such an extent that in almost every part of the world commodities are consumed that are produced in other parts of the world. Here again human ideals and the feelings of the human soul have not kept pace with the world's requirements that have become evident. Everywhere we see how urgent is the demand of modern times for a world economy, for arrangements by which a world economy could be rendered possible. *SF 132-135*

Spiritual Worldview

How can we align our inner moral values with this outer call for altruism in economic life? We must foster a spiritual worldview that elevates human beings above the demands of personal self-interest. If we allow a spiritual worldview to penetrate our minds, hearts and wills, we will be able to cultivate a motivation for work that replaces self-interest with concern for others.

A bald economic theory can never act as a force to counteract the powers of egoism . . .

There is only one thing which can be of any use; and that is a spiritual world conception, which, of its own self, through that which it has to offer, can make a living home in the thoughts, in the feelings, in the will – in one's whole soul, in short. *ASQ 37-38*

We see that, in fact, what the deepening of the spirit offers us can bring every one of us what enables us, at our modest post, to work together from our sphere on the great social task. For this, progress will not be achieved by abstract regulations, but rather in the aggregate of what individual souls do . . . Just as our social misery has its basis in personal self-interest, in our ranking within the social order – so only a world view that raises the ego above personal self-interest can be of any help. Strange as it may seem, nourishment does not come only from our work; rather nourishment, instead of need, suffering, and misery, comes from spiritual scientific deepening. *SSSQ, FSL 14*

Human beings create social illness. Social relations and structures are a reflection of the thoughts and feelings that lie within human souls. If these thoughts and feelings are elevated by an all-encompassing spiritual view of the world, then this will affect outer arrangements in a positive way. Outer social change and progress are possible only to the extent that we are able to nurture healthy social impulses within our own souls.

If souls are ennobled and made more acute by a world view that goes into the spiritual, then the circumstances and outer relationships, which always mirror what human beings think, will follow. Human beings are not determined by outer conditions, rather these conditions, to the extent that they are societal, are made by human beings. If people are suffering due to circumstances, then they are in truth suffering from what their fellow human beings are doing to them. And all the misery that comes from industrial development – anyone seeking the truth must admit this – comes solely from the fact that human beings did not find it necessary to apply the same spiritual force they used for beneficial outer progress to the betterment of the lot of those people who are being exploited for the very implementation of this progress. *SSSQ, FSL 13*

Community Spirit and Spiritual Mission

In order to be motivated to work for one's community rather than for oneself, community members must have sufficient appreciation for their community, which is something that mere abstract ideals cannot provide or cultivate. The community needs a spiritual mission, and its members need to sense a living, active community spirit.

If people work for others, they must find in those others the reason for their work; and if people work for the community, they must perceive and feel the meaning and value of this community, and what it is as a living, organic whole . . .

> *The whole communal body must have a spiritual mission . . . All the vague progressive ideas, the abstract ideals, of which people talk so much, cannot present such a mission. If there is nothing but these as a guiding principle, then one individual here, or one group there, will be working without any clear comprehension of what use there is in their work, except its being to the advantage of their families, or of those particular interests to which they happen to be attached. In every single member, down to the least, this Spirit of the Community must be alive and active.* ASQ 35

The Influence of an Independent Cultural Life

We have reached a stage in human evolution in which many people yearn to work out of a higher purpose. Although the desire for profit is not in reality a fundamental aspect of the human soul, the profit motive has become increasingly strong because economic life and related political interests now intrude and infringe upon the cultural life of society.

If there is to be any hope of healthy social transformation, the three areas of social life, the cultural-spiritual, the political or rights, and the economic, must be separated [more on the threefold social organism in the next chapter]. Economic life must be limited to economic processes (the production, distribution and consumption of goods and services). At the same time, we must foster and protect an independent cultural life in which we can develop an understanding of society, and a love for the contribution of each individual's work to the whole of society. Out of this love and understanding, we can begin to develop principles to replace striving for personal profit.

> *It should be obvious that a new incentive to work must be created the moment there is any thought of eliminating the old incentive of egotistical gain . . . This [large] part of humanity no longer wants to be led to work by economic compulsion. They want to work out of motives more befitting human dignity . . .*
>
> *If the economic system is to be organized in a way that can have no effect on our will to work, then our will to work*

must be stimulated in some other way. The threefold social order recognizes that at the present stage of human evolution, the economic sphere must limit itself exclusively to economic processes . . .

It aims at establishing within an independent, self-sustaining cultural life a realm where one learns in a living way to understand this human society for which one is called upon to work; a realm where one learns to see what each single piece of work means for the combined fabric of the social order, to see it in such a light that one will learn to love it because of its value for the whole. It aims at creating in this free life of spirit the more profound principles that can replace the motive of personal gain. Only in a free spiritual life can a love for the human social order spring up that is comparable to the love an artist has for the creation of his or her works. If one is not prepared to consider fostering this kind of love within a free spiritual-cultural life, then one may as well renounce all striving for a new social order. Anyone who doubts that men and women are capable of being brought to this kind of love must also renounce all hope of eliminating personal profit from economic life. Anyone who fails to believe that a free spiritual life generates this kind of love is unaware that it is the dependence of spiritual and cultural life upon the state and the economy that creates desire for personal profit – this desire for profit is not a fundamental aspect of human nature. *RSO 80-82*

Rights Life and the Will to Work

An independent and democratic rights sphere promotes healthy social transformation by enabling people to feel and experience the worth and equality of individuals in a community, regardless of their position in life or personal attributes. In a social organism in which people work and cooperate as equals, genuine relationships form. Only out of such relationships can a true feeling of community be developed. This feeling for community can activate one's will to work on behalf of society rather than out of personal interest.

And just as the free spiritual life will create the impulses for developing individual ability, the democratically ordered life of the legal sphere will provide the impulses for the will to work. Real relationships will grow up between people united in a social organism where each adult has a voice in government and is co-equal with every other adult: it is relationships such as these that are able to enkindle the will to work "for the community." One must reflect that a truly communal feeling can grow only from such relationships, and that from this feeling, the will to work can grow. For in actual practice the consequence of such a state founded on democratic rights will be that each human being will take his or her place with vitality and full consciousness in the common field of work. Each will know what he or she is working for; and all will want to work within the working community of which they know themselves to be a member. RSO 83

You see, so long as religious impulses dominate the entire social life of humankind, egotism does no harm. This is a most important point, notably for an understanding of the social and economic life. Human beings may be ever so egotistical, but if there is a religious organization . . . such that in spite of their egotism individuals are fruitfully placed in the social life, it will do no harm. Egotism does begin to play a part in the life of people, however, the moment human rights and labor emancipate themselves from other social impulses or social currents. Hence, during the historical period when labor and rights are becoming emancipated, the spirit of humanity strives unconsciously to come to grips with egotism, which now begins to make itself felt and must in some way be integrated with social life. This striving culminates in nothing other than modern democracy – the sense for the equality of human beings – the feeling that each must have influence in determining legal rights and in determining the labor that one contributes. RE 32

> *In the spiritual life we receive according to our desires. In the sphere of rights we make a claim to something we need in order to secure a satisfactory human life as an equal among equals. And in the economic sphere is born that which unites people in terms of feeling: that is, solidarity or brotherhood. The more this sense of solidarity is cultivated, the more fruitful economic life becomes. And the impulse towards solidarity arises when we establish a certain connection between our property and another's, between our need and another's, between something we have and something another has, and so on.*
>
> *Here we are brought back to two fundamental elements of human life. Capacities belong to the human power of imagination because, since we must act consciously, our capacities in the first instance arise out of our power of imagination, our thought-will. Of course, the power of imagination must be continually fired and filled with enthusiasm, by feeling, but feeling alone is powerless if the fundamental imagination is absent. Therefore, the question of a person's efficiency or practical skill brings us in the last instance to the question of imagination. It becomes evident . . . that care must be taken to enable people to realize their power of imagination in social life. The other element that has to be allowed free play has more to do with the will. Will power, which is connected with desire, the craving for something or other, is a fundamental force in the human being.* SF 59-60

Labor as a Rights or Equity Issue Rather Than an Economic One

Labor should not be treated as a commodity to be bought and sold in the marketplace. Only the regulation of goods and services, the results of human labor, should concern economic life. A contract between an employer and employee ought to be based on an equitable division of the goods or services produced. The idea that a wage is the price of labor is a false one. Labor itself is a matter of rights and should be fully protected by an independent legal or political system. Removing labor from the economic sphere will help society shift the economy from self-interested drives to concern for others.

Consider how far people have fallen away from right thinking! For this reason they often find things absurd that must, nevertheless, be said because they are true. Let us suppose that some people give themselves up to sports from morning till evening, that they make it their occupation. They expend exactly the same labor-power as people who chop wood, and in exactly the same manner. What is important in this context is the use of one's strength in working for the community at large. Athletes do not do this; the most that can be said of them is that they make themselves strong; only, as a rule, they do not turn their strength to account. Generally, it is of no importance to the community whether people engage in sports, by which they tire themselves as much as by chopping wood. Chopping wood, however, is of some use. All this is to say that the use of labor-power has no importance socially, but what results from such use has a meaning in social life. We must look at the result of the application of labor. That is valuable to the community. Hence, the only thing that can be of value in economic life is the product of labor-power, and the only thing with which the administration of economic life can have any concern is the regulation of the comparative values of products. Labor must lie quite outside the economic sphere. It belongs to the sphere of equity, of which we shall speak tomorrow, in which every adult human being has a right to make him or herself heard, on equal terms with every other human being. The manner and duration and the kind of work will be determined by the legal conditions prevailing between the people involved.* *SF 42-43*

Workers have realized that goods belong in commerce but labor does not. If you take goods to the market, you can sell them and return home with the proceeds, but if you sell your labor, you cannot simply take your money and go home; you have to show up and work. *FTSF 10*

---

* Editor's Note: Labor-power refers to the productive powers of workers, or more specifically, their capacity or ability to work.

Let us turn for a moment to what is perhaps one of the most discussed topics nowadays and a principal source of the errors that find their way into economic science. People talk of "wages," and they talk of them in such a way as to make them look like the price of labor. If the so-called wage earners have to be paid more, they say that the price of labor has gone up. If they have to be paid less, they say that labor is cheaper. They actually speak as though a kind of sale and purchase took place between the wage earners who sell their labor and those who buy it from them. But this sale and purchase is fictitious. It does not in reality take place. *RE 79-80*

It is not merely a sin against the social order, but a sin against the truth, if, for example, daily work proceeds on the assumption that human labor-power (I have often said this here) is a commodity. It can be made to seem so, indeed: but this seeming results in pain and suffering for human society, and sets the stage for convulsions and revolutions in economic life. *IASQ 52*

I have often pointed out how in modern times labor-power has become a commodity. Ordinary wage contracts are based on that; they derive from the assumption that labor-power is a commodity, and they are determined by the amount of labor that the worker renders to the employer. A healthy relationship will arise only under the following conditions: the contract must by no means be settled in terms of so much labor; the labor must be treated as a rights-question, to be fixed by the political state; and the contract must be based on a division of the goods produced between the manual workers and the spiritual workers. Such a contract can be based only on the goods produced, not on the relationship between workers and employer. That is the only way to put the thing on a healthy footing.

People ask: whence come the social evils that are associated with capitalism? They say these evils come from the capitalist economic system. But no evils can arise from an economic system: they arise first of all because we have no real labor laws to protect labor; and further because we fail to notice that the way in which workers are denied their due share amounts to a living lie. But what does this denial depend on? Not on the organization of economic life, but on the fact that the social order permits the individual capacities of the employer to be unjustly rewarded, at the workers' expense. The division of proceeds ought to be made in terms of goods, for these are the joint products of the spiritual and the manual workers. But if you use your individual capacities to take from people something that ought not to be taken, what are you doing? You are cheating them, taking advantage of them! One need only look these circumstances straight in the face to realize that the trouble does not lie in capitalism, but in the misuse of spiritual capacities. IASQ 66-67

Fostering Altruism by Overcoming Labor as a Commodity

When owners or managers of businesses treat labor as a commodity, they are not motivated to provide adequate support for their workers. This treatment of labor as a commodity is a vestige of ancient slavery, when the whole human being was literally bought and sold. Today, just part of the human being is bought: his or her labor.

Take a look at ancient Greece. What was work in those days? Workers stood in an entirely different relation to their master. At that time, work was slavery. Workers could be compelled by force to work. What they received from their master was their living. But their master took the proceeds of the work; it had nothing whatever to do with the particular relation of the workers to their master. They had to work; moreover, they were maintained under precarious conditions; they were not compensated for the things they did. There we have labor under duress, without pay . . .

Look at today's situation. Today we have jobs for which workers are partly compensated – partly. What they bring in flows as profit into the pockets of the entrepreneur . . . So we have labor that is half compelled and half voluntary. SPS 59-60

Greek civilization unfolded on the basis of slavery . . . It was Christianity which freed people from slavery and led them

> *to recognize, at least in principle, that all human beings are equal before God, as to their soul. For this was the principle which uprooted slavery out of the social order of humanity . . . One thing has been retained, namely the possibility in our social order for a part of the human being to be bought and sold as a commodity . . . The salient point of the social question . . . is the fact that human labor-power can be paid for. This too creates at the very foundation of all our social order the character of egoism. For egoism cannot but prevail . . . if, to obtain what they require for their own needs, people must sell their labor. They are obliged to earn money for themselves.* *FSDT, Lecture 5*

When people have to sell their labor to meet their needs in life, self-interest motivates their work, and egoism prevails.

> *I have previously stated publicly: human beings already live by the principle of egoism as soon as they live according to the principle: I must be paid personally; I must be personally compensated for the work I do. Or concealed egoism: all of you must be personally compensated, since the work you do must also be paid for.* *TEL, FSL 10*

> *Now, on the basis of our current mode of thinking, there is an attitude on the basis of which what we have been talking about seems downright absurd. Why? Because today one is convinced that a great part, far and away the greatest part, of human life must be based on egoism. To be sure, in theory and words one won't agree, but in practice one will soon admit this. And one will admit it in the following way: One says it is altogether natural that people should be compensated for their labor, that workers personally receive payment for their work – and yet this is nothing more than the extension of egoism into economic life. We are living out of egoism as soon as we live by the principle that we must be personally compensated, that I must be paid for the work I do . . .* *SSSQ, FSL 13*

If work and income can be separated, our labor can become a free or voluntary offering to society based on the needs of our fellow human beings, out of a spirit of love. Our labor will become a loving sacrifice, having nothing to do with self-interest or compensation. In turn, we will receive support and sustenance thanks to the free sacrifice of others in the community. This shift is crucial for positive social transformation. Only in this way will the altruism inherent in the division of labor be met with an equivalent altruism in our motivation for work. Only such a shift will allow us to stand in harmony with human evolution, which is moving from slavery, to wage slavery, to freedom.

> *This is the next and necessary stage – after the overcoming of slavery – it must be made impossible for anyone's labor to be a commodity. This is the true salient point of the social question . . . In future, people will only buy and sell commodities – outer objects, things separate from human beings themselves – while (as I wrote already in my essay on "Theosophy and the Social Question" which appeared in 1905) one person will work for another motivated by brotherly love.*
>
> *It may be a long way to attain this end. Yet this and this alone will solve the social question. Those who do not believe today that this must come about are like those who would have said, at the time of the origin of Christianity: "There must always be slaves." Even as they would have been wrong at that time, so likewise today those are wrong who say: "Labor must always be paid for." At that time it seemed unimaginable that a certain number of people should not be slaves. Not even Plato or Aristotle could conceive of such a thing. Today the cleverest of people cannot conceive of a society in which labor would have quite another value – quite another meaning – than that of earning money. Needless to say, even then the product will proceed from the labor; but the product alone will be able to be bought and sold. Socially, this very fact will be the salvation of humanity.* FSDT, Lecture 5

> *The course of human evolution calls for the eradication of paid labor and its replacement by free or volunteer labor*

instead of working for a living so one's needs can be met. This can be done only if work and income are separated, if I give over what I produce to others and my needs are met through society.

And the course of evolution leads in the direction of completely voluntary work . . . Just as Greek laborers did their work under the compulsion of their master and a present-day laborer works under the compulsion of wages, just so in the future only freedom will obtain. In the future labor and compensation will be completely separated.

That will constitute the health of social conditions in the future. You see it already today. Work will be a voluntary performance out of the recognition of necessity, out of the realization that it must be done. People will perform it because they will look at a person and see what that person needs. What was labor in antiquity? It was tribute; it was performed because it had to be performed. And what is the labor of the present time? It is based on self-interest, on the compulsion that egoism exerts on us. Because we want to exist, we want our labor to be paid for. We work for our own sake, for the sake of our pay. In the future we will work for our fellow human beings, because they need what we can provide . . . We will clothe our fellow men; we will give them what they need – as a completely free activity. From this, compensation must be completely separated. Labor in the past was a tribute, in the future it will be sacrifice. It has nothing to do with self-interest, nothing to do with compensation. If I base my labor on consumer demand, on what humanity needs, I stand in a free relation to labor, and my work is a sacrifice for humanity. Then I will work with all my powers, because I love humanity and want to place my capacities at its disposal.

That has to be possible, and is possible only when one's living is separated from one's labor. And that is going to happen in the future. No one will be the owner of the products of labor. People must be educated to do voluntary work, one for all and all for one . . . *SPS 60-61*

Now, from all that I have presented to you as examples . . . this question will be obvious to you. "How can the situation be otherwise if money is really only a means for acquiring power?" This is already answered in that fundamental social principle I introduced last week because that is a peculiarity of what I introduced to you as a sort of social science taken from the spiritual world. It is just as certain as mathematics . . . what I introduced to you as a social science derived from spiritual science is much like the theorem of Pythagoras . . . So it is with the fundamental principle I introduced to you as underlying social science and social life. Everything that people acquire in such a way that it is received in exchange for their work within the social system has an unwholesome effect. A wholesome condition results within the social system only when human beings have to support their life, not by their own work, but from other sources within society. This seemingly contradicts what I have just said, but only seemingly. What will render work valuable will be the fact that it will no longer be remunerated . . .

The goal toward which we must work . . . must be that of separating work from the provision of the means of existence. I have recently explained this. When people are no longer recompensed for their work, then money will lose its value as a means for acquiring power over work. There is no other way of overcoming the misuse that has been perpetrated with mere money than by forming the social structure in such a way that no one is recompensed for his or her work, and that the provision of the means of existence comes from an entirely different source. It will then naturally be impossible to use money for the purpose of compelling anyone to work . . .

In the future money must never be the equivalent of human labor, but only of inanimate commodities. Only inanimate commodities will be acquired in future by means of money, not human labor. CT 59-60

Every institution in a community of human beings that is contrary to this [fundamental social] law will inevitably engender in some part of it, after a while, suffering and want. It is a fundamental law which holds good for all social life with the same absoluteness and necessity as any law of nature within a particular field of natural causation. It must not be supposed, however, that it is sufficient to acknowledge this law as one for general moral conduct, or to try and interpret it into the sentiment that everyone should work for the good of others. No – this law only finds its living, fitting expression in actual reality, when a community of human beings succeeds in creating institutions of such a kind that those who are active within them can never claim the results of their own labor for themselves, but these results all, down to the last fraction, go wholly to the benefit of the community. And each individual, again, must be supported in return by the labors of others. The important point is, therefore, that working for others, and the goal of obtaining a certain income, must be kept apart, as two separate things. *ASQ 33*

Ways to Overcome Paid Labor

In a healthy economy, an employee will be seen as the employer's collaborator in the production of goods, rather than as an object of exploitation for the employer's maximum personal gain. A helpful image in any effort to decommodify labor is that of the entrepreneur and worker as parts of a supply chain in which the worker produces something which the entrepreneur then purchases. The entrepreneur's knowledge of the market and other entrepreneurial expertise then add value to the product.

The social relationship between the worker and the entrepreneur is significantly different, depending on whether labor is treated as a commodity that is sold to the entrepreneur or whether the workers and owners function as independent contractors, each providing essential services in an economic supply chain.

The production of goods comes about through the collaboration of the employer and employee. The worker receives one part of the equivalent value of these goods, the employer the other. It is the product of this collaboration which enters economic circulation. For the goods to be produced, a legal relationship is necessary between worker and employer. But capitalist economics can turn this relationship into one determined by the employer's economic power over the employee. In a healthy social organism it must be clear that work itself cannot be paid for – work cannot receive an economic value as if it were a product. Only the product itself, the result of the work, can be assigned an economic value in relation to other products. The nature and extent of the work which a person carries out in service of society must be determined by his or her capacities and the requirements of human dignity. This can only occur if work is regulated by the political state independently of economic management. *TSR 53*

We cannot really exchange labor for anything because between labor and anything else there is no possibility of reciprocal determination of value. We may fancy that we are paying for labor; we may even actualize this fancy by letting in the wage nexus. But we do not really do anything of the sort. In reality, even in the labor or wage nexus, it is values that are exchanged. Workers produce something directly and deliver a product, and it is this product that the entrepreneur [Unternehmer] really buys from them. In actual fact, down to the last penny, the entrepreneur pays for the products that the workers deliver. It is time we began to see these things in their right light. Entrepreneurs buy products from workers; and after they have bought the products it is their business to impart to them a higher value, by making use of the conditions present in the social organism and by their own enterprising spirit. It is really this that gives them their profit. They gain on the transaction because, having bought the commodities from the workers, they are able by their "knowledge of the market" (we must not shirk unpleasant expressions) to enhance the value of the commodities. *RE 80-81*

I have already said that the wage laborers do not in reality receive what is generally understood by the idea of "wages," but they really sell the products of their labor for dollars and cents to the business manager, and thus receive payment. It is only through their expert knowledge of the market that the managers give the proper value – or at any rate a higher value – to that which they buy from the laborers. Economically considered, the profit is not extracted from the labor as a surplus value. By thinking in terms of economics we cannot possibly arrive at such a judgment. We can arrive at it, at most, by a moral judgment. The business profit occurs because the laborers are in a less favorable social situation. The products the laborers sell have less value at the point where they sell them than at the point where the managers sell them, who are in a different position – they know the circumstances far better, and can sell at a greater advantage. The worker's relation to the manager resembles that of a man who goes to the market and buys a commodity for a given price. He must buy it there, for the simple reason that his circumstances will not allow him, let us say, to buy it anywhere else. Another person may perhaps be able to buy it for less at another place. The two cases are exactly the same. Economically speaking, what exists between the manager and the wage laborer is simply a kind of market.

It does make a certain difference, undoubtedly, whether I am fully conscious that this is the case, or whether I imagine that I am paying the laborers for their labor. You may think the difference merely theoretical, but let such a view of things – or two such views, the one and the other – become real. Let them be realized, and you will see how the economic relationships change under the influence of the one view or the other. What happens between human beings is, among other things, the result of their mental outlook, of the ideas they entertain. As our mental outlook changes, it changes the course of events. *RE 98-99*

To highlight a healthy relation between work and income, Rudolf Steiner offers examples of what could be called salary arrangements, to the extent that payment of funds is a general amount not specifically tied to quantity of time worked or number of goods produced. However, unlike our usual understanding of salary, in Steiner's example, economic support comes before work is completed. In this way, money is given to meet the individual's needs, and is not directly connected to the work. To be clear, although Steiner's example looks at state employees specifically, he was in no way suggesting that every worker should be a paid employee of the state.

> *. . . you will find in the beginning of my booklet ("Anthroposophy and the Social Question") . . . something which ought to work as a social axiom. I endeavored to point out that no form of social structure can flourish in which the principle of direct payment for human labor is introduced . . . Human beings must not be paid for their labor. Their labor belongs to humanity, and their means of existence must be created along other channels, not through payment for their labor. I should like to say, my dear friends, as I have already said in this little book, that if the principle of militarism (minus the state) could be carried over to this sphere of the social order, a very great deal would be gained. But behind this must be the insight that it immediately produces unhealthiness in social life when human beings are so placed into society that they are paid for their labor according to whether they do much or little. People must derive their means of existence from a society quite differently constituted. Soldiers receive their maintenance [salary], then they have to work; but they are not paid directly for their work, but because, as human beings, they hold a certain position. That is the point. That, my dear friends, is the most essential social principle: that the product of labor should be completely separated from the salary, at least in a certain sphere of social relationships. So long as this is not clearly perceived, we shall not realize anything really social . . . For in a healthy society the product of labor must be completely separated from the provision of a salary. Civil servants, if they did not become bureaucrats through a deficiency of ideas, soldiers, if they did not become militarists through poverty of ideas, are in a certain respect – please do not misunderstand me, I say "in a certain respect" – the ideal of social relationships. And it is no ideal social relationship, but the very contrary, for a person to work, not for the community but for him or herself. That, my dear friends, is the introduction*

of the principle of selfishness into society. Those who only understand egoism and altruism in a sentimental sense, understand nothing. But they know the truth who see, in a practical manner, with their healthy human understanding, without sentimentality, that every society must of necessity collapse if people work only for themselves – or if, in other words, they see what it is that is purely egoistic in the social order.

That, my friends, is a law which works as surely as the laws of nature work, and one simply must know it . . . The work of the community must be so organized that the product of labor belongs to society, and so that the means of subsistence are created not as the reward for labor, but through the structure of society. *HBFJSQ, Lecture 8, 19-21*

THREE

The Threefold Social Organism

The health of the social organism depends upon its articulation into three independent spheres: a spiritual-cultural sphere, a legal or rights-sphere, and an economic sphere. RSO 13

There must be Liberty in the spiritual and judicial domain, the domain of religion, education and jurisprudence. There must be Equality in the administration, in the government, the services of public security. There must be Fraternity in the economic domain. FSDT 58

THREE

The Threefold Social Organism

Rudolf Steiner identifies human society as a living organism, which is threefold in nature. The three domains of human social life that form this living organism are the cultural/spiritual life, rights or political life, and economic life. In order to promote greater health in each domain and in society as a whole, we must work to make our outer structures and inner attitudes harmonious with this threefold reality and the principles that govern each domain. Steiner's sociology seeks to guide us toward this harmony by providing a comprehensive framework for understanding social life, diagnosing its illnesses, and prescribing healing gestures.

Social threefolding harmonizes any apparent contradictions among the great social ideals of the French Revolution: liberty, equality, and fraternity. These ideals can seem contradictory when imagined in the context of a centralized state, or a society in which the three streams of social life are muddled together chaotically. However, they become attainable and harmonious when each of the three domains of the social organism is self-determining, with its own dynamics, administration, and governing principles. Each domain or 'limb' draws its strength from one of the French ideals, so that freedom or liberty becomes the basis of an independent cultural life, equality becomes the basis of an independent rights or political life, and fraternity (brotherhood, solidarity, mutuality) becomes the basis of an independent economy. Unity of the social organism is possible when each of the separate domains works collaboratively but contributes its own unique qualities for the good of society.

For more than a century, people have talked about equality, liberty, and fraternity as the three great social ideals or impulses for humankind. The highly intelligent people of the nineteenth century, who proved that these ideals could not possibly be achieved had been hypnotized by the idea of the centralized state, and therefore saw these ideals as contradictory. But now it is time to implement these ideals and to take up these threefold social impulses, which can only be done in the context of the threefold social organism. In a self-determining domain of cultural and intellectual affairs, individual capacities must develop on the basis of freedom. In the sphere of rights, which includes employer-employee relationships, the prevailing principle must be the inherent equality of all human individuals. And the economy must be governed by the true sister-and-brotherliness that can flourish only in cooperative associations, whether of consumers or producers.

Liberty, equality, and fraternity will each be able to prevail in one of the members of the threefold body social. Liberty will thrive in cultural and intellectual affairs, equality in a democratic sphere of rights, and fraternity in economic activity. *FTSF 18*

. . . Liberty in spiritual matters; Equality in the State (for if you will, one third may continue to be called so); and Fraternity in relation to the economic life. I know well-written books which rightly emphasize that the three ideals, Liberty, Equality, and Fraternity contradict one another; it is true, Equality decidedly contradicts Liberty. Very clever writers said this even in 1848 or even earlier. If we muddle everything together these things contradict one another. There must be Liberty in the spiritual and judicial domain, the domain of religion, education and jurisprudence. There must be Equality in the administration, in the government, the services of public security. There must be Fraternity in the economic domain. In the economic domain we have property, which must however be correspondingly developed in the future. In the domain of public security and administration we must have Equity or Right. In the domain of spiritual life and jurisprudence we must have Liberty. When divided into a trinity, these things are not in contradiction with one another. For here the things that

contradict one another in thought are still in accordance with reality, because in the reality they are distributed to the different domains. Mere thought burrows for contradictions; but reality lives in contradictions. We cannot grasp reality if we cannot grasp the contradictions, follow them and deal with them in our thoughts. *FSDT Lecture 2*

At the end of the eighteenth century, under circumstances different from those we live in now, the call for a new social structure arose from the underground depths of human nature. The motto of this urge to reconstruct society rang out as: Liberty, Equality, Fraternity. Anyone examining the realities of human evolution with an open mind and healthy common sense will easily understand all that lay behind this call. But during the nineteenth century some clever thinkers tried very hard to show the impossibility of realizing ideals of fraternity, equality, and liberty within a unified social organism. They believed that these three impulses would inevitably be at odds with each other. The clever point was made, for instance, that realizing equality would render individual freedom impossible. One can do no other than agree with those who pointed out this contradiction – and yet, at the same time, our human sensibility leads us to sympathy with every one of these ideals!

This contradiction is due to the fact that the true social significance of these three ideals only comes into its own when we understand the necessity of a threefold structuring of the social organism. The three 'members' of society should not be cobbled together and centralized in an abstract parliamentary bill or other theoretical form, but should be a living reality. Each of the three members should be self-determining, centered within itself; and only through the dynamics of their separate yet collaborative working can the unity of the social organism come about. What seems to be paradoxical then becomes a living unity. People will only grasp the true nature of the social organism when they are able to perceive how it can embody fraternity, equality and freedom through a living, threefold structure. Then they will see that collaboration in the economic sphere depends on brotherliness arising through economic associations. In the second sphere, that of civil rights, where we are dealing with purely human relationships between people, the ideal of equality should be striven for. And in the sphere of spirit or mind, which has relative autonomy within the social organism, the ideal of freedom can be realized. Seen in this light, these three ideals are real, attainable values. They cannot be realized, though, in a chaotic society where these three streams are muddled and mingled, but only in a healthy, threefold social organism. Nor can an abstract, centralized social order make liberty, equality, and fraternity real. Each separate member of the social organism must draw its separate strength from one of these impulses only, and then each will be able to contribute its own quality and life to collaboration with the others. *TSR 60-62*

Healthy Social Life is Threefold

Within the human being, there are also three aspects to social life. In order to best contribute to the well-being of the community, individuals must be able to develop their unique talents and capacities, to live and work in peace and harmony with their fellow human beings, and to find and pursue work that will serve the community. In this way, the question of a healthy social life consists of three corresponding and interrelated questions or perspectives: the cultural, legal, and economic.

If we contemplate life itself, we shall find that human social life is threefold. Three aspects are clearly distinguished in all individuals when we consider them as members of human society. If they are to contribute their share, as they certainly must, to the well-being of the social order in modern society, if they are to add to the welfare of the community by cooperating in the production of values, of commodities, they must first of all possess individual capacities, individual talents, abilities. In the second place, they must be able to live at peace with others and to work harmoniously with them. Thirdly, they must be able to find their proper place, from

> *which they can further the interests of the community by their work, by their activity, by their achievements.*
>
> *With respect to the first of these, individuals are dependent on human society for the development of their capacities and talents, for the training of their intellect, so that the educated intelligence in them may become at the same time their guide in their physical work.* *SF 17-18*

> *In these lectures we shall have to learn to look at the social question as a cultural question, as one of law, of the state or politics, and as an economic question.*
>
> *The spirit must give the answer to the question: How can human beings be made strong and capable, so that a social structure may arise without the present evils, which are unjustifiable [such as human exploitation, wealth inequity, and political conflicts]?*
>
> *The second question is: Under the advanced conditions of the present economic life, what is the political system or system of equity, which can lead people to live in peace again?*
>
> *The third is: What social structure will enable individuals to find the place from which they can work for the human community and its welfare, as well as their nature, their talents and capacities permit? We shall be led to the answer by the question: What credit can be attached to the personal value of a human being? Here we see the transformation of the economic system out of new conditions.*
>
> *A cultural, a political, and an economic problem are all contained in the social question, and we shall see that the smallest detail of that question can only appear in its true light when we look at it as a whole, fundamentally, in these three aspects: cultural, legal-political, and economic.* *SF 23-24*

The health of the whole of society is dependent upon separating culture, politics, and the economy. Administrative representatives of these three domains need to come together to work out common issues, in a manner similar to the diplomacy and collaboration that takes place between heads of state. In this way, each domain would have a healthy balance of autonomy and influence, unlike our current society wherein these domains are muddled together and can overtake each other with their influence and power. While healthy boundaries and relations between domains do not in themselves guarantee perfection or happiness, they are an important prerequisite for the individual's development of a meaningful existence.

> *The health of the social organism depends upon its articulation into three independent spheres: a spiritual-cultural sphere, a legal or rights sphere, and an economic sphere. Far from dividing people into three social strata, the articulation will allow them to participate in all three spheres according to their interests as whole human beings. The separation will be such that in the cultural or legal spheres, for instance, no decision can be made concerning problems arising within the economy. In the unitary state, where the three systems are intertwined, an economic group will have the power to legalize its interests and declare them public rights. In the threefold organism this can never happen, because economic interests can play themselves out only within the economic cycle, and there will be no possibility of impinging on the legal sphere.*
>
> *The greatest possible guarantee that one sphere of the threefold organism cannot be violated by another lies in their union, effected by the total corporate body consisting of the delegates of the three central administrations and agencies. For these central administrative committees will have to deal with actual developments within their own spheres. They will not arrive at a situation where, for instance, the rights sphere or the cultural sphere would be impinged upon by the economic, because this would place them in opposition to the developments taking place in their several spheres. Should, however, the influence of one department over another become necessary, the factual basis for such influence can lie only in the sphere of common interest and not in the individual group's interest.*
>
> *No one should cherish the illusion that any social institution could ever create an "ideal situation." What can be attained, however, is a viable, healthy social organism.*

Anything beyond that must be found through something other than social development. It is not the task of this articulation to guarantee "happiness," but rather to find the living conditions needed by a healthy social organism. Within it, however, people must be able to seek what they need to lead a dignified human existence. Nor does the healthy physical organism create from within itself the kind of culture which only the soul can unfold from its own depths; but a diseased organism prevents the soul from doing so. Thus a healthy social organism can only provide the prerequisites necessary for all that human beings must nurture and develop through their own capabilities and needs.

Anyone who descries as utopian or as mere ideology what reveals itself to be a guideline for social development, and wants to leave everything to evolution, resembles a person who becomes indisposed because he sits in an unventilated room and refuses to open a window while waiting for the stale air to renew itself.

The merger of cultural life and economics with the state would rob democracy of its real foundations. Anyone desiring genuine democracy will insist on granting the cultural and the economic spheres self-determination. *RSO 13-14*

. . . In the healthy social organism, therefore, alongside the economic system and independent from it, a separate realm must exist in which the life of rights and legal regulation between people unfolds and is cared for. But this life of rights is something intrinsic to the political realm, to government and the state. If people carry the interests which they serve in the economic realm into the legal structure and government of the state, the laws and rights which come about as a result will only express these economic interests. If, therefore, the constitutional function of the state is ruled by economic factors, it will lose the capacity to regulate the legal relationships between people. Its measures and organizational forms will have to serve the need for commodities, and will thus become divorced from the impulses which should sustain rights and legal regulation . . .

> *This complete separation of the life of rights from economic life is one rooted in the real nature of human life. Of course, people involved in economic life also have awareness of their rights. But it is on the basis of these latter alone, uninfluenced by economic interests, that they will administer legal matters; they will keep all such matters within the realm of political and legal jurisdiction, which will have no direct involvement in economic life. Such a political state will have its own legislative and administrative bodies, both structured to promote a modern awareness of human rights. It will be based on the impulses in human consciousness which are nowadays referred to as democratic. The economic realm will also form its own, separate legislative and administrative bodies, in line with purely economic factors. The necessary exchanges between the administrators of the legal and economic spheres will take place along lines similar to the negotiations between the governments of different countries. This structure, and clear distinction between spheres of activity, to exert the right kind of influence on each other. As things are at present, this is hindered by the fact that one sphere tries to develop aspects within itself which should really flow towards it from another.* TSR 46-48

National and International Relations

Within a given country, the administrations of each of the three domains – cultural, political, and economic – need to meet together to discuss mutual concerns. On an international level, each domain is free to interact and collaborate independently with representatives of the corresponding domains of other countries. This freedom of relationship can help promote peace between nations, because national boundaries become secondary to shared interests.

> *These three [sectors] should confront one another just as independent states do today. They should deal with one another through representatives, ordering their mutual relationships, but in themselves they should enjoy independent sovereignty.* FSDT Lecture 3

> *The internal structure of the healthy social organism also results in a threefold structure of international relations. Each of the three realms will have an autonomous relationship to the corresponding realm of other social organisms. Relationships between the economic spheres of different countries will not be directly influenced by relationships between their respective political spheres. And likewise, the relationship between the political spheres of different countries will, within certain limits, develop in complete independence from economic relationships.*
>
> *Since this independence is there from the start of such relationships, they will have a balancing, calming effect upon one another whenever disputes or conflicts arise. Mutual interests between different social organisms will ensure that national boundaries are of only secondary importance where human cooperation and coexistence are concerned. The spiritual, cultural spheres of separate countries will be able to develop relationships with one another that are based only on a shared life of the mind and the spirit . . . The people of one language region will not come into unnatural conflict with those of another as long as they do not try to assert their own culture through political or economic means.* *TSR 103-104*

Nationalism grows within our individual souls as a natural bond with others who share a common identity, such as blood ties or language. This happens instinctually on the basis of self-centered commonality. As such, nationalism reveals itself as the highest level of egoism. However our feeling for internationalism can only emerge when we consciously develop love and understanding for all humankind, in reverent recognition of our differences. In this way, internationalism leads us to conscious concern for the well-being of all of humanity. Feelings of internationalism gradually permeate us through understanding-borne love. This loving understanding of the universality of humanity and our common needs, is the proper basis of production in a world economy.

> *. . . We become national, because the feeling of nationalism arises out of our own nature. Nationalism is a blossom*

on the growth of the individual human being who is of the same blood as his tribe, or is bound by other ties to his people. Nationalism grows naturally in people. It grows in them like bodily growth. They do not possess internationalism in this way. Internationalism is rather comparable to the feeling we acquire when we contemplate the beauty of nature; through this contemplation we are impelled to love, to revere, to understand, because it has become a reality to us, because it impresses itself on us, because we give ourselves up to it freely. Whereas we grow into our own nation because we are, so to speak, members of it, we learn to know other nations. They work on us indirectly through our knowledge of them, our understanding of them. We learn little by little to love them with understanding; and our feeling for internationalism grows in proportion to our learning to love and to understand mankind in its different peoples in their various countries. There are two absolutely distinct sources in human nature from which arise, respectively, nationalism and internationalism. Nationalism is the highest development of egoism. Internationalism is what permeates us more and more as we give ourselves to a wide understanding of human nature. We must regard the common life of human beings all over the civilized globe in this light, especially if we wish to come to a clear understanding of the conflicting element in these impulses, nationalism and internationalism. SF 132

. . . Human wants are international, only they comprise the opposite pole of that which is spiritually international. The internationality of the spirit must furnish the understanding, must permeate with love our understanding of other nationalities, and must be able to expand that love to internationalism in the sense already indicated. Egoism is equally international. Internationalism will only be able to establish a connection with world production when the latter springs from a common spiritual understanding, from a common spiritual conception of unity. Understanding of universal consumption will never arise out of the egoism of peoples. Only from a universal spiritual perception can

> *the capacities develop that proceed, not from egoism, but from love, and that, therefore, can govern production. What is the cause of the demand for a world economy? Owing to the growing complexity in the conditions of human life everywhere, and the consequent increasing similarity of human needs, it becomes ever more evident that human beings everywhere have the same wants.* SF 144

Transgressing Boundaries as a Main Cause of Social Problems

One of the primary causes of social problems is the transgression of one domain of social life into another. Domination of cultural and political life by economic interests is particularly strong in today's world. By wielding economic power over culture and politics, the capitalist has gained untold legal and other advantages and caused untold harm to cultural life and to human rights, including those of workers.

The solution to this problem is not to strip entrepreneurs of their creative freedom; the development of individual talent and initiative in the business world is crucial. Instead, economic influence on politics must be eliminated, and our legal system must be strengthened in favor of human rights. This can be achieved only by creating healthy structures and arrangements between the three domains of the social organism.

> *Whereas spiritual life has partly emancipated itself, the political organization has completely merged itself in the course of recent centuries with the powerful interests of the economic body. It has happened unnoticed, but in reality the two have become one. Economic interests and needs have found expression in public laws, and these are often held to be human rights. When scrutinized, however, they are found to be only economic and political interests and wants in the guise of laws. While, on the one hand, spiritual life demands its power, we find, on the other, that confusion has arisen in regard to the relation between legal and economic conditions. Large masses of the population throughout the civilized world*

include in their demands for the solution of the social problem a further fusion of the legal and economic organization . . .

Thus we see the necessity of thoroughly investigating the connection between law and politics and the economic life at present. Free spiritual life has partly emancipated itself and demands restitution of its original powers, but if the legal system continues to be ever more closely bound up with the economic system, the whole social organism will be thrown into disorder. SF 109-110

People ask: whence come the social evils that are associated with capitalism? They say, these evils come from the capitalist economic system. But no evils can arise from an economic system: they arise first of all because we have no real labor laws to protect labor; and further because we fail to notice that the way in which the worker is denied his due share amounts to a living lie. But what does this denial depend on? Not on the organization of economic life, but on the fact that the social order permits the individual capacities of the employer to be unjustly rewarded, at the worker's expense. The division of proceeds ought to be made in terms of goods, for these are the joint products of the spiritual and the manual workers. But if you use your individual capacities to take from someone something that ought not to be taken, what are you doing? You are cheating him, taking advantage of him! IASQ 66-67

Undoubtedly, along with the modern private capitalist form of industrial economy there have arisen social evils – evils that embrace the widest range of social life; but is this in any way a proof that they are a necessary consequence of this industrial system? An industrial system can, in and of itself, do nothing beyond putting people into life situations that enable them to produce goods for themselves or for others in a more or less efficient manner. The modern industrial system has brought the means of production under the power of individual persons or groups. The achievements of technology were such that the best use could be made of them by a concentration of industrial and economic power.

So long as this power is employed in the one field – the production of goods alone – its social effect is essentially different from what it is when this power oversteps its bounds and trespasses into the fields of law or culture. It is this trespassing into the other fields that, in the course of the last few centuries, has led to the social evils that the modern social movement is striving to abolish. Those who possess the means of production acquire economic power over others. This economic power has resulted in capitalists allying themselves with the powers of government, whereby they are able to procure other advantages in society, oppressing those who are economically dependent on them – advantages which, even in a democratically constituted state, are actually of a legal nature. This economic domination has led to a similar monopolization of the cultural life by those who hold economic power.

The simplest thing would seem to be to get rid of this economic predominance of individuals, and thereby do away with their dominance in the spheres of rights and spiritual culture as well. One arrives at this "simplicity" of social thought when one fails to remember that the combination of technological and economic activity afforded by modern life necessitates allowing the most fruitful possible development of individual initiative and personal talent within the business community. The form production must take under modern conditions makes this a necessity. Individuals cannot bring their abilities to bear in business if in their work and decision-making they are tied down to the will of the community. However dazzling the thought may be of individuals producing not for themselves but collectively for society, its justification within certain bounds should not hinder one from also recognizing the other truth: that collectively, society is incapable of giving birth to economic schemes that can be realized through individuals in the most desirable way. Really practical thought, therefore, will not look to find the cure for social ills in a reshaping of economic life that would substitute communal production for private management of the means of production. Rather, the endeavor should be to forestall evils

> *that may spring up along with management by individual initiative and personal talent, without impairing this management itself. This is possible only if neither the legal relationship among those engaged in industry, nor that which the spiritual-cultural sphere must contribute, are influenced by the interests of industrial and economic life.*
>
> *It cannot be said that those who manage the business of economic life can, while occupied by economic interests, preserve sound judgment on legal affairs and that, because their experience and work have made them well acquainted with the requirements of economic life, they will therefore be best able to settle legal matters that may arise within the workings of the economy. To hold such an opinion is to overlook the fact that a sphere of life calls forth interests arising only within that sphere. Out of the economic sphere one can develop only economic interests. If one is called out of this sphere to produce legal judgments as well, then these will merely be economic interests in disguise. Genuine political interests can only grow upon the field of political life, where the only consideration will be the rights of a matter. And if people proceed from such considerations to frame legal regulations, then the law thus made will have an effect upon economic life. It will then be unnecessary to place restrictions on individuals with respect to acquiring economic power; for such economic power will only result in their rendering economic services proportionate to their abilities – not in their using it to obtain special rights and privileges in social life.* *RSO 24-26*

Just as the inappropriate intrusion of economic interests into cultural life and politics creates illness in the social organism, so too does the inappropriate intrusion of political or cultural interests into the affairs of other domains.

Over the last few centuries, the three domains of social life have largely fused together into a single unified state. Contemporary social unrest is due to the fact that many people are struggling – often unconsciously – for a clear separation of the three domains of the social organism. Social threefolding will not damage the fundamental unity of the organism, because all human beings will have interests and influence in all three spheres, and the administrators of each domain can collaborate to harmonize their working relationships.

> *. . . An economy that governs the rights of human beings, and educates them according to its own interests, reduces the person to a mere cog in the economic machinery. It stunts the human spirit, which can develop freely only when it unfolds according to its own innate impulses.*
>
> *It stunts, too, those relations with our fellows that stem from our feelings, and refuse to be influenced by economic considerations – relations that are striving rather to be governed in accordance with the equality of all regarding what is purely human. When the political sphere or the sphere of rights controls the development of our individual abilities, it weighs on this development like a crushing burden. For the interests that arise out of these spheres must naturally produce a tendency to develop such abilities according to the government's needs and not according to their own proper nature, however good may be the original intentions to allow for individual characteristics. Such a legal or political sphere also imposes an alien character upon economic matters. Those subject to this kind of political system become, through constant tutelage, spiritually cramped and economically hampered in the pursuit of interests inappropriate to their own nature.*
>
> *A spiritual life that attempted to determine legal relations on its own terms would inevitably be led from the inequality of human abilities to inequality in the law. It would be false to its own nature if it were to allow itself to be determined by economic interests. Under such a spiritual culture, people would never come to a true consciousness of what, in reality, the spirit may be for human life, for they would watch the spirit degrade itself through injustice and falsify itself through economic aims.*
>
> *What has brought humanity to the present state of affairs in the civilized world is that during the last few centuries these three spheres have in many respects grown together*

into a single, unified state. And the cause of the present unrest is that an enormous number of people are struggling (while unconscious of the real nature of their striving) toward a de-limitation of these three spheres of life into separate systems of the social organism, so that the spiritual-cultural life may be free to shape itself according to its own spiritual impulses; that the sphere of rights may be built up democratically through the interaction (direct or representational) of people on equal terms; and that the economic life may extend solely to the production, circulation and consumption of commodities. *RSO 85-86*

Just as the legal sphere (the administration of the state) is regulated within the autonomous legal system of the social organism independent of the economy, so shall the life of spirit (the educational system) guide itself in perfect freedom within its independent spiritual organ of the social community. For just as a healthy economic life in the social organism cannot be fused with its legal system (where everything must be based upon the decisions of all co-equal adults), it is impossible for the spiritual life to be administered according to laws, regulations and controls that proceed from the opinions of all people who have merely come of age. The spiritual life requires a self-administration guided only by the best educational insights available. Only under such self-administration is it possible for the individual abilities latent in a community of people to be nurtured truly for the benefit of social life.

Anyone who examines impartially the real factors at work in present-day society can only conclude that the health of the organism requires its division into three independent systems: a spiritual, a legal and an economic. The unity of the organism will not thereby be endangered in any way, for this unity is securely grounded in reality by the fact that each human being has interests within all three parts of the system, and that (notwithstanding their mutual independence) the central authorities at the head of each will be able to harmonize their various measures. *RSO 56-57*

Cultural Freedom Begins with Educational Freedom

In a healthy society, individual capacities, developed through education and other cultural activities, are able to offer themselves to the needs of society at large. However, this is not possible if cultural life, and the educational system in particular, are harnessed to the interests and dictates of the economy or the state. Similarly, economic and political interests will undermine their own foundations and potential for progress if they attempt to control education and the broader intellectual and cultural life of society. With this awareness, the movement for social threefolding strives for a separation between school and state.

Although it was appropriate for the state to oversee the education of citizens at an earlier point in history, that time has passed. It is now essential that cultural life, including education, assume an independent basis. Those who mistake for freedom the slavery of state-run education hinder social transformation.

> *Today's social chaos has evolved because a cultural life that is so filtered, so abstract, loses all its impetus. It is now up to us to place cultural life on its own foundation once more, so that it can flourish again. We must find the way from spirit that is nothing but a thought, back to the creative spirit. An independent cultural life will be strong enough to come alive again. A spiritual, cultural life held in check by the leash of the church, or preserved and protected by the state, or staggering under the burden of commerce and the economy, cannot become fruitful for mankind. Only a free and independent spiritual life of culture can do so.* INE 42

> *All that comprises society in terms of economic life and rights awareness is also influenced by something which comes from a third source: the individual capacities of individual people. This realm encompasses everything from the highest spiritual achievements to a person's greater or lesser physical aptitude for the work he or she does, which serves the social organism. What derives from this source must flow into the social organism in a quite different way from that in which*

goods are exchanged or political rights and justice are dispensed. The social organism can only take up these individual capacities in a healthy way by allowing them free rein, and making them dependent solely on free human receptivity. If the human efforts and achievements arising through such capacities are artificially influenced by economic or political life, then they are deprived to a large extent of their vital essence. They can only flourish through their own innate power and effectiveness. If economic conditions or political organization determine the reception of such individual achievements, they are not freely received. But it is only through such open receptivity that they can enter the fabric of society in a healthy way. The life of the spirit and of the mind, with which the development of other individual capacities is so intimately interconnected, can only develop in a healthy way when it relies upon its own impulses, and when it establishes sympathetic connections with others who receive what it creates. *TSR 54-55*

. . . The state's control of education has been regarded for a long time as something entirely beneficial for humanity's progress. And people with socialistic ideas can hardly imagine society not educating the individual on its own terms, to serve it.

So people have little inclination to recognize something essential: that what might once, at an earlier stage of human history, have been right and proper can become misplaced and wrong at a later stage. It was a necessary stage in the development of human, social relationships for the circles which in medieval times oversaw education and culture to be relieved of this function, and for the state to take control. But to perpetuate this is a serious social error.

The first section of this book [Towards Social Renewal] *aims to demonstrate this. Within the framework of the state, cultural and spiritual life has grown towards freedom; but it cannot become fully free within these strictures. It needs to become autonomous. By its very nature, spiritual life is now asking to be a fully independent sector of the social organism. Education, from which all spiritual and cultural life emerges and develops, must be administered by the educators, without any interference from political or economic quarters.* *TSR 3-4*

The movement for the threefold social [organism] strives for the complete disassociation of the educational system from government and industry. *RSO 75*

[Comment from an audience participant] "Amongst us, the State really interferes very little in anything we may choose to do as regards our school-system."

[Rudolf Steiner's Response] Let me say to you, that people who talk in this way are the very best testimony to the necessity of emancipating our spiritual life. People who still have some sense of how unfree they are, are people for whom one can find much more use. But the people, who no longer have even a sense of their own lack of freedom, who take the State's educational ideas, that have been pumped into their heads, to come from their own inner freedom, and have not the faintest notion of how far this public-educational slavery extends – these are the people really, who are the drag upon everything. It is a question of taking hold of things by the right end. And people who, without knowing it, take slavery for freedom, are the people who, naturally, hinder us from moving forwards. *TOBS, Lecture 2*

While an independent cultural life will not be trouble-free, independent education, with teachers whose judgment is free of influence from other domains, will provide the best possibility for children to develop capacities that can be of real service to society. Consequently, the economic and political domains will then receive benefits otherwise unavailable to them.

One might object that even such a self-governing cultural and spiritual life will not avoid every pitfall, and will also be far from perfect. But we are not asking for perfection. All anyone can do is strive for the best that is possible. A child's developing capacities will truly come to serve

> *society only if those people oversee his education whose judgment is based on independent and purely educational perspectives. How far a child can be helped forward in one way or another is a decision that can be made only within an independent cultural community. And how to implement such decisions is also a matter for such a community alone. From such an independent source the state and the economy can then receive a strength and vitality which would be unavailable if they themselves shape cultural life according to their own perspectives.* TSR, 4

Education plays an instrumental role in overcoming the antisocial tendencies living within us. The cultivation of social sensitivity is as important for social health as the transformation of outer structures that promote antisocial behavior. Teachers must be free of constraints from other domains of society or they will lose touch with reality, unduly swayed by one influence or another, and will be in no position to cultivate social sensitivity in students.

> *. . . The antisocial tendencies of our time have arisen because people's social sensitivity and awareness is not developed through their education. Social sensitivity can only be developed through a kind of education that is guided and governed by people who are socially sensitive themselves. We will not begin to make headway with the social problems of our times until we see that the way in which we think about education and cultural life is a vital part of the equation. Antisocial tendencies are not only created through economic structures but also through people behaving in antisocial ways within these structures. And it is antisocial to let young people be educated by teachers who, by having the aims and content of their activity externally and artificially forced upon them, have become divorced from reality.* TSR, 5

The Economy and the Political State

If it is to function in a healthy manner, the economic sphere must accept what the democratic rights domain determines to be just and fair. This does not mean, however, that the state should control economic life any more than the rights domain should be controlled by economic interests. Rather, the healthy role of the rights or political domain is to provide the economic domain with the appropriate legal conditions necessary to operate fairly and without exploitation.

> *. . . In order to see clearly in the social question, the great error must be overcome . . . that we only need to revolutionize economic conditions and then everything will follow automatically. That error has arisen in consequence of the all-powerful modern development of economic life alone. It is as if people were under the influence of an idea, as if they were under the suggestion that economic life is the only power. As long as this suggestion holds sway they will never find the solution of the social problem. They will give themselves up to illusions, especially in proletarian circles. They will try to extract from the economic system what they call a just distribution of property. But this will only be achieved when there are people in the social organism with the ability to promote institutions through which economic needs can be satisfied. That can only happen when it is understood that the revolutionizing of the economic system is not the only thing necessary to satisfy the requirements of social life. People must first answer the question: Must not something else be there alongside the economic body in order that the economic life may be built up continuously in a social manner by people who have grown social in political and in cultural life? This is the truth that we must oppose to error and dogma, and those who look to economic life for the means of restoring health to the social organism must look instead to the spirit and to justice. There must be no vague dreams of justice growing out of the economic system; we must cultivate right thought in accordance with realities, and we must do so because justice and the consciousness of justice have retreated in later times before the advancing economic flood. For a social construction of society, we need the creation of a genuine political organism with the social impetus necessary for it.*
>
> *SF 73-74*

However, just as in a natural organism one single organic system would destroy itself through its specific activity if there were no other systems to keep it in balance, so does one function of the social organism need to be kept in balance by another. Work within the economic sphere would, over time, inevitably lead to comparable damage, unless it were counteracted by the political system of laws that must rest on a democratic basis, just as the economic life cannot. In the sphere of democratic law-making, politicking is appropriate. What is done there has the effect within economic activity of counteracting its innate tendency and causing damage. If one were to harness economic life to the administration of the state, one would deprive it of its efficiency and freedom of movement. Those engaged in economic work must receive the law from somewhere outside of economic life, and only apply it in economic life itself. *RSO 92*

On the one hand, economic life is subject to natural conditions (such as climate, geography, mineral resources, etc.), on the other it is also dependent on the legal and political conditions which the state creates between the people and groups of people engaged in the economy. Economic activity is thereby conducted within certain confines. Just as nature provides certain preconditions and resources which cannot be dictated by economic life, which are simply 'given,' so people's legal and political rights in a healthy social organism should be seen as something untouched by economic considerations, as something which has an autonomous, self-regulated existence. *TSR 48*

. . . When parliaments are composed of representatives of economic interests, majorities can always be found to pass resolutions affecting those interests and to make laws that have nothing whatever to do with that feeling for justice that exists between one person and another.

. . . The impulse for the organization of the threefold order must . . . demand in the most emphatic manner, the separation of politics, and the groundwork of the law, from the administration of economic affairs, of the economic circuit . . .

> *. . . What results as just and equitable from the resolutions taken on the basis of the democratic State is introduced into the economic sphere by those who are occupied in industry. But it is not their work to initiate this spirit and to make laws. They receive the law and carry it out in economic life.* SF 65-67

Implementing Social Threefolding

It is possible to begin to implement social threefolding immediately by forming economic associations. *[See Chapter 5 for more on economic associations.]* These new economic forms can exist side by side with old forms of business and interact with them. Over time, the merits of the associative way of working will reveal themselves, and the old ways will fall away.

In working with threefold ideas, perseverance is required in order to penetrate to the root causes of social problems. In the cultural domain, as the ideas of threefolding take hold, a true social intelligence can be awakened. This new intelligence can guide individuals toward a healthier society, with meaningful contributions to the three domains of social life. Constructive social change will be possible only when attention is directed beyond the outer institutions, the symptoms of problems, to the human beings who have designed and inhabited those institutions.

> *People who depend on their accustomed lines of thought will say, "These are very fine ideas, but how are we to make the transition from present conditions to the threefold system?" It is important to see that what has been proposed here can be put into practice without delay. One need only begin by forming such associations. Surely no one who has a healthy sense of reality can deny this is immediately possible. Associations based on the idea of the threefold social order can be formed just as readily as companies and consortia were formed along the old lines. Moreover, all kinds of dealings and transactions are possible between the new associations and the old forms of business. There is no question of the old having to be destroyed and replaced artificially by the*

new. The new simply takes its place beside the old; the new will then have to justify itself and prove its inherent power, while the old will gradually crumble away.

The threefold idea is not a program or system for society as a whole, requiring the old system to cease suddenly and everything to be "set up" anew. The threefold idea can make a start with individual enterprises in society. The transformation of the whole will then follow through the ever-widening life of these individual institutions. Because it is able to work this way, the threefold idea is not utopian. It is a force adequate to the realities of modern life.

The essential thing is that the idea of a threefold order shall stimulate a real social intelligence in the people of the community. The economic viewpoint shall be properly fructified by the impulses that come from the independent cultural and political spheres. The individual shall contribute in a very definite sense to the achievements of the community as a whole. Through the role the individual plays in the independent cultural life, through the interests that arise in the political and legal sphere, and through the mutual relations of the economic associations, his or her contribution shall be realized.

Under the influence of the threefold idea, the operation of social life will in a certain sense be reversed. Presently, one must look to the increase of one's capital or wages as a sign that one is playing a satisfactory part in the life of the community. In the threefold social order, the greatest possible efficiency of common work will result because individual faculties work in harmony with the human relationships founded in the legal sphere, and with the production, circulation and consumption regulated by the economic associations. Increase of capital, and a proper adjustment of work and the return upon work, shall appear as a final consequence of these social institutions and their activities.

The threefold idea would guide our transforming and constructive power from mere attempts at reform of social effects into the sphere of social causes. Whether one rejects this idea or makes it one's own will depend on summoning

> *the will and energy to work one's way through to the realm of causes. If one does this, one will cease considering only external institutions; instead, one's attention will be guided to the human beings who make the institutions.* RSO 47-49

The time has come to cultivate reunifying forces that can overcome the separateness brought about by the division of labor. Once social life is divided into the three independent realms of culture, politics, and economy, vibrant reunifying forces will flow from them to heal unhealthy social divisions.

> *. . . Modern life has brought about a division of labor in many spheres, for outer methods and institutions demand it. The effects of division of labor must be balanced by vital mutual relations among people in the community. Division of labor separates people; the forces that come to them from the three spheres of social life, once these are made independent, will draw them together again. This division of society has reached its zenith. This is a fact of experience, and it gives our modern social life its stamp. Once we recognize it, we realize the imperative demand of the age: to find and follow the path that leads to reunion.* RSO 49

All discussion about social threefolding will seem nonsensical until social life is liberated into its health-bringing threefold arrangement. The idea of threefolding will make sense only to the degree that the three systems actually have become separated. Our first task, then, is to liberate cultural and economic life from the chains of state control.

> *We must be wary of the people who are forever saying "But how about this, and how about that!" for the fact of the matter is, that we shall first be able to begin to discuss things sensibly, when we are a bit further on with the separation of the three systems; when we actually have thrown ourselves so completely into the [publicity] for the threefolding of the body social, that a sufficiently large number of people in economic life definitely know: "Nothing we can say has any sense, so long as we still continue to reckon on the whole of our economic life being arranged for us by the state. Only in*

> *proportion as we manage to free ourselves, will discussion begin to have any sense. Until then, everything we may say is nonsense." – And, in the same way, there is just as little sense in discussing reforms in the spiritual life, until it is clear, that one can't even begin to converse on the subject, before one is actually living in a free spiritual system. One must at least be fully aware, that so long as one is living in a spiritual system which is dependent on the state, all one may say can have no sense, – that, so long as this is the case, one cannot reform anything.* TOBS, Lecture 2

At the same time, for true social transformation to take hold, conscious feelings and sensibilities for the threefold nature of social life must arise in human beings. Such feelings for the social future of humanity must be fostered in the education of children. These sensibilities are as important as learning to add, subtract, multiply, and divide.

> *One might think that this book is underpinned by the belief that the social organism should be 'built up' on the basis of a lifeless theory 'lifted' from science. But that is as far as possible from my intention. I am suggesting something quite different: that the present crisis of mankind is asking for certain feelings and sensibilities to arise in every single individual; and that the stimulus for these feelings should be provided by the education system in the same way that all pupils learn the four processes in mathematics. The old social forms, which existed up to now without the conscious involvement of human feeling, will no longer be effective in the future. The evolutionary impulses trying to enter human life anew from the present day onwards consist partly in the need to develop the sensibilities of each individual in the same way that certain basic skills are already expected. From now on people will need to develop a healthy sense for the way in which the social organism should work if its forces are to be life-giving ones. People must come to feel that it is actually unhealthy and antisocial to be involved in this social organism without such feelings.*

Nowadays we often hear about 'socialization' as a necessary ingredient of our times. However, this socialization will not heal the social organism, will be mere quackery, perhaps even initiate a process of destruction, if human hearts and souls do not come to be informed by a knowledge – even if only instinctive – of the need for a threefold social organism. If it is to have a healthy effect, the social organism must develop three distinct members or systems. TSR 41

The Relation of the Physiological and Social Organisms

Rudolf Steiner developed a picture of the human physiological organism that is threefold. He identified three unique yet interrelated systems: the nerve-sense system centered in the region of the head, the rhythmic system centered in the chest region, and the metabolic system centered in the lower part of the body and the limbs. In a similar way, we can think about the social organism as three independent, yet interrelated systems. In both the physical and the social body, there is no overall centralization. In fact, the whole organism can be sustained only when each of the three systems works harmoniously with the others while at the same time preserving its autonomy. The aim of social threefolding ultimately is not to divide the areas of social life, but to find how they can be brought together in healthy harmony, just as the human body is healthy when its three systems work together harmoniously.

I would like to use a comparison to try to describe the impulses underlying a comprehensive, multifaceted observation of the social question. But please remember that this is no more than a comparison, as an aid to understanding how the social organism can grow healthier. If we look at the most complicated natural organism, the human organism, we can observe that it is composed of three systems that work alongside one another, each with a certain degree of independence. One can characterize each of these as follows: firstly the system that consists of nerves and senses. We could also call it the head organism, since nerves and senses have their central focus in that most important part of the human organism.

Secondly we must recognize what I would like to call the rhythmic system. This consists of breathing, blood circulation, and all that is expressed in rhythmic processes of the human organism.

The third system consists of all the organs and functions that are connected with metabolism as such.

These three systems contain everything which, properly organized, sustains the healthy functioning of the human organism . . . I am convinced that biology, physiology and all of science will, in the very near future, develop a view of the human organism in which these three functions – head system, circulatory or rhythmic system, and metabolic system – are seen as each preserving a certain autonomy in order to sustain the whole human organism, and that there is not, therefore, any absolute centralization. Also that each of these systems has a particular relationship to the outer world – the head system through the senses, the circulatory system through the breathing, and the metabolic system through the organs of digestion and movement . . . Healthy thinking, feeling, willing and wishing about the social organism can only develop when people are aware – even if only instinctively – that this social organism must be structured in a threefold way, just as the human organism is. TSR 38-40

The social organism is articulated like a natural organism. Just as the natural organism must take care of the process of thinking through its head and not through its lungs, so the social organism must be organized into systems. No one system can assume the work of the other; each must work harmoniously with the others while preserving its own integrity.

Economic life can only prosper if it develops according to its own laws and energies as an independent system within the social organism, and if it does not let confusion upset its structure by permitting another part of the social order – that which is at work in politics – to invade it. On the contrary, the political system must function independently alongside the economic system, just as in the natural organism breathing

> *and thinking function side by side. Their wholesome collaboration can be attained only if each member has its own vitally interacting regulations and administration. However, beneficial interaction falters if both members have one and the same administrative and regulatory organ. If it is allowed to take over, the political system is bound to destroy the economy, and the economic system loses its vitality if it becomes political.* *RSO 146-147*

> *The three members of the social organism must stand in the right relation to one another, so that they may work on one another in the right way.*
>
> *This is the real meaning of the threefold nature of the social organism – not the splitting apart of the three members; the splitting apart is always there. The point is rather to find how the three members can be brought together, so that they can really work in the social organism with inherent intelligence, just as the nerves and senses system, the heart and lungs system, and the metabolic system, for example, work together in our physical organism.* *RE 129*

We can develop a new way of thinking about the social organism by working with a true understanding of the threefold human being. We would, however, arrive at wrong conclusions if we were to try to force a strict analogy between the two organisms. Rather, the kind of thinking that is needed for an understanding of the social organism can be awakened by the kind of thinking needed for the study of the human organism.

Strict analogy based on materialistic physiology might lead us to conclude that the head system relates to the cultural life, the rhythmic system to the life of rights, and the metabolism to the economy, but we would be mistaken. In fact, a deeper study of the human organism reveals that the nerve-sense system is in a constant process of dying off. It needs life-giving nourishment from the metabolic processes. In like manner, the economy on its own brings destructive processes into social life and needs nourishment from an independent cultural-spiritual life if it is to be sustained. Just as the head system depends on the metabolism for life-giving forces, so too does the health of the economy, and ultimately all of social life, depend on an independent cultural life.

> *One can learn [impartiality] through the study of conditions which of their own nature elicit impartial judgment, and in which thinking therefore becomes its own corrective. The human organism affords such conditions.*
>
> *Of course, if only the conventional scientific concepts are applied as correctives, they will not go far. In many respects, these concepts lack the kind of force necessary to strike deep into the facts of nature. Yet if one tries to keep to nature herself, and not merely to these concepts of nature, one will be in a better position to learn impartiality than one would be amid party views. Despite the good will of many natural scientists who have endeavored to overcome materialist convictions, the usual concepts of natural science are today still strongly imbued with materialism. A spiritual contemplation of nature will shed this materialism; and spiritual contemplation of nature will provide means for the kind of training in thought which, among other things, makes it possible to comprehend social organisms.*
>
> *The idea of the threefold social order does not simply borrow facts from natural science and transplant them into the field of social life. It uses the study of nature only as a way of gaining the ability to observe social facts impartially. This should be kept in mind by those who learn about the idea in a superficial fashion – the threefold idea talks of a threefold division of social life in much the same way as one might talk of a threefold division of the natural human organism. Anyone who studies seriously the characteristics of the human organism will be made aware that the one cannot be simply transferred to the other. However, the method of study one is obliged to use on the human organism will awaken the kind of thinking that will enable one to find one's way among the social facts.* RSO 125-126

> *What really matters is to gain a clear understanding of social relations in this world. Real understanding of the*

natural threefold order of the human organism, of the way the human organism is an organism of nerves and senses, a rhythmical organism, and a metabolic organism, as shown in my book Von Seelenrätseln [Riddles of the Soul], *leads to a way of thinking that can also apply to social life. People of little understanding will say: 'You are using analogy in applying the threefold order of the human body to the social organism.' This is nonsense of course. Analogy is not the method used in* Towards Social Renewal. *All I said was that if people succeeded in letting their thinking escape from the strait-jacket put on it by modern scholarship and particularly public opinion, they would free their thinking to the extent that it will be possible to think sensible thoughts concerning social issues. The kind of thinking that puts the human brain side by side with the liver, examining everything as though it were of the same substance, will never come to sensible conclusions.*

Using external analogies we might say: The social organism is threefold by nature and so is the human organism. The head is the organ of mind and intellect; it should therefore be compared with the cultural and intellectual life in the threefold organism. The rhythmical system establishes harmony between different functions in the action of the heart, in respiration – that would be the rights sphere in the social organism. Metabolism, the most physical, material aspect – something mystics tend to look down on to some extent, though they say they also have to eat and drink – would be compared to the sphere of economics.

This is definitely not the case, however. I have repeatedly pointed out on other occasions that in reality things are very different than mere analogy would make them to be. It cannot be said, for instance, that summer is comparable to the waking state for the earth and winter to a state of sleep. The reality is different. In summer the earth is asleep, in winter it is awake. I have gone into this in detail.

The same applies if we consider the real situation in comparing the social and the human organism. The economic sphere of the social organism actually compares to the activities of the human head. As to the sphere of rights, the legal sphere, people were quite rightly comparing this, the middle realm, with rhythmical activities in the human organism. The life of mind and intellect however has to be compared with the metabolism. This means that economic life has to be compared with the organs that serve the mind and intellect, and the cultural and intellectual sphere of the social organism with the metabolic organs. There is no way round this. Economic life is the head of the social organism; cultural life is the stomach, liver and spleen of the social organism but not of the individual human being. It is of course too much of an effort for anyone whose thinking is in a strait-jacket to make distinctions between social life and the life of an individual person.

Again the essential point is that spiritual science prepares us to see things as they really are and not to produce analogies and elaborate symbolism. We will then arrive at important conclusions. We shall find, for example, that we can say: But in that case economic life, if it really is the head in the social organism, will have to live on the rest of the organism, just as the head does in the human organism. In that case we cannot say morality, religious life and the search for knowledge are ideological elements arising from economic life. Quite the contrary, in fact. Economic life is dependent on cultural life, on the metabolism of the social organism, just as the human head depends on respiration, on stomach, liver and spleen. We then come to see that economic life arises out of cultural and religious life. If we did not have a stomach we could not have a head. Of course we also could not have a stomach if we did not have a head, but it is the head after all that is fed by the stomach, and in the same way economic life is fed by cultural life and not the other way round. The socialist theories that now threaten to spread through the whole of the civilized world are therefore quite erroneous, a dreadful superstition. No one has thought to look for the truth in recent centuries; on a purely emotional basis everyone has been promulgating the kind of truth their class and point of view suggest to them. Now at last it is realized that it is a total delusion to see historical evolution as the product of the modes and relations of production. The idea is now to compare the actual facts and not to talk in analogies. Now a realistic view is taken and it is realized that if the stomach is undermined in the human organism, the head will suffer. In the same way there can be no sound metabolism in the social organism and economic life must fall into decline if morality, religious life and intelligent thought are undermined in the social organism. Nothing in fact depends on economic life; primarily everything depends on the views, the ideas, the cultural life of humankind.

The head is always dying – I have spoken of this in other lectures – and we only maintain the head organism because it is constantly dying and the rest of the organism rebels against this. The same applies in the sphere of economics. Economic life is constantly bringing death and decay into the progress of history; rather than generating everything else, it brings about the death of everything. This element of death constantly has to be counterbalanced by what the cultural organism is able to produce. The situation is therefore exactly the other way round. Anyone speaking in materialistic terms and saying economic life is the basis for progress is not speaking the truth. The truth is that economic life is the basis of something that is always dying in stages, and the mind and spirit have to make up for this dying process. To proceed the way people are now proceeding in Russia is to help the world to its death. The only possible outcome of proceeding in this way is to help the world to its death, for the simple reason that the laws of death are inherent in the things that are being done there.

You can see the eminent social importance of these things. We have now been working in anthroposophy for twenty years, and all the time I have tried to make it utterly clear and apparent in all kinds of lectures that what matters to us is not the cultivation of a philosophy full of inner self-gratification, a kind of spiritual snobbery, but to develop the most important impulse that is needed in the present age. *PEM, 61-64.*

True Social Renewal Requires a Change in Thinking

The social question is first and foremost a cultural one, in that it concerns transformation of the human mind.

> *The emptiness of modern intellectual life is the first aspect of the social question that we have to recognize . . .*
>
> *. . . The social question must in its first aspect be treated as a spiritual-cultural question. One question, above all, stands out before us today in letters of flame. How must the human mind be changed, in order that it may learn to master the social question?* SF 12-13

FOUR

Economic Science

[The nature of the evolution of economic life upon the Earth] consists of a series of successive stages, but one in which the earlier stages continue to exist side by side with the later . . . The phenomena of primitive phases of economic life are still here today, side by side with those that have attained a higher stage . . . But the more primitive processes are constantly penetrating into the more highly evolved ones. *RE 130*

FOUR

Economic Science

Rudolf Steiner used a descriptive, phenomenological approach to economic science. He insisted on the necessity of this approach because economic life is not a fixed entity, but rather a process which unfolds in perpetual movement. The economy involves an untold number of factors, including the thinking, feeling and willing of human beings, who themselves are ever-changing. Economic thinking must strive to be comprehensive, with its basis in the observation and description of phenomena from as many points of view as possible. Economic science that is based on dogmatic, fixed concepts can only partially grasp the living reality of economic life. Theory and concepts must arise from the totality of social and economic phenomena and must constantly be verified and modified by further experiences.

> *In economics you need a method of characterizing, whereby one seeks to find the concepts by coming from various starting points, holding them together, and letting them culminate as concepts. In that way one arrives at a definite concept. In a certain sense this will probably be one-sided since one can never survey the whole range of the facts, but only have a certain sum of experiences. Now go over the phenomena once again with the concept and try to verify it. Then you will see that this is really a modification. So through characterizing you arrive at a concept that you modify as you verify it, and then you arrive at a perception of it according to economics. You have to work to arrive at perceptions.* RE 187-199

> *You say "the esoteric aspects of the social question" are logically sound in themselves. They are not at all – neither*

they nor any of the other things! By this I am emphasizing that I did not want to speak purely from the economics point of view, but also from the social point of view. The whole style and position taken by these writings is of course determined by that, so that they cannot be evaluated at all from the pure economics aspect. At the most, that could be done with certain essays on threefolding. But I don't find them logically grounded in themselves at all, because, carefully enough, I gave only guidelines or examples, or really only illustrations. *RE 190*

All one can say is this: it is necessary for our consideration to first take the economic point of view as a basis. This has only a heuristic value, a value for research, for investigation. But if you want to find an exhaustive economic theory in accord with reality, you will not be able to avoid characterizing the economic effects from every angle . . . in economics one should not stress one thing out of the whole range of manifestations, but should go through the whole range. One needs to realize that we begin to think in terms of economics because we can then help those who cannot do so. But one must also realize that economic thinking must give rise to the demand that it be quite total in nature, a thinking that is very inclusive. It is much easier to think juristically. Most economists think very juristically. *RE 195*

Particularly in the sphere of economics the first concepts and ideas that we must develop cannot but be a little complicated – and for a quite objective reason. You must imagine the economic process, considered even as a world economy, as a thing of perpetual movement. As the blood flows through the human being, so do goods, as merchandise or commodities, flow by every conceivable channel through the whole economic body. *RE 15*

. . . Inasmuch as the economic process consists in movement and everything must be brought about in it by movement, we must place the human being in it everywhere. For an

objective science of economics this may be uncomfortable; the human being is a kind of incommensurable magnitude and is changeable; we have to reckon with the human being in so many different ways. But there is no getting away from it, this is the fact; and we must reckon with the human being in many different ways. *RE 122*

In the thinking you develop as a member of the social economic struggle, what is constantly happening – however paradoxical this must seem to you – is that another person is thinking along with you, a more profound human being within you. The moment you feel yourself to be a member of an economic structure, a more profound person is taking part in your thoughts. You become committed to combine external factors of life by means of thought. You have to think out: What will the price of such and such be? How do I obtain this or the other product? Your thoughts jump around over the surface of outer facts; the essence of your thought is not spiritual but belongs to external material things. And precisely because external material things live in your thinking, precisely because you have to experience in thought and not merely instinctively like an animal what is taking place in the life of the economy, this is why another more profound person is constantly reflecting within you on these things, and carrying them further in a way only he can do, so that they come through to a conclusion and find their relationship to other things. *EASQ 28*

. . . a living thing may realize itself in a variety of ways. By the act of grasping it livingly, you give it the possibility to realize itself in the most varied ways, just as living human beings can use their capacities in various ways. This is the essence of a non-dogmatic concept. To make such concepts your own, especially in economics, is to see how well these things enter into real life. Only on this foundation will you be able to make proper use of what is given in the so-called economic science of today out of quite good, but only partial, observations. *RE 170-171*

The Evolution of Economic Life

Over centuries, economic life has evolved from local agricultural private economies (i.e. businesses) to national economies and on to international economies. At each stage, more isolated economies have advanced and expanded by trading with other similarly developed economies (farms with other farms and businesses, nations with other nations, etc.). The means of exchange has seen a parallel evolution, from a direct exchange of commodities, to a financial system, to a system of credit. At the same time, as is the case with earth's evolution, the most primitive forms of economy continue to exist embedded within more evolved economies. Although primitive forms remain separate from their more advanced counterparts in the animal kingdom, in economic life, primitive and advanced forms continually interpenetrate.

National economies arose as a result of the gradual joining together of private economies. As such, elements of the old private economies were still preserved. At the same time, however, they created fundamentally new social structures, with new regulatory systems and methods of exchange. The same process has unfolded with the appearance of international economies with greater levels of differentiation and complexity. It is essential that economic science take this evolution and complexity into account. Adam Smith and other early economists failed to do so because their views were based on the notion that the developing national economies of their day were nothing more than private economies on a large scale.

> *. . . [The nature of the evolution of economic life upon the Earth] consists of a series of successive stages, but one in which the earlier stages continue to exist side by side with the later. Similarly we may say that the lowest organic forms now living are somewhat like the earliest living creatures of earthly evolution. Thus, in a sense, the most primitive creatures are still here, existing side by side with the highest creatures that have evolved up to this time. There is a difference, but there is also a marked resemblance in the forms. So it is in economic life. The phenomena of primitive phases of economic life are*

still here today, side by side with those that have attained a higher stage. But in economic life there is another peculiarity. While in the animal kingdom, for example, the more primitive forms can live literally side by side in space with the more highly evolved, in economic life the more primitive processes are constantly penetrating into the more highly evolved ones. We might very well compare it with those cases where bacteria penetrate into higher organisms, except that in economic life it is infinitely more complicated. Nevertheless, we can detect certain underlying structures, and from these we can take useful examples that will help us to bring our line of thought to its conclusion.

The more primitive forms of economic life must be conceived as private agricultural economies on a large scale.

Now if we trace the further course of evolution, we see how private economies gradually passed over into national economies, which again at a certain time – at the beginning of the modern period – tended to become state economies. The way it happens is characteristic. Private economy – initiative in private business – gradually passes over into the hands of government departments, and thus the fiscal administration grows increasingly into industrial organization.

We observe, as I said, how private economies were gradually joined together. It generally happened on a rather large scale. Private economies grew into something that could be called economy on a larger scale – national economy; and in this way a new social structure was created. Yet, within the new, the element of private economy was still preserved. The more primitive phase of evolution was still there as an insertion into the new. What is it that arises at this stage in the true sense of national economy? It is a mutual exchange between the several private economies. The exchange is regulated in many different ways. The regulation hovers like a kind of cloud over it all. The exchange, the trade or commerce between so many private economies, is the essential thing that arises with this welding of private economies into a national economy. What is the outcome? We saw yesterday that in the process of economic exchange each of the parties has an advantage, or can have an advantage. The result is, therefore, that the single economies that join together for the sake of mutual exchange (the essential thing in all economic life) profit by so doing. Once more, then, the single economies, the single businesses, gain an advantage by joining together. They profit by this connection simply because they can now exchange with one another. We can draw up a statement. We can calculate how much the one private economy or business will gain by means of the other private economies with which it is now connected. Each party gains an advantage, and the gain of each and all becomes significant for the entire economy.

At the time when the modern science of economics was founded, that particular stage had been reached. National economies had taken shape out of the private economies. This must be borne in mind if we wish to understand the economic ideas of Ricardo or Adam Smith. Only on this foundation can we understand the thoughts that they evolved about "political economy," as they called it. It was this working together of private economies that they actually saw and upon which they based their views. In Adam Smith you can see again and again how he thinks from the point of view of private economy or private business, and from that draws his conclusions. At the same time he has before him the picture of their joining together into a national economy. Yet even in their ideas about this latter process, the older economists retained to a large extent a way of thinking based on private business. Such were the views at which they commonly arrived; they treated national economy like an analogy of private economy. Thus the fertility, the prosperity of a national economy, as they conceived it, lay in the fact that one national economy would exchange with another, would come into mutual interchange with another, and would thus derive profit and advantage. Mercantilism, for example, was based on the advantages arising from such exchange between national economies. *RE 130-133*

. . . We read in the literature of political economy that long ago in Central Europe and until the end of the Middle Ages the old system of natural economy was in use. This was built up on the mere exchange of commodities, and its place was taken by the financial system, in which current coin represents commodities and in which only the commodity value is actually exchanged for money. But there is something new making its appearance in social life which seems likely to take the place of the financial system. This new element is everywhere at work, but it passes unnoticed as yet. Anyone who can see through the mere figures in his checkbook and ledger, and can read the language of these figures, will find that they do not merely represent the value of commodities, but that the figures often express what we may call the conditions of credit in the newest sense of the word. What a person can do because someone believes him or her to be capable of it, what can awaken confidence in the person's capacity, this, strange as it may seem, begins to appear more and more frequently in our dull, dry, business life. Look into business books and you will find that over and against the mere money values, mutual confidence, belief in human capacity is beginning to be evident. In modern business books, when we know how to read them, a great change is expressed, a social metamorphosis. When it is said that the old natural economy has given place to the financial system, it must now be added that, in the third place, finance is giving way to credit. *SF 22-23*

Historically, of course business capital, and indeed trade itself, is essentially the very first commercial activity that must come about. Even today in primitive villages you find relatively little business capital. The village craftspeople do not earn any more than the farmers. The merchants on the other hand are able to set money aside, and therefore are in a position to make loans. And so it goes on, because no capital is created unless it is negotiable. Business capital arises only as a third stage; this is so connected with local customs that no rational grounds for it can be found at all. *RE 257*

From World Trade to World Economy

By the late 19th century, when economic relations had developed to the farthest corners of the globe, there was a shift from world-trade between national economies to a single integrated, interdependent world economy. Single economic units no longer simply exchanged raw or finished products, but now actually shared in the production of goods. This industrial collaboration on the world stage is the defining feature of the closed-domain world economy.

> *Now, with the last third of the nineteenth century, there was a transition from world trade to world economy. It is a very remarkable process, this passage from world trade into world economy. Definitions are of course inexact, for these transitions tend to take place in successive stages; but, if we want a definition, we must say that at the stage of world trade the economic life of the world is characterized by single national economies exchanging with one another. This traffic quickens the whole process of exchange and thus essentially alters prices – alters the whole structure of economic life. In all other respects, economic life is carried on within the several territories. By contrast, it may be called "world economy" when the single economic units not only exchange their products with one another, but when they actually work together industrially. For example, partially manufactured products may be sent from one country to another for their manufacture to be continued there. That is a radical example of what I mean by their working together industrially. So long as it is merely a question of raw products, the account will continue to show a condition of pure trade. This cannot yet be described as an actual working together in industrial life. But when all factors in human life (in so far as they are affected by economics), that is to say, when all production, all distribution, all consumption – not merely production alone or consumption alone – are fed from the entire world; when all things are intricately interwoven and fed from the entire world – then we have world economy.* RE 135

Consider now the former national economies, then you see that they are simply adjacent to one another. Even earlier the situation was that they were quite separate from each other. That economic situation existed at a time when lands could still simply be conquered. It does not depend on the distances involved. You can think about France when it was still uncultivated, and the Franks who were passing through discovered the empty lands. That leads to quite different economic conditions than when one comes into a comparatively closed region with a greater culture. The Visigoths had a different destiny because they invaded a region that was more advanced economically. And the greatest example of separated national economies that then react on one another is the relationship between England and its colonies, especially India. There separate national economies were combined into a common area through conquest, also through peaceful conquest. That is the first situation. The second is when the territories are adjacent and have independent national economies. And the third is where a closed area is created because nothing can be adjacent to it in an economic sense – because total wastelands are not to be considered in this connection. Now we just need to be aware that we are in a tremendous time of transition, and that the most vital thing is the worldwide promotion of the world economy to which we must adjust ourselves. This new understanding of everything in economics is what everything depends on. *RE 246*

As with the development of any living organism, economic life will grow weaker over time if it is not improved and strengthened. Historically, this was achieved through the merger of like economies: neighbor with neighbor, region with region, nation with nation. It is no longer possible to strengthen and rejuvenate by means of merger, because there is not another world economy with which to merge.

. . . And through the rise of this world economy, certain advantages that existed formerly for the national economies are lost.

Let us look back once more. When private economies join into a national economy, they gain on the whole; they derive advantages. Every single one derives advantages . . .The fact is that the single private economies or businesses have the same characteristic as every living organism; their life tends in the course of time to become weaker and weaker. It is a universal law, and it applies equally to economic life. An economic life that is not being constantly improved always deteriorates . . .

When the businesses join together, they gain the corresponding advantage, though of course it varies from one case to another. And we may say that whatever the single economies have lost in the course of time is amply compensated for by their joining into national economies. Indeed, it is usually more than compensated. Moreover, whatever the national economies have lost in the course of time is amply made up by world trade and the transition into world economy. But when world economy is once achieved, what then? With whom can it exchange? This, in effect, is what has happened. We have seen the economic life of the entire earth gradually merging into world economy. And at this point the possibility of reaping further advantages by merger is at an end. *RE 135-136*

The great challenge for the future of economic science is to find ways to bring health and rejuvenation to our closed-domain interdependent world economy. One important question is how to bring harmony to the friction that is caused by the fact that individual nations, with their interests and demands based in nationalistic egoism, still exist as separate entities within the world economy. If the world economy is to have a healthy basis, impulses must be cultivated that lead all nations to take an interest in each other. Only when such a unity exists among the people of the world will it be possible to forge a healthy, unified world system of production, distribution and consumption.

To conceive what world economics really means, we must see clearly, to begin with, that at the frontiers of the domain of world economy (if we may use the expression) the conditions will be quite different from those of economic domains bordering on one another. Relatively speaking, a world economy exists today; and therefore, relatively speaking, a science of world economy will have to follow. The domain of world economy borders on nothing else, and this makes it necessary for us to observe still more precisely those economic processes that emerge within a closed economic domain, independent of its external frontiers. The cardinal problem for modern economics to solve is the problem of the closed economic domain – a self-contained domain of one giant economy. Today the very smallest question – even the price of breakfast coffee – is influenced by the economic life of the entire earth. If it is not so, it means that progress is only partial. This state of affairs is actually on the way, and our thinking will have to follow. *RE 137-138*

Let us see what would be the position of this Commonwealth, which also in the single state today is undoubtedly a demand of the future, with regard to the international problem. How does this international problem present itself to us, especially with regard to the economic system? We can see that though a universal demand exists for a world economy, the single nations stand separate within the circuit of the whole world economy. These separate nations, apart from the other historical causes of their existence, are held together for a time by the feelings arising out of the egoism of the community. Even in the highest part of the life of a nation, in literature, art, science, religion, it is the imagination arising out of egoism which holds the groups of people together. The groups thus held together take their place in the sphere of world economy, and in the course of the nineteenth century they have asserted themselves with particular energy, and ever more and more decidedly up to the beginning of the twentieth century, when the climax was reached. We might describe what really happened by saying that while other interests, which bore a much greater resemblance to those of the old despotic order of society, formerly prevailed between the nations, the principle of exchange and barter became even more prominent, precisely in the mutual intercourse of nations. This condition of things, therefore, reached its height at the beginning of the twentieth century. Just as production and consumption were carried on in the various states, so what was supplied to other states or was derived from them was absorbed into the egoism of the various states. Thus value was attached only to that in which the single state, as a nation, was interested. The reciprocal economic relations established between the states were absolutely dependent upon the commercial principle ruling the system of trade in regard to the distribution of commodities. In this sphere, but on a large scale, it was especially evident how the mere system of trade must lead ad absurdum, and the fact that this actually came to pass was one of the chief causes that led to the disaster of [World War I].

That this great opposition existed between the demand for a world economy and the influence of the various states against its realization is now becoming ever more and more evident. Instead of promoting a world-economy, these states closed their frontiers, shut themselves off by imposing customs and duties and by other measures, and laid claim to every advantage that might result from a world economy, seizing all for themselves. This led to the crisis which we call the catastrophe of the World War. There were, of course, other causes of the disaster, but this is one of the chief causes. Therefore it is important to understand that the very first step towards the improvement of international relations is to be able to carry on commerce across frontiers, but on different principles from those on which the present system of exchange is based.

Just as every single person who wishes to share in the work of the community must take an interest in production and consumption wherever it is carried on, just as every member of the community must be interested in the whole sphere of the economy – consumption, production and distribution – so in every country in the world impulses must prevail that would lead to a genuine interest in every other country. Nothing resembling the chance conditions of the present market could prevail among the peoples of the earth, but a real inner understanding would prevail among them. *SF 136-138*

How can a uniform principle of production be created to meet this uniform demand, one that will actively promote a world economy? It can be created through our upward striving to the spiritual life, to a true spiritual perception, which is powerful enough to create a common world production for the common world consumption. Then the balance can be struck, because unity in the spirit will work towards unity of consumption, towards unity of substance. Then the balance will be struck in the distribution of goods as mediator between production and consumption. Thus we must be able to look into the human soul, if we would understand how, over the whole civilized world – in reality out of many organisms – one uniform organism may arise. In no other way can this uniform organism be built up, this uniform organism that must be such that, in accordance with social demands all over the world, a true organic bond may be created between production and consumption, so that the piece of bread, or the coal required for the single household, or for the single person, may truly correspond with the social demands that are now making themselves felt in the subconsciousness of the human race. *SF 144-145*

Constant Fluctuations within the World Economy

A new economic science for our time must begin with the conscious embodiment of the principle of interdependence in economic processes at all levels. To do this we must make space for the diverse perspectives of all participants in economic life, as well as recognize the constant fluctuations that occur within and among various economic factors and parties. Economic science therefore cannot simply apply the concepts and methods of natural science to the economy. Modern economic life is more complicated, variable, and unstable than the most complex natural phenomena, and therefore is less able to be grasped by fixed, static concepts.

In the economic sphere, above all, we must not think shortsightedly, but think all things in connection. We must think things in connection with one another, as a whole . . .

. . .The economic process can find its reflection only where judgments, proceeding from those who stand in the most varied spheres, are working together. *RE 101*

. . . in the real economic process things are in perpetual movement. It is relatively simple to form concepts of the phenomena of nature – even the most complicated – as compared with the ideas that we require for a science of economics. Infinitely more complicated, variable, and unstable are the phenomena in economics than in nature – more fluctuating, less capable of being grasped with any defined or hard and fast concepts. In effect, an altogether different method must be adopted. *RE 19*

Fundamentally speaking, therefore, we have not yet attained a true science of economics. With the concepts to which we have grown accustomed thus far, we cannot truthfully answer the question, for instance, "what is value?" Or, "what is price?" Whatever has value must be considered as being in perpetual circulation; likewise we must consider price, which corresponds to value, as something in perpetual circulation. If you ask about the simple properties of carbon, you will still know absolutely nothing of what goes on in the lungs, for example, although carbon is also present in the lungs. For the whole configuration of carbon becomes quite different in the lungs. In the same way, iron, when found in the mine, is something altogether different from what it is in the economic process. Economics is concerned with something quite different from the mere fact that it "is" iron. It is with these unstable, constantly changing factors that we must reckon. *RE 11-12*

Economic life in the world economy is a living process, and our concepts must therefore have the same mobility as the process itself. For example, for the concept of price, we must observe how it fluctuates with place and time. We might then be able to determine some of the conditions in which a price emerges in that particular place and time. A price is always specific to particular conditions. There can never be a fixed definition of how a price is determined.

> *Thus, our ideas in economics must be quite mobile. We must rid ourselves of the habit of constructing concepts with the intention of defining things once and for all. We must realize that we are dealing with a living process, and must transform our concepts within the living process. But what the economists have tried to do is to grasp such things as value, price, production, consumption, and so forth, with ideas such as they had in ordinary science. And these were of no use.* *RE 11*

> *In all economic theories of modern times, this has been the difficulty: they have always tried at the outset to hold fast what is really fluctuating . . . the point is that even those of considerable insight have stumbled again and again over this obstacle in developing their theory of economics. They have tried to observe things that are always in a state of flux as if they were at rest.* *RE 26*

> *. . . Economics must stand firmly on a basis of reality. In economics we can speak only of the conditions existing at a given time and at the actual place to which we are referring. Those who desire the progress of humanity will come to the conclusion that things can be different. To begin with, however, things must be observed in their immediate reality at the particular moment. From all this you will see how impossible it is to approach such a thing as price – a most important concept in economics – by seeking to grasp it with a sharply defined idea. We can make no progress in economic theory by this means; quite other ways must be adopted. We must observe the economic process itself.* *RE 17*

> *To begin with, we can say little more than that we must observe how the price fluctuates with place and time. Then, perhaps, we can trace some of the conditions through which*

at a given place a given price actually emerges as it does. But there can be no such thing as a general definition stating how the price of a thing is composed: that is an impossibility. Again and again one is astonished to find price discussed in the commonly found works on economics, as though it were possible to define it. We simply cannot define it, for a price is always concrete and specific. Precisely in economic matters, it is impossible to get anywhere near the realities with definitions. RE 16

Picture-Thinking

What is required in order to perceive true economic realities? We must endeavor to think in pictures. Whereas current economic science promotes abstract understandings and inherited interpretations of reality, imaginative thinking is mobile and malleable, and works in response to immediate realities. To create vivid imaginative pictures of economic life, we must enter into the phenomena of production, trade, and consumption by drawing deeply on direct perception and experience. What will result are approximate, but useful and dynamic concepts, which can be expanded and corrected by others and remain useful even when conditions change. Pictorial thinking transcends the traditional dichotomy of theory versus practice. It brings a feeling experience to the economic process, out of which we can translate our perceptions into action.

The method of economics is a very inconvenient method because in reality it involves having to put together the concepts from infinitely many factors. You have to work toward economic imaginations! Only with those can you make any progress. If you have them and they approach something, then they modify themselves on their own, whereas with a fixed concept it is not so easy to modify it. RE 188

It is simply not true that we can grasp anything of the economic process by working abstract concepts into it. Only by working imaginative perceptions into it can we grasp anything of it. For instance, we may have the imaginative perception of peas on their way from the market stall to the mouths of people. That is one definite picture. Or we may have the imaginative perception of peas being used as money. That is another picture. Even in economic science we must work toward such pictures, taken from what is immediate perception. This means, in other words, that to act rightly in the economic sense, we must make up our minds to enter into the events of production, trade, and consumption with picture-thinking. We must be ready to enter into the real process; then we shall get approximate conceptions – only approximate ones, it is true – but conceptions that will be of real use to us when we wish to take an actual part in the economic life. Above all, such conceptions will be of use to us when what we do not know by our own sensibility (supposing we ourselves have not arrived through sensibility at the corresponding pictures) is supplemented or corrected by others who are connected with us in associations. There is no other possibility. Economic judgments cannot be built on theory; they must be built on living association, where the sensitive judgments of people are real and effective; for it will then be possible to determine out of the association – out of the immediate experiences of those concerned – what the value of any given thing can be. *RE 125-126*

This is the great difficulty that besets the formation of economic ideas. You cannot form them in any other way than by conceiving things pictorially. No abstract concept can enable you to grasp the economic process; you must grasp it in pictures. Nonetheless, it is just this that makes the intellectual world so uneasy today – this demand, no matter in what sphere of thought, that we should pass from the mere abstract concepts to ideation of an imaginative kind. Yet we can never found a real science of economics without developing pictorial ideas; we must be able to conceive all the details of our economic science in imaginative pictures. And these

> *pictures must contain a dynamic quality; we must become aware of how such a process works under each new form that it assumes.* RE 124-125

> *Sometimes farmers, for example, who do not have the remotest notion of economic concepts – yet who have attained a certain age and have simply observed the conditions of the market in their district – know with precision, without relying on any theoretical concepts, what the picture signifies when they give a certain sum of money for a horse or plough. Of course they may make a mistake, but you may do that even if you have studied the logic of economics! But the mistakes will not be the most important thing. The picture that is composed in their minds – the picture of a certain sum of money and a plough – calls forth in them the immediate feeling that they can still afford to give a little more money, or else that they cannot. They see this directly out of their feeling-experience. Now even in the most complicated economic process, this feeling-experience must not be eliminated. That is thinking in pictures.* RE 125

When the cultural domain of social life operates independently and on the basis of freedom, our inherent power of imagination flourishes. The realization of this power is necessary for the healthy, full development of all human capacities, including the capacity for economic thinking.

> *. . . Capacities belong to the human power of imagination because, since we must act consciously, our capacities in the first instance arise out of our power of imagination, our thought-will. Of course, the power of imagination must be continually fired and filled with enthusiasm, by feeling, but feeling alone is powerless, if the fundamental imagination is absent. Therefore, the question of a person's efficiency or practical skill brings us in the last instance to the life of imagination. It became evident to many persons that care must be taken to enable people to realize their power of imagination in social life.* SF 59

Economics and the Color Spectrum

An economic science for our time must come to terms with the whole range of economic life, beginning with the pre-economic extraction of resources and moving through to the abstract world of banking and finance. Steiner uses the image of the color spectrum as an analogy for this broad range of economic activity. Living contemplation of this image of the color spectrum in relation to economic life can lead us to deeper understanding.

> *If you call to mind your studies of physics, you will remember that the physicist speaks of the "spectrum." This band of colors is created with the help of the prism: red, orange, yellow, green, blue, indigo, violet. So far (from the red to the violet), the spectrum appears luminous. But, as you know, before the area that shows a luminous effect, what we call the infrared rays are assumed to exist; and, beyond the violet, the ultraviolet rays . . .*
>
> *I have, however, mentioned the matter here because there is a valid analogy. Consider for a moment not the economy of people, but, let us say, the economy of sparrows or the economy of swallows. They too, after all, have a kind of economy. But this – the economy of the animal kingdom – does not reach far up into the human kingdom. Even in the case of the hamster we may indeed speak of a kind of animal capitalism. The essence of animal economics is that nature provides the products, and the animal as a single creature takes them for itself. Humanity does indeed reach down into this animal economy; but we have to emerge from it.*
>
> *The true human economy may be compared to the part of the spectrum that is visible as light. What reaches down into nature would then be comparable with the part of the spectrum that extends into the infrared. Here, on the one hand, for example, we come into the domain of agriculture, of economic geography, and so forth. The science of economics cannot be sharply defined in this direction: it reaches down into a region that must be grasped by very different methods. This is one side of the situation.*

On the other hand, under the influence of the very complicated relations of today, it has gradually come to pass that our economic thinking fails us once more in another direction. Just as light ceases to appear as light, as we go on into the ultraviolet, so does human economic activity cease to be purely economic [as amassed capital and banking]...

Now from this you will see that people did not even possess the necessary concept to enable them to define the science of economics and set it in its proper place within the whole domain of knowledge. As we shall presently see, it is a curious thing, but this region alone (which we have compared to infrared light) – this region, which does not yet actually reach up into the sphere of economics – this alone is intelligible to the human intellect. We can consider with ordinary thinking how to grow oats or barley, and so forth; or how best to obtain ore in mining. Basically, that is all that we can really think about with the intellect as we have grown accustomed to apply it in the science of modern times. *RE 8-11*

Viewing the Economic Process from the Inside

To truly understand economic life, we need to develop mobility in thinking that can enable us to fully perceive, feel, and grasp economic processes from within them. Whereas the natural scientist remains outside the processes being observed, we ourselves stand within economic life and must therefore observe its processes from the inside. An economic science cannot penetrate to the reality of economic life if it remains outside economic processes, in the abstract, with indifference to the environment and those involved.

For many centuries humankind has grown accustomed to sharply outlined concepts, but such are inapplicable to a living process. Today we are called upon by the facts of life to welcome movement into our concepts, so as to penetrate the economic processes with conscious understanding – but we cannot do so. This is what we must attain: mobility of thinking, so as to be able to think a process through to its end quite inwardly. True, in ordinary science we also contemplate

> *processes, we "think them through," if you will; but we always see them from outside, and that is of no avail in economics. To contemplate the economic process as the chemist contemplates chemical processes, from outside, you would have to go far up above the earth in a balloon. Economic processes are distinguished by the fact that we ourselves are in them; therefore we must see them from within. We must feel ourselves within the economic processes, just like a being that is inside a chemist's retort where something is being concocted with a great generation of heat. The being in the retort, that I am now comparing with ourselves, cannot of course be the chemist. The being would have to be taking part in the heat, boiling with it, as it were. The chemist cannot do this; to the chemist the whole thing is external. In natural science, we stand outside the process . . .*
>
> *The economic process is different, however; we ourselves partake in it inwardly at every point. Therefore, we must understand it inwardly as well.* *RE 52*

This inner, subjective understanding of what is actually happening in economic life can only occur when we come to know it experientially. Furthermore, we must avoid the temptation to apply judgments and decisions formed in one context to all situations. We must recognize that decisions or judgments made with regard to a particular region or situation may not necessarily be applicable to other circumstances. General economic theories are of no help.

> *. . . in practical economic life there is no other effective way of knowing what is going on in trade, for example, except to be engaged in trade oneself. You must be in the midst of it, you must be trading. There is no other way. There are no theories about it. Theories may be interesting, but the point is not that you should know how trade goes on in general, but that you should know how the products circulate in the process of trade in Basel and its immediate neighborhood. If you know that, you do not thereby know how they circulate in the Lugano district. The point is not that we should know about things in general, but that we should know something in a particular region.* *RE 102*

. . . it is necessary in economics to start out from a certain subjective understanding of what is happening out there in the world. But in economics this subjective element again becomes easier for one than it is in biology. As a human being one stands (since one is not a June bug when one is studying it), of course, one always stands outside, and must do so; whereas one stands outside to a much lesser degree when considering something in the sphere of economics.

One can always summon so much humanity that one can have a good understanding of the worker as well as of the business person. That is a common human concern, and that takes the place of what is outer perception in biology. RE 212

Elements of a New Method for Economic Science

Economics can be either a theoretical or a practical science. It becomes practical when theoretical knowledge is used to do something concrete in the world. Economists also engage in practical economics when they observe and address the conditions that cause particular economic events, rather than tinkering with indicators or theory-based manipulations. One essential element of a new economic science is an appropriate weaving together of the theoretical and the practical.

Now, if we wish to arrive at any knowledge in economics, it is undoubtedly necessary to make observations. We have to make observations, just as we must observe the readings of the barometer and thermometer to ascertain the state of air and warmth. So far, economics is a theoretical science. At this point, nothing has yet been done. We achieve something only when we are really able to act under the influence of this theoretical knowledge. RE 29

. . . If we feel cold in a room, we do not go to the thermometer and try by some mysterious method to lengthen the column of mercury. We leave the thermometer alone and stoke the fire. We get at the problem from quite a different angle; and so it must be in economics too. When it comes to

action, we must start from quite a different angle. Only then does it become practical. We must conclude, therefore, that the science of economics is both theoretical and practical. The point will be how to bring the practical and the theoretical together.

Here we have one aspect of the form of economic science.
RE 30

In order to inform a healthy, reality-based economic science, we must recognize the true significance of two key features of modern economic life: value and price. First, economists must forgo their abstract manipulations of value and price and address the true underlying conditions which cause their constant fluctuations. Rudolf Steiner offers two examples of such an approach: adjust the number of employees involved; and increase efficiency of production. In this way, underlying conditions are altered in a healthy direction, and values and prices adjust accordingly. When price and value are approached in this manner, there is a healthy blending of the practical and the theoretical.

In economic science, as I explained yesterday, one is essentially trying to take hold of something that is always fluctuating, namely, the circulation of values and the mutual interplay of fluctuating values in the forming of price. Bearing this in mind, our first need is to discover what is really the proper form of the science of economics. A thing that fluctuates cannot be taken hold of directly . . .

Let us take an example from life. For certain purposes we use a thermometer. We use it to read various degrees of temperature, which we have grown accustomed, in a certain sense, to compare with one another. For instance, we estimate 20° of warmth in relation to 5°, and so on. We may also construct temperature curves. We plot the temperatures, for instance, during the winter, followed by the rising temperatures in summer. Our curve will then represent the fluctuating level of the thermometer. We do not come to the underlying reality, however, until we consider the various conditions that determine the lower temperature in the winter, the higher temperature in the summer months, the temperature in one district, the different temperature in another, and so forth. We have something real in hand, so to speak, only when we refer the varying levels of the mercury to that which underlies them. To record the readings of the thermometer is in itself a mere statistical procedure. In economics it is not much more than this when we merely study prices and values, and so forth. The procedure begins to have a real meaning only when we regard prices and values much as we regard the positions of the mercury – as indications, pointing to something else. Only then do we arrive at the realities of economic life. Now this consideration will lead us to the true and proper form that economic science must have. *RE 28-29*

Another essential element of a new method of economic science is a thorough understanding and recognition of the Fundamental Social Law. *[This law of social life is fully examined in Chapter Two, The Fundamental Social Law.]* In the future, the economy will need to be based on the principle of altruism, rather than on that of self-interest, if society is going to evolve towards social health and renewal. The very nature of the division of labor demands this. Economic science must be able to see economic life through the lens of the Fundamental Social Law, in order to accurately assess imbalances and recommend the appropriate new forms and procedures.

. . . The other aspect [of the form of Economic Science] is one to which I drew attention many years ago, though it was not understood then. It was in an essay I wrote at the beginning of the century, which at that time was entitled "Theosophy and the Social Question." It would have had real significance only if it had been taken up by politicians, and if they had acted accordingly. But it was left altogether unnoticed; consequently, I did not complete it or publish any more of it. We can only hope that these things will be more and more understood, and I hope these lectures will contribute to a deeper understanding . . .*

* Editor's Note: Published as "*Anthroposophy and the Social Question.*"

> *... let us regard this as a line of thought that will lead us to the true form of economic science. The facts themselves will, of course, have to be considered again later ...*
>
> *This point of view could easily be taken as idealism, but I ask you to observe once more that in this lecture I am speaking neither idealistically nor ethically, but from an economic point of view. What I have just said is intended in a purely economic sense. It is neither God, nor a moral law, nor an instinct that calls for altruism in modern economic life – altruism in work, altruism in the production of goods. It is the modern division of labor, a purely economic category, that requires it.* *RE 30-36*

One of the most important goals of new economic thinking is to separate work from income, so that motivation for work is based on the needs of the community rather than self-interest.

> *... In recent times our economic life has begun to require more of us than we are ethically, religiously, capable of achieving. This is the underlying fact of many a conflict. Study the sociology of the present day and you will find that the social conflicts are largely because as economic systems expanded into a world economy it became more and more necessary to be altruistic, to organize the various social institutions altruistically, while, in their way of thinking, people had not yet been able to get beyond egotism and therefore kept on interfering in a clumsy, selfish way ...*
>
> *One of the first and most essential economic questions, therefore, comes before us. How are we to eliminate from the economic process this principle of working for a living? Those who to this day are still mere wage earners – earners of a living for themselves – how are they to be placed in the whole economic process, no longer as such earners but as people who work out of social necessity?* *RE 36-37*

To a certain degree, egoism or self-interest is appropriate with regard to the motivation of the consumer; everyone has legitimate needs in this regard. Economic science must ask how producers can develop altruism as active concern for the needs of consumers.

> *Even if economic life were governed by its own conditions, and an attempt were made to understand it, it would still be necessary to point to the two impulses in the human soul just mentioned. What we have called the threefold human life element in these lectures leads us back to these two impulses in the human soul. Think of the economic system, for instance; consider how it pervades the whole national and international life of humanity. . . Let us examine this economic system. We are compelled to recognize its origin in human wants, in consumption. The satisfaction of these wants is really the whole task of economic life. Production and distribution of commodities, administration, human intercourse, and so on, are necessary to supply human requirements. Here again we may ask what element of human nature lies at the root of requirement, of consumption. Egoism is at their root. It is important that this fact should be properly understood. If it is understood, no one will feel impelled to ask with regard to economic life, "How can we overcome egoism?" but rather, "How is it possible for altruism to meet the just demands of egoism?" Perhaps this question may sound less idealistic, but it is the true question.* SF 133

FIVE

Economic Associations

The judgments that have to be formed in the economic life must be formed out of immediate, concrete situations . . . For definite domains or regions . . . associations must be formed . . . From the most varied branches of the ecnomic life, there must be the representatives of the three things that occur in it – production, consumption, and distribution. RE 102

The "market" relationship must be superseded by associations that regulate the exchange and production of goods through an intelligent consideration of human needs. RSO 41-42

FIVE

Economic Associations

Characteristic Features and Dynamics

A healthy economic life within a threefold social organism would be based on freely-formed economic associations of producers, distributors, and consumers. These associations would allocate resources, facilitate trade, and establish prices based on the experiences and perspectives of representatives from all aspects of economic life. Business relations would be based on contracts, on mutual agreements, entered into by members of an association or groups of associations. In this way, direct insight, collective intelligence, and mutual understanding would guide economic processes, rather than the chance of the market or the commands of the state.

> *The judgments that have to be formed in economic life must be formed out of immediate, concrete situations. And that is possible only in this way. For definite domains or regions (whose magnitude, as we have seen, will be determined by the economic process itself), associations must be formed, in which all three types of representatives will be present alike. From the most varied branches of economic life, there must be representatives of the three things that occur in it – production, consumption, and distribution.* RE 102

> *Within the economic circuit, as I explained yesterday, associations must be formed. Representatives of the different occupations should meet; producers and consumers should come together. The purely business operations and measures which take place should be based upon contracts entered into by the association. In the economic world everything should*

rest on contracts, everything should depend upon mutual service rendered. Corporations should carry on business with other corporations; expert knowledge and efficiency in particular branches should have the decisive voice. SF 66

So we see that human reason will take the place of chance, that, as the result of the arrangements that will come into existence, the price will express the agreements arrived at, the contracts entered into. Thus we shall see a revolution of the market accomplished by the substitution of reason for the prevailing forces of the market. SF 47

The "market" relationship must be superseded by associations that regulate the exchange and production of goods through an intelligent consideration of human needs. RSO 41-42

Specialized knowledge and down-to-earth objectivity can lead to a general harmony of interests within such an association. Not rules and regulations, but people themselves determine production, circulation and consumption of goods, through their direct insight and interests. By active participation in this associative way of working, people can develop the insights and skills they need for it; and goods can circulate at their proper value by means of contracts which balance one interest against another. TSR 8-9

In the future, when economic life is independent, the emphasis will be much more on distribution and consumption among people. Associations will be formed that will regulate production in accord with consumption. T-S 08-09

In the context of social threefolding, an economic association would not be a legally-constituted organization or business. Rather, it would be a freely-formed collaborative of participants in the various aspects of economic life. All members of the association contribute their expertise, and decisions are made by mutual agreement. The size and scope of associations will be determined by the actual conditions of the domain under consideration and must function as purely economic entities, free of government interference or political influence.

An association is not an organization and not a combination. It comes into being through the conflux of the individuals within the economy. The individuals do not have to adopt something handed down from a central body, but are able to contribute knowledge and ability they have in their own field. From a collaboration in which all give of their best, and where what is done springs from the agreement of many – only from such associations does economic life in general derive. *TBEW 179*

Economic life strives to organize itself in accord with its own nature, to become independent of government institutions and political ideas. But it can only do this if associations are formed along purely economic lines, composed of consumers, traders and producers. Actual conditions would naturally regulate the scope of such associations. If they were too small, they would be too costly; if too big, they would be too unmanageable and difficult to oversee. Each association would adjust to actual needs in regulating its trade with others . . . *TSR 8*

Evolution of the Role of the Individual and the Need for Associations Today

The individual's role in society has evolved over the course of history. If we turn to medieval times, we see that social arrangements were ordered according to the will of a single ruler or despot. The will of the community was a projection of the will of this single powerful individual. With the advent of the division of labor and the rise of capitalism, individual initiative, expressed as competing interests, became prominent in economic life. Community life was no longer ordered by the will of a single ruler, but now was dominated by the clashing of opposing interests and motivations, which still exists today in our system of trade. A healthy economic life for our time is made possible by the development of a conscious collective will, which is based on free agreements between individuals, businesses, and other institutions.

Let us go back to a time before the end of the Middle Ages. We find a condition of things extending into the latter part of medieval times, especially in civilized Europe. We find society in a condition that we may call a social order of might. This society of might or despotism arose in the following way, to give one example of the manner in which such changes are brought about. Some conqueror, with his train of followers, settled in some locality, and these followers became his workmen. Then, since the leader was looked up to on account of his individual qualities, his abilities, a social relationship was brought about between his power and that of those whom he had once led, and who afterwards became his servants or his workmen. Here the model for the social organism, which took its rise in one person or in one aristocratic group, passed on to the community at large, and lived on in that community. The will of the community was to a certain extent only the reproduction or the projection of the single will in that society of might, of despotism.

Under the influence of modern times, of the division of labor, of capitalism, of technical culture, this despotic order of society gave way to the system of trade, of exchange, which, however, carries on the same impulses among individuals and in the whole life of the community. The commodity produced by the individual becomes merchandise, which is exchanged for something else. For financial economy is, in reality, so far as it consists in a transaction between individuals or groups, neither more nor less than a system of trading. Social life is a system of trading. Whereas under the old despotic system, the whole community had to do with the will of a single individual, which it accepted, the system of trading, under which we are still living, and from which a great part of the population of the world is striving to extricate itself, has to do with the will of one individual opposed to the will of another. The collective will of the community arises, as if by chance, only out of the cooperation of one single member with another. Springing from intercourse between one individual and another, the economic community takes shape, together with wealth, and the element we recognize in plutocracy. In all this there is something at work that has to do with the clashing of individual interests with one another . . .

But, out of the deepest human impulses of our day, this trading system strives to pass, especially in the domain of economic life, into a form which I might call, even if the term is inadequate, a Commonwealth. The Society of Traders must be transformed into a Commonwealth.

What form will the Commonwealth take? Just as the individual will, or the will of an aristocracy, which is also a kind of individual will, continues in a sense to work in the whole community so that the impulses of individuals only represent an extension of the will of the one; just as the trading system had to do with the clashing of one individual will with another, so the economic order of the Commonwealth will have to do with a kind of collective will, which then in reverse fashion works back on the individual will. I explained in . . . [a previous] lecture how associations of the various branches of production with the consumers will be called into existence in the sphere of economic life, so that everywhere there will be a combination of producers with consumers. These associations will enter into contracts with other associations. A kind of collective will then arises within larger or smaller groups. This collective will is an ideal for which many socialists yearn, but they visualize the matter in a [very] confused, by no means reasonable, manner. Just as in the society of despotism, of power, the single will worked in the community, so a common will, a collective will must work in the future Commonwealth.

[But] how will that be possible? As we know, it must arise through the co-operation of single wills. The single wills must achieve a result that is not a tyranny for the individual, but within which everyone must be able to feel him- or herself free. What must be the content of this collective will? In it must be contained what every soul and everybody can accept, something with which they are in agreement, with which they can grow familiar. That means that the spirit and soul living in the individual human being must also live in the collective will of the Commonwealth. This is possible only

> *when those who build up the collective carry in themselves of their own will, in their intentions, in their feelings and in their thoughts, a complete understanding of the individual. Into that collective will must flow all that is felt by the individuals as their own spiritual, moral, and bodily nature. This is imperative.* SF 121-124

Participation in economic associations provides encouragement for overcoming narrow, self-interested behavior, and for seeking the common interests of all participants in the economic process – producers, distributors, and consumers. The whole economic process will be reflected in the economic interests of the individuals participating in the associations. Consequently, the needs of all participants will be reflected in economic decision-making. Associations reestablish communication between producers and consumers, who have been separated by the market.

> *What are the sole conditions under which world economy is possible? Of a truth, this question can only be answered after we have first turned our attention to the form that the social order of the future must take from the present time on, if the order of the Commonwealth takes the place of the old despotic order – that of might – and of the present method of trade. The Commonwealth is the social order in which production will be carried on by associations, through contracts with other associations.*
>
> *If this should really come about, where would the real difference lie between such a community, and the mere trading system of society, the ruling system today?*
>
> *The difference shows itself in the fact that in the trading system the individual or the single group has, for the most part, to do with another individual or another group. What are the common interests of individuals or groups in their mutual relations? At present, whether they are producers or consumers, their production and consumption are divided from one another, as if by a chasm, by the chances of the market. [And] the chances of the market are the means of bringing about the distribution of commodities and*

of facilitating commerce. Whatever may be our opinion regarding the justification or otherwise of the domination of capital, or of labor, and the like, that is, regarding the significance of capital and the significance of labor, it must be admitted that the essential fact in our system of exchange is that the distribution of commodities should be the ruling factor. Distribution is the link between production and consumption; when these are sundered from each other by the abyss of the market, there is no means of communication between them through the exercise of intelligence.

What will take the place in the Commonwealth of the system of distribution now prevailing? The whole domain of economic life will be drawn into the sphere of interest of every producer. Whereas it is now the interest of the producer to find out how he can procure and dispose of his products, which, however, he does out of self-interest, it will be necessary for every producer in the Commonwealth to have a full interest in consumption, distribution, and production. That is to say, it will be necessary that the entire economic process be reflected in the economic interests of the individual. This must be the essential point in the social order of the Commonwealth. *SF 135-136*

Informed, Transparent, and Freely-Formed Agreements

The management of an economy that produces in response to the needs of the community must be based on contractual agreements that arise out of free, informed initiatives of those involved, with no political influence or compulsion intervening in the process. It is important that such agreements enable the best possible use of the skills and capacities of individuals in service to the community. In order to do this, they must arise out of the associative working of producers, distributors, and consumers in response to real needs, rather than according to the abstract demands of an unregulated market. The forming of such free, informed, need-based agreements is the essential work of economic associations in a threefold social organism.

That democracy and a social form of life represent two impulses struggling to realize themselves within present-day human nature is an insight that has escaped entirely the vast majority of participants . . . Both impulses will continue to cause unrest and destruction in public life until institutions are provided within which they can unfold themselves; but the social impulse that must live in the economic process cannot, because of its essential nature, manifest itself democratically. The aim of this social impulse is that people engaged in economic production should pay attention to the legitimate needs of their fellows. The kind of management that this impulse demands is one that regulates the economic process on the basis of what individuals engaged in it actually do for one another. What they do, however, must be based upon contractual agreements that arise from the economic positions of the individuals concerned. If these contractual agreements are to have a social effect, two things are necessary. First, these agreements must originate as a free initiative of those concerned – an initiative that is based on insight. Second, these individuals must live in an economic body that enables one through such agreements to convey in the best possible way the services of each to the community. The first demand can be fulfilled only when there is no sort of political influence intervening between those working within the economy and their personal relationship to the sources and interests of economic life itself. The second demand will be satisfied when agreements are made not according to the demands of an unregulated market, but rather according to the conditions that result when branches of industry associate with each other and with associations of consumers as dictated by real needs, so that the circulation of goods is managed as these associations see fit. Such associations represent a model for determining how, in each particular case, economic activity should be governed contractually.

There can be no politicking when the economy is run in this way. There is only the competence and skill of each person in some special branch of industry, and the structuring of these to the best possible social advantage. What is done in an economic body of this kind is decided not by counting votes, but by the voice of real needs: it will necessarily concern

> *itself with finding those most competent to perform certain tasks, and then conveying products to the consumers deemed appropriate by the cooperating associations.* RSO 91-92

Economic Judgments Via Living Associations

The economic process can never be grasped in its totality by a single human being. It is very different from a scientific system, the understanding of which can be aided by the application of abstract theory. A true reflection of the economic process can only be found in the collective judgments and intelligence of a group of people working in the various areas of economic life, under conditions specific to a particular time and place. Economic judgments must therefore flow from living associations. Only out of the resulting practical insights is it possible for decisions and innovative solutions to arise that are based on an understanding of real, living conditions.

> *. . . the economic process is very different from a scientific system. A scientific system in its totality can be contained in a single human being – perhaps only in outline, but still, it can be contained within a single human being. The economic process, in contrast, can never take place in its totality within a single human being. The economic process can find its reflection only where judgments, proceeding from those who stand in the most varied spheres, are working together.*
>
> *The only possibility of arriving at a real judgment on these things – not a theoretical but a real judgment – is by way of association . . .*
>
> *But in practical economic life there is no other effective way of knowing what is going on in trade, for example, except to be engaged in trade oneself. You must be in the midst of it, you must be trading. There is no other way. There are no theories about it. Theories may be interesting, but the point is not that you should know how trade goes on in general . . . but that we should know something in a particular region.* RE 101-102

> *. . . Economic judgments cannot be built on theory; they must be built on living association, where the sensitive*

judgments of people are real and effective; for it will then be possible to determine out of the association – out of the immediate experiences of those concerned – what the value of any given thing can be.

Strange as it may sound, it is not possible to determine theoretically wherein the value of a product may consist. We can only say that a product enters into the economic life as a whole through the several parts of the economic process; and its value at a given place must be judged and estimated by the association. *RE 126*

We see, therefore, that at a given moment of its evolution the economic process gives no real information of itself. The "before and after" must always be taken into account; but the "before and after" cannot be taken into account unless they are based on the judgment of people who join together in association and who are able to have a corresponding insight into the past and the future. We have to build the economic process on the insight of those whose feet are planted within the economic process. *RE 108*

We shall learn to think about how we relate to other people simply through the fact of having to handle all kinds of wares on the economic level, and doing this as a community living in a particular territory. *EASQ 27*

Insight, Collective Consciousness, and Group-Born Intelligence

The gathering of insights out of the experiences of the individual members of an association is not a sufficient basis for economic judgments and decisions. There must be present a sense for the community, and the economic process, as a whole. This interest in the other, an objective community spirit, will arise out of the very nature of the economic associations. A group-generated collective consciousness will unfold through the sharing of perspectives of the individual members of the associations. Expressions of legitimate individual needs can be brought together to create a picture of mutuality, from which sound economic judgments and community-spirited solutions can arise.

. . . You may even found associations whose members have a great deal of economic insight; yet, if something else is not contained within the associations, all their insight will be of little avail. Something else must be contained in the associations, and will be contained in them once the necessity of such associations is recognized. There must be in them a community spirit – a sense of community, a sense for the economic process as a whole. Those individuals who immediately use what they buy can do nothing other than satisfy their own egotistic sense. Indeed, they would live very poorly if they did not satisfy their own egotistic sense. As an individual in economic life, one cannot say, if someone offers a coat for 40 francs, "Oh, no, that price does not suit me; I will give you 60 francs for it!" That will not do; at this point the individual within the economic process can do absolutely nothing. But the moment the life of associations enters the economic process, it is no longer a question of immediate personal interest. The wide outlook over the economic process will be active; the interest of the other person will actually be there in the economic judgment that is formed. In no other way can a true economic judgment come about. Thus we are impelled to rise from the economic processes to mutuality, the give-and-take between one person and another, and furthermore to what will arise from this, the objective community spirit working in the associations. This will be a community spirit, not proceeding from any "moralic acid" but from a realization of the necessities inherent in the economic process itself. *RE 127-128*

The economic process can be sound only when such a wise self-active intelligence is working within it. This can happen only if human beings are united together – human beings who have the economic process within them as pictures, piece by piece; and, being united in the associations, they complement and correct one another, so that the right circulation can take place in the whole economic process. *RE 127*

Theoretically, no one will want to deny that a larger sense of responsibility is necessary in the present-day world of busi-

ness and economic affairs. To this end, associations must be created that will work to confront individuals with the wider social effects of all their actions. RSO 50

Balancing Egoism and Love in Economic Life

Two fundamental forces in the soul, egoism or self-interest, and altruism or love, are acknowledged and continually balanced through the workings of economic associations. *[See Chapter Two, The Fundamental Social Law, for a discussion of egoism and altruism in economic life.]* The meeting of human needs is the origin and task of economic life. The expression of these needs through consumer demand is a legitimate form of egoism. To meet these needs in a healthy way, we need to draw upon the other soul force of love or altruism. Associations of producers and consumers can provide a vehicle for hearing and understanding the real needs of their fellow human beings. At the same time, participants in associations can experience what it means for others to hear and meet their needs. Producers, by understanding the lives of their fellow human beings, are motivated to devote themselves to producing in a way that corresponds to real needs in the community. Distribution of products and services can be regulated according to a close observation of the real needs of consumers. Economic institutions must provide the means for creative and productive people to work out of altruism and love in their desire to meet the needs of others.

Even if economic life were governed by its own conditions, and an attempt were made to understand it, it would still be necessary to point to the two impulses in the human soul just mentioned. What we have called the threefold human life element in these lectures leads us back to these two impulses [Egoism and Love] in the human soul. Think of the economic system, for instance; consider how it pervades the whole national and international life of humanity. Let us examine this economic system. We are compelled to recognize its origin in human wants, in consumption. The satisfaction of these wants is really the whole task of economic life. Production and distribution of commodities, administration, human intercourse, and so on, are necessary to supply human requirements. Here again we may ask what element of human nature lies at the root of requirement, of consumption. Egoism is at their root. It is important that this fact should be properly understood. If it is understood, no one will feel impelled to ask with regard to economic life, "How can we overcome egoism?" but rather, "How is it possible for altruism to meet the just demands of egoism?" Perhaps this question may sound less idealistic, but it is the true question.

When we turn our attention to production by which consumption is satisfied, we see at once that something else is necessary. Producers are of course at the same time consumers. Those whose business it is to produce must have an understanding not only of the process of production, but also of the life of their fellow human beings, so that they can devote themselves to the work of production in a manner corresponding to their needs. Producers must be able, indirectly or directly through institutions of which we have spoken, to see what people need for their consumption. They must then devote themselves unselfishly and with understanding to some kind of production for which they have the capability. It is only necessary to describe this, and people will be forced to see that the real motive power of production is self-sacrificing love towards human society, even though the sphere in which it manifests may appear dry and uninteresting. [And] nothing constructive will ever be said regarding the actual solution of the social problem until it is understood that production can only be regulated in a social manner by the creation, through the spiritual and equity organizations, of a source from which unselfish love for the various branches of production can flow into the human soul, because of the producers' interest in others and in life.

Between these two – consumption governed by egotism, and production in which love is the ruling principle – there is the distribution of commodities, holding the balance between them. Today this is brought about through the rise and fall of the market, through supply and demand, but in future times associations of people will substitute intelligence for the fluctuation of the market. People will be there who will make it their task to regulate production in conformity with their observation of the needs of consumers. So that the market will consist in commodities that the associations, already mentioned, will be able to produce, these associations having first studied and observed intelligently the needs of consumption. All catchwords in this department of life will be discarded, and the attention will be given wholly to realities. Who has not seen that in modern times something has arisen that was bound to appear as a result of the continual widening of our human horizon all over the world? Instead of the national economies of the past, limited to small territories, we have a world economy. It is true that so far this world economy is only the stage of a sort of demand, though it has developed to such an extent that in almost every part of the world commodities are consumed that are produced in other parts of the world. Here again human ideals and the feelings of the human soul have not kept pace with the world requirements that have become evident. Everywhere we see how urgent is the demand of modern times for a world economy, for arrangements by which a world economy could be rendered possible. *SF 132-133*

Answering the Need for Constant Price Corrections

As a living organism, economic life is in a constant state of movement, and subject to various forces and disturbances. Constant corrections are required, especially in regard to price determination. By taking hold of the economic process from within, associations, instead of relying on the chances of the market, are able to make appropriate adjustments to prices on the basis of collaborative insight into real facts regarding the nature of human needs and how to meet them.

Today my main purpose was that we should acquire concepts that point to the true relationships in the economic process. These true relationships are again and again being diverted, by falsified processes, into a mode of operation that introduces constant disturbances into the economic process. To continually smooth out and compensate for the disturbances is one of the essential tasks of economics. People keep on saying that we ought to get rid of the damages in economic life. They are inclined to have at the back of their minds the notion that then everything would be all right and earthly paradise would begin. That is no different than saying, "I should like once and for all to eat so much that I need never eat any more." I cannot do that; I am a living organism wherein ascending and descending processes must constantly be taking place. Such ascending and descending processes must likewise be present in economic life; there must be the tendency on the one hand to falsify prices by the formation of rent, and on the other hand the tendency to lower prices on the side of business capital. These tendencies are present at all times, and we must understand them in order to obtain, as far as possible, those prices that represent a minimum of falsification.

To this end it is necessary, by direct human experience, to take hold of the economic process, as it were, in the nascent state – to be within it at all times. The individual can never do this; nor can a society above a certain size (such as the state, for example). It can be done only by associations, which grow out of economic life itself and which are therefore able to work out of the immediate reality of economic life. The greater the technical accuracy with which we study the economic process, the more we are led to acknowledge that the required institutions must grow out of economic life itself. They will then be able to observe the kind of tendencies that are at work, and to understand how these tendencies can be counteracted. *RE 90*

And how is the essential fact of an economic life that is to be based only on knowledge of facts and on practical ability – this "settling of prices" – to be achieved? It must not be decided by the chances of a free market as has been the case hitherto in both national-economy and world-economy. By means of the associations which will come into being to suit the circumstances existing between the various branches of production and consumption – associations which will be composed of people whose position is justified by their knowledge of facts and practical ability – we shall obtain organically and rationally what is nowadays attained through crises in the chances of a free market. POT 131-132

An essential task of associations is to regulate the distribution of labor in response to real needs for particular products. When the price of a product is too high, not enough workers are employed in its production to meet the need for it. When the price is too low, too many workers are employed in relation to need, one result of which is that workers are not able to receive adequate support. If associations regulate the distribution of labor on the basis of an understanding of real human needs, the price of a commodity will correspond to the true value attached to it by the community [See Chapter Nine, The Fundamental Social Law, for a discussion of Price].

You create something real if you regulate the labor – that is to say, the number of people engaged in a certain kind of work. The price depends on the number of workers engaged in a given field of work. To try to regulate these things bureaucratically, through the state, would be the worst form of tyranny. To regulate through free "associations" that arise within the social sphere, where everyone can see what is going on – either as members, or because their representative sits on the association, or they are told what is going on, or they see for themselves and realize what is required – that is what we must aim for. RE 65

For this purpose [meeting the needs of consumers], and following the principle of association, it will be possible to produce a supply of commodities corresponding to the needs which have been investigated. That is, arrangements must exist with persons who can study the wants of consumers. Statistics can only give the present state of affairs. They can never be authoritative about the future. The needs for the time being must be studied, and, in accordance with these, measures must be taken to produce what is needed.

When a product shows a tendency to become too expensive, that is a sign that there are too few workers engaged on it. Negotiations must then be carried on with other branches of production to transfer workers from one branch to another where the need lies, in order that more of the lacking products may be supplied. If a commodity tends to become too cheap, that is to say, to earn too little profit, arrangements must be made to employ fewer workers on that particular product. This means that in the future the satisfaction of the needs of the community will depend on the way in which people are employed in industry. The price of the product is conditional on the number of persons engaged in its production. But, through these arrangements, the price will really correspond to the value attached to the commodity in question by the community in accordance with its requirements. *SF 46*

. . . if at any point a certain kind of commodity becomes too cheap or too expensive, those concerned must be able truly to observe the fact. The mere fact in itself is not the point. When, through experiences that can grow only out of the concerted counsels of the associations, they are able to say, as a result of such experiences, "Five units of money for so and so much salt are too little or too much – the price is too low or too high," then and then only will they be in a position to take the necessary steps.

If the price of a commodity becomes too low, so that those who produce it can no longer receive sufficient remuneration for their excessively cheap services and their excessively cheap products, it will be necessary to assign fewer workers to this particular commodity. Workers will therefore have to be diverted to another kind of work. If, on the other hand, a commodity becomes too expensive, workers will have to be led over into this branch of production. In this way, the associations will always be concerned with a proper employment of people in several areas of economic life. We must be clear on this. A real rise in the price of a given economic article indicates the necessity for an increase in the number of those who are working on this article, while an undue fall of price calls for measures to divert workers from this field of labor to another. In reality we can speak of prices only in relation to the distribution of people among the several branches of labor in the given social organism. RE 64-65

From Profit Motive to Satisfaction of Human Needs

The elimination of profits in the evolution of economic life as described is justified. However, it is unjustified to use egoism as an argument for eliminating profit from economic activity, for there must be something in the current economy that can serve to indicate whether there is a need for a particular manufactured item. In the modern form of economics, the only indicator of this need is the fact that the item yields profits. An item can be manufactured if it yields profits that, in the economic context, are sufficiently large. An item that yields no profits must not be produced because it will upset the price balance of items in circulation. Profits may represent what they will in ethical terms; in conventional economic terms, they represent an indicator for the need to produce an article.

The further evolution of economics does require the elimination of profits, but for the following reason: because they make the production of articles dependent on accidents of the market, of which the spirit of the age demands that they be abolished. One clouds one's judgment if one argues against profit because of its egotistical nature. Real life demands that within any field one must mount arguments appropriate to the particular situation. Arguments drawn from another field of life may be perfectly true in themselves, but they cannot guide one's judgment toward the real facts.

What is necessary for economic life is that profits as indicators should be replaced by groups tasked with establishing a rational correspondence between production and consumption that will abolish accidents of the market. The change from profits-indicator to a rational coordination of production and consumption, if correctly understood, will result in the elimination of the motives that have hitherto clouded judgment on this issue by removing them to the legal and cultural spheres. RSO 96-97

. . . The consideration that lies at the root of the matter in this sphere is that the yielding of profit is at present the one and only thing enabling someone to produce a certain commodity, because it will have a certain value in the community. The remodeling of the market, which today operates in this way, will follow as soon as a real principle of association finds a place in our social life. Then it will no longer be impersonal supply and demand – having nothing to do with the human being – that will determine whether a commodity shall be produced or not. Then, from those associations, by the will of those working in them, other persons will be brought in whose business it will be to find the relation between the value of a manufactured commodity and its price. We may say that the value of a commodity does not come under consideration. It certainly gives the impulse to the demand, but the demand in our present social conditions is extremely doubtful because there is always the question whether there are sufficient means available to make the demand possible. We may want things; if we do not possess the means to satisfy our wants, we shall not be able to create a demand. What is essential is that a connecting link be formed between human needs, which give the commodities their value, and the value itself, because the commodity we need acquires its human value always in accordance with that need. Institutions must arise out of the social order that form a link between the value attached to the commodities by human needs, and the right prices. The prices are now fixed by the market in accordance with the known purchasing power of potential buyers. A truly social order must be guided by the fact that those who quite justifiably must have commodities must be able to pay for them, that is, the prices must fit the value of the commodities and correspond to it. Instead of the present chaotic market, there must be an arrangement by which tyrannizing over human needs and interference with consumption is eradicated. *SF 45-46*

When consumer needs replace returns or profits as the determinative factor in initiating production, profits will be understood to be the healthy result of having met expressed and justified needs in an efficient manner. Returns will no longer be the primary driving force of production. What is produced will be the result of the direct will of those who meet and work out production priorities through interaction and negotiation within associations.

. . . It has gradually come to be the custom in questions of national economy altogether, to take only things like 'supply and demand' into account, or questions of that kind: conditions of the market, of trade, of exchanges, and so forth. And what is really meant by it always is something purely abstract, which figures as 'returns.' And when one comes to examine the way in which people to a very large extent think about economic problems today, they really think about these things only so far as to take into account the factor of returns. And in consequence, the whole of economic life comes to be looked at more or less one-sidedly, since everything in the products of economic life that has to do with consumption is left out of account. Consumption is simply left to proceed, I might say, automatically from whatever one may get as returns from anything. What one looks at, in going into any sort of business, is the amount it brings in, not the kind of consumption that is connected with the particular business. One doesn't take into account in the least any special qualification of the article, insofar as it is an article of consumption; from the national-economy aspect, one considers it solely on the side of returns, not on the side of consumption. People think that everything is to be found out by studying the returns side: how certain business conditions develop, whether favorable or unfavorable, how upward or downward tendencies develop in economic life, and so on. If one altogether neglects, however, to give any economic thought to the other, to the consumption side, the result is that consumption gradually becomes anarchic; it runs wild; and one gradually loses all possibility of coping with consumption . . .

. . . To people who are merely bent upon getting returns, what they are producing and what they are paid for is a matter of indifference, so long as they get their money;

> *money is abstract in economic life, and for money they can get everything. But what is needed, is to bring our general economy into a form in which it depends in an honest way upon the human will, not in a dishonest way. How can it be brought to depend in an honest way upon the human will? By means of associations. When you have associations, then all that takes place in economic life proceeds from the direct will of the people joined together in these associations; the transactions that take place in economic life will then be transacted between the different associations; then you will have transactions between live people, and what is produced will be the proceeds of this kind of transaction between live people, one with another, in the associations. When it is a question of starting a factory, people will not consider it merely from the point of view of how much 'returns' it will yield under the existing market conditions; but they will start from a collective insight into what is needed. This requires no government regulation: that would only tie the whole thing up in red tape; what it requires is the practical knowledge of the people actually engaged in the various businesses and the various branches of business; and this provides the means of finding out whether a particular business enterprise is needed. If it is needed, then one may proceed to production, and people can make their earnings by it too. It will be done by way of the associations; and in this way everything will become eliminated which might acquire an unhealthy influence.* *TOBS 13-17*

> *This is the only sound principle of economics . . . Up to now, production was geared to profits; in the future, production will have to be geared to consumption.* *T-S 9*

A New Relation of Management and Investors to Workers

When workers' rights are properly upheld in an independent rights domain, new possibilities arise for collaborative relations between workers and management. Moreover, freed from having to fight for their rights, workers can participate in associations with dignity, while receiving their due share of the combined efforts of production. When the work of the associations is thus limited to purely economic issues, the harmful effects of capitalism can be mitigated.

> *When blue collar and white collar workers meet with each other, they need only consider economic issues because legal matters will be dealt with separately under the state's jurisdiction. Blue collar workers will be able to associate freely with the manager of the business, because only the division, on economic principles, of that which they have earned together will be allowed; there will be no economic compulsion resulting from the greater economic resources of the manager. The associative structuring of the economic body will place the blue collar workers' contractual relationship to the business manager in a totally different light. Up to now, they have been forced to fight against the interests of the business manager, but in their new associative role they will share in the fruits of production . . .*
>
> *An individual business cannot be socialized; socialization happens only when the production of economic value that a separate business contributes to the total economic life has no antisocial effect. As a result of such genuine socialization, the capitalist system will lose its harmful tendencies. (In my book,* Towards Social Renewal, *I have described how capital must function within a healthy threefold organism.) It should be clear by now that one cannot "do away" with capital, since capital is nothing other than the means of production working for the community. It is not capital itself that is harmful, but rather capital in private hands, especially if this private ownership is able to control the social structure of the economic body.* *RSO 10-11*

Associations can enable lenders/investors and workers to overcome the gulf that arose between them with the advent of the financial economy. Uniting all participants in economic life under the principle of association establishes an environment for facilitating the borrowing and lending of money and the creation of credit. *[For an elaboration of how economic associations will facilitate the giving and receiving of credit, see Chapter Eight on Credit.]*

> *. . . money transactions are carried on quite independently of those who produce commodities. Money emancipates us in a certain sense from the actual economic process, just because it itself becomes an economic process. This is extremely significant. [For] in the old natural economy, one individual depended on another. People were forced to work together, to bear with one another. They had to agree on certain arrangements, otherwise economic life could not go on. Under the financial system, capitalists are, of course, also dependent on those who work, but they are quite alien to these workers. How close was the tie between consumers and producers in the old natural economy in which actual commodities were dealt with! How remote is the one who transacts business in money from those who work in order that his money may yield interest! A deep gulf has opened between one human being and another. They do not get near to each other under this financial system of economy. This is one of the first things to be considered if we wish to understand how the masses of workers (no matter whether they are intellectual or manual workers) can again be brought together with those who also make business possible by lending capital. This, however, can only be done through the principle of association, by which people will again unite with each other as human beings. The principle of association is a demand of social life, but a demand such as I have described it, not one resembling those that often figure in socialistic programs.* *SF 39-40*

Associations in Relation to Gift Money and Cultural Life

Participants in economic associations are in a position to directly observe that a productive and socially responsible economic life depends on the development of human capacities and skills. An understanding and appreciation of the importance of a vibrant cultural life can inspire associations to ensure that a sufficient amount of money flows into cultural life and education. Rather than letting surplus capital stagnate, associations can direct it to the support of cultural life and institutions.

> *. . . When one day associations begin to understand something of the influence of the free spiritual-cultural life on the economic process, we can give them a very good means of regulating the economic circuit. I mentioned this in my book* Towards Social Renewal. *The associations will find that when free spiritual-cultural life declines, too little is being given freely; they will grasp the connection. They will see the connection between too little giving and too little free spiritual-cultural work. When there is not enough free spiritual-cultural work, they will realize that too little is being given. When too little is being given, they will notice a decline in free spiritual-cultural work.*
>
> *. . . the capital that presses to be invested, the capital that tends to march into mortgages and stay there, must be given an outlet into free spiritual-cultural institutions. That is the practical aspect. Let the associations see to it that the money that tends to get tied up in mortgages finds its way into independent spiritual-cultural institutions.* *RE 78*

Implementing Economic Associations

As has been discussed, it is not necessary to tear down the old system before beginning to form a new associative economy. Technically speaking, it is not any more difficult to establish economic associations and affiliated businesses than it is to set up a traditional business in the current market economy. Moreover, associated initiatives can do business not only amongst themselves but also with traditional businesses. The old style of doing business will fade away as the socially advanced associative approach expands.

> *People who depend on their accustomed lines of thought will say, "These are very fine ideas, but how are we to make the transition from present conditions to the threefold system?" It is important to see that what has been proposed here can be put into practice without delay. One need only begin by forming such associations. Surely no one who has a healthy sense of reality can deny this is immediately possible. Associations based on the idea of the threefold*

social order can be formed just as readily as companies and consortia were formed along the old lines. Moreover, all kinds of dealings and transactions are possible between the new associations and the old forms of business. There is no question of the old having to be destroyed and replaced artificially by the new. The new simply takes its place beside the old; the new will then have to justify itself and prove its inherent power, while the old will gradually crumble away.

The threefold idea is not a program or system for society as a whole, requiring the old system to cease suddenly and everything to be "set up" anew. The threefold idea can make a start with individual enterprises in society. The transformation of the whole will then follow through the ever-widening life of these individual institutions. Because it is able to work this way, the threefold idea is not utopian. It is a force adequate to the realities of modern life. *RSO 47-48*

In working towards a threefold social organism, we should not be trying to create new realities based on utopian concepts; we should be coming to grips with what is already there. Institutions already in existence, consumers, producers, entrepreneurs – everything already in existence, needs to come together in associations. There is no need to ask how to create associations. The question to ask is: 'How can existing economic organizations and institutions be integrated in associations?' *RSSB 161*

It is really tragic that no understanding is found in our time for what is, after all, so simple and so sensible. The moment there is a real understanding, the changes can be made – not even by the day after tomorrow, but by tomorrow. It is not a question of radical changes, but of seeking for the proper associative union and cooperation in each case. You need only summon the will and the understanding to do it. This is what touches one so painfully, for, after all, economic thinking does to some extent coincide with moral and religious thinking. To me, for instance, it is quite unintelligible how this way of tackling the economic problem could have been entirely missed by those who are officially in charge of the religious needs of the world. There can be no doubt that during recent times it has become clear that economic facts are no longer being mastered. The facts have gone beyond the capacities of human beings to grasp them. Today we stand before this question: How can the situation be mastered, how shall we grapple with it? It must be mastered by human beings, by human beings in association. *RE 102-103*

SIX

Economic Values

There are indeed no other ways in which economic values are created. Either nature is modified by labor, or labor is modified by spirit (human intelligence/mind). *RE 22-23*

A commodity has not merely the value we attach to it through our requirements and the personal importance we give to these requirements, which is then transferred to the commodity; it has also an objective value in itself. It has an objective value to the degree that it is durable or the reverse, lasting or perishable; to the degree that by its nature it is more or less serviceable, plentiful, or scarce. *SF 105-106*

SIX

Economic Values

The Economic Process as Context for Economic Value

Economic value must be determined and characterized within the context of the overall economic process. As a product circulates through the economy, its value changes in response to innumerable circumstances and conditions. Therefore, to understand how economic values are created and quantified, the entire process of economic circulation must be examined.

> *Whatever has value must be considered as being in perpetual circulation; likewise we must consider price, which corresponds to value, as something in perpetual circulation. If you ask about the simple properties of carbon, you will still know absolutely nothing of what goes on in the lungs, for example, although carbon is also present in the lungs. For the whole configuration of carbon becomes quite different in the lungs. In the same way, iron, when found in the mine, is something altogether different from what it is in the economic process. Economics is concerned with something quite different from the mere fact that it "is" iron. It is with these unstable, constantly changing factors that we must reckon . . .*
>
> *You can never develop concepts of economics in reference to mere external reality. No, you must always develop them in reference to the economic process as a whole. And within this process, each thing is continuously changing. Therefore we must speak of the economic process of circulation before we can arrive at such things as value, price, and so forth.*
>
> *In the economic theories of today, you will observe that they generally begin with definitions of value and price. That is quite wrong. First it is necessary to describe the economic process.* *RE 11-12*

Origin of Economic Values: Labor Transforming Nature

Keeping in mind that the value of a product constantly changes as it circulates through the economy, we can consider where and how economic activity begins and how values first arise. At the foundation of economic life, land or nature, or a product of nature, is transformed by human labor for the sake of placing the resulting product into economic circulation. *[See Diagram 1 below.]* Agriculture and mining are examples of this most basic form of economic activity. To begin with, the substance in question has no value as such, but receives its value from the human labor which works upon it to make it available for consumption. Similarly, human activity or exertion of effort does not itself have value in the economic sense, but contributes to the creation of value when it is directed toward the transformation of nature for the purpose of consumption. In addition, when an individual only performs labor to directly meet his own needs, this labor is not economically significant. Labor has economic significance only when it is employed to meet the needs of others.

> *Obviously the first stage in the process – in the taking over of the nature-product by human labor – is direct work on the land. Therefore, when all is said, we must always look upon*

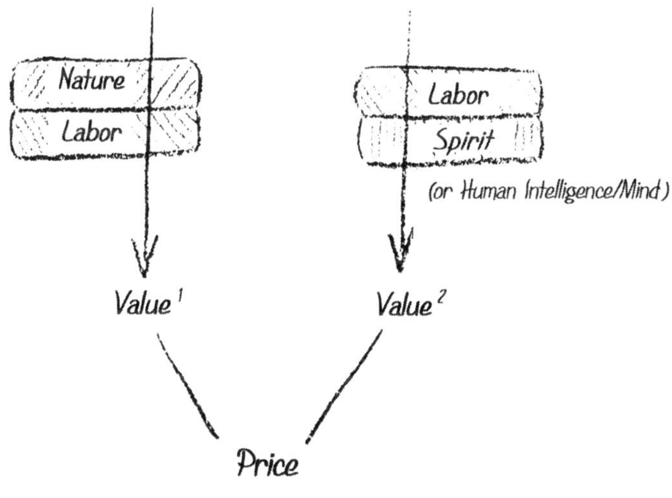

Diagram 1. RE 21

the cultivation of the land – in the widest sense of the term – as the starting point of economic life. RE 159

In the first place, human labor must set to work on nature, transforming nature's products. A product of nature thus receives the stamp of human labor; as transformed by human labor, it receives an economic value. In economics we are not dealing with the substance; the substance, as such, has no economic value. Coal, as substance, lying in mines under the earth, has no economic value; nor would it gain an economic value if it walked of its own accord from the mine into the house of the person who uses it for heating. What turns the substance into a value is the labor that has been impressed upon it; that is to say, all that had to be done to bring it to the light of day, to prepare the mines themselves, to transport the coal, and so forth. It is only the human labor impressed upon the substance of the coal that gives it economic value, and this is all that we must concern ourselves with in economics. RE 42

I do nothing special for the economy when I try to define work for itself. Above all, I must myself be clear about the fact that work as such becomes an economic category only when I bring it to bear upon a product of nature. RE 207

The one thing that matters is how labor enters the economic process. It is a matter of the fact, for everything being considered, that everywhere nature is changed by human labor; and only in so far as nature is transformed by human labor do we create real economic values from this one side. If, for instance, we find it necessary for our physical health, having worked upon nature in some way, to dance a little or to do eurythmy in the intervals, all this may of course be judged from another standpoint; but what we do in the intervals cannot be described as work or labor in the economic sense, nor can it be regarded as in any way a factor creating economic values. Seen from another side, it may well be creating values, but we must first get our concepts pure and clear concerning economic values as such. RE 22

It is very easy to arrive at a concept of work in relation to economics. You arrive at it when you have a product of nature before you that has been changed through human activity for the purpose of being consumed. *RE 234*

. . . The moment, however, that human beings no longer provide merely for themselves or for their nearest kindred but for one another, human labor, properly so-called, comes into consideration. Indeed, the moment we no longer use nature's products just for ourselves, but we stand in some relation to other human beings and trade goods with them, what we then do in relation to nature becomes labor. Here we arrive at the one aspect of value in the economy. It arises in this way. Human labor is expended on the products of nature, and we have before us in economic circulation products of nature transformed by human labor. It is only here that a true economic value first arises. As long as the product is untouched, at the place where it is found in nature, it has no other value than it has, for instance, for the animals. But the moment you take the very first steps to put the product of nature into the process of economic circulation, the transformed nature-product begins to have economic value. We may therefore characterize this economic value as follows. An economic value, seen from this one aspect, is a product of nature transformed by human labor. Whether the human labor consists in digging or chopping, or merely moving a product of nature from one place to another, is irrelevant. If we are seeking the determination of value in general, then we must simply say: one value-forming factor is that of human labor, transforming a product of nature so as to pass it into the economic process of circulation. *RE 20*

Value Creation through the Human Spirit, or Intelligence Transforming Labor

The second type of value creation emerges when labor becomes more efficient in the creation of products for human consumption and use. In this way, labor is transformed and given value by human intelligence or inventiveness, that is, by the human spirit. *[See Diagram 1, pg. 147.]*

Now there is an altogether different possibility for economic value to arise. It is that we turn our attention to labor as such, and we take labor as the given thing. To begin with, as you have seen just now, this labor, economically speaking, is something totally neutral and irrelevant. Yet it becomes an economic value-creating factor the moment we let it be directed by human intelligence (the human mind, or spirit). I must now speak in a somewhat different sense from before. Even in the most extreme cases, you can imagine something that would otherwise not be labor at all being transformed into real labor by human intelligence . . . Through spirit – by intelligence, reflection, perhaps even speculation – labor is given a certain direction, and the various units of labor are brought into certain mutual relations.

We may say that here we have the second aspect of the value-forming factors in economics. Here labor stands in the background, and in the foreground stands spirit, which directs the labor. Labor shines through spirit (or human intelligence), and this again creates economic value. As you will soon see, these two aspects are present everywhere. Having shown in this diagram [See Diagram 1, pg. 147.] *how an economic value emerges when we have nature appearing through labor, if we now wish to represent diagrammatically what was just explained, we shall have to put labor in the background and in front of it spirit, which gives it a certain modification . . .*

These are the two essential poles of the economic process. There are indeed no other ways in which economic values are created. Either nature is modified by labor, or labor is modified by spirit (human intelligence/mind). RE 22-23

The intellect can deal merely with the arrangement and organization of the work. Then in some circumstances one is not dealing with any object . . . That is a secondary concept. Work is human activity that is performed in order to make a nature-product consumable. In the context of economics, that is work. This you must now regard as the ultimate concept. Now the intellect can come along and organize the work. But in the course of things, that which you now want to grasp as a coherent economic process can simply separate itself from the nature-product. It can consist in the mere organization, the mere arrangement of the work. RE 234-235

Fluctuating Character of Economic Values

The importance of avoiding abstract definitions of value becomes clear from the examination of the two main ways that value is created – by labor transforming nature products and by the intelligence of the human spirit transforming or organizing labor. Economic realities can be grasped fully only when we look behind the value itself to the factors that created it. We must look to concrete indicators such as the quantity, accessibility, and quality of the nature products available in a given region, and the cleverness or ineptitude of people managing labor in the workplace. Once a value goes into circulation, it must be allowed to fluctuate as part of the living economic organism.

So you see there can be no question of arriving at a definition of economic value. Once more you need only consider on how many circumstances – on the cleverness or stupidity of how many different people – the modification of labor by the spirit in any given instance will depend. There is every kind of fluctuating condition. RE 24

Consider this for a moment: nature appears to us through human labor. Suppose we obtain iron at a given place under extraordinarily difficult conditions. The value that is thus produced through human labor is a modified object of nature. If at a different place iron is produced under far easier conditions, it may happen that an altogether different value will result. You see, therefore, that we cannot grasp the reality in the value itself; we must go behind the value. We must go back to what creates the value. Here alone can we gradually find our way to the more constant conditions on which we can exercise a direct influence. The moment you have brought the value into economic circulation, you must let it fluctuate with the economic organism as a whole . . . We must always go back to the real origins whence the economic process is nourished, on the one hand, and by which, on the other hand, it is regulated – nature on the one hand, spirit on the other. *RE 25*

Consumer Needs and Value Creation

The question of the determining factors in value creation must also be examined from the consumer side of economic activity. Because economic production must meet the specific needs of consumers, products or services that do not meet human needs will have no value, regardless of the amount of labor and intelligence expended in producing them. From the perspective of human need, the value of a product is affected by the tastes, desires, and bodily needs of the consumer, as well as the amount a consumer is willing to exchange in order to possess the product. Legal conditions in the form of ownership rights also affect value whenever a commodity owned by one person is sought by another person. Commodities also have an objective value, depending on such factors as durability and availability.

What determines the value of a commodity that can satisfy our requirements? In the first place we must have some personal need for the commodity in question. But let us examine how the need is determined. To begin with, it has, of course, to do with our bodily nature. For our bodily nature determines the value of the various material commodities. But even material goods are variously valued, according to the kind of education and requirements of the individual person, but where spiritual and intellectual products are concerned – and these are often inseparable from the sphere of the material, physical goods – we shall find that the method of valuing any commodity whatever is absolutely determined by the whole make-up of the human being, and the amount and kind of work he or she is willing to perform in order to possess that commodity. Here we see that it is the spiritual or intellectual element in the human being that determines the value of a commodity, or of any sort of merchandise.

Secondly, we see that the goods being exchanged between one person and another are limited by the conditions of ownership, and that means neither more nor less than that they are limited by legal conditions. Whenever a person tries to obtain a commodity from another, he or she touches in some way the other's rights to the commodity in question, so that economic life with its circulation of commodities is permeated throughout by all sorts of legal conditions.

In the third place, a commodity has not merely the value we attach to it through our requirements and the personal importance we give to these requirements, which is then transferred to the commodity; it has also an objective value in itself. It has an objective value to the degree that it is durable or the reverse – lasting or perishable; to the degree that by its nature it is more or less serviceable, plentiful, or scarce. All these things condition an objective, actual economic value, the determination of which demands an objective expert knowledge, and the production of which requires an objective technical capacity. But these three determinations of value are brought together into a unity in the commodity. *SF105-106*

Socially Correct Value

Steiner introduces into the discussion of value creation an ethical or social element, which he characterizes as the socially correct value. This means that the value of a product must equal the value of all products needed by those who are engaged in its production until they are able to again produce a similar product. *[This idea is expanded upon in the discussion of True Price in Chapter Ten, Price Formation.]*

The socially correct value of a piece of goods can only be determined by comparison with other goods. Its value must equal the value of all other goods needed by the producers to fulfill their own requirements until the time when they can again produce a similar piece of goods. This they must do while considering all those requirements necessary in the interest of other people. (Herein must be included, for instance, the needs of their children and what they must contribute for the support of persons incapable of working, etc.) *RSO 12*

Consumption, Elimination of Value, and Value-Creating Tension

Having examined the continual creation and increase of values on the production side of the economic process, we must also examine the continual elimination of values through consumption. Value creation and the devaluing or elimination of a commodity is an ongoing process consistent with processes in any healthy organism. Overproduction is not healthy for the economy.

> *You see, then, that devaluation can also take place in the economic process, which as I said, you can therefore regard as an organic process – an organic process in which spirit constantly intervenes. There must be – or rather, there is – constant devaluation. As values proceed on their way from nature through labor to capital, they will be accompanied by a continual process of devaluation.* RE 58

> *. . . when values are created that are not destroyed in an appropriate way, although they are there to be destroyed, then a disturbance of the economic process also occurs. The process is disturbed by too much production. The process is disturbed simply because, put picturesquely, there is too much in the stomach of the economic life.* RE 205

> *A simple reflection will show you that consumption is exactly the opposite pole to production. We have been trying to find, on the one hand, the values that arise in the economic process within the sphere of production. Consumption, on the other hand, consists in a continual elimination of these values. In consumption they are constantly being used up; that is to say, consumption consists in a constant devaluation of the values. It is this that plays the other important part in the economic process – this constant devaluation of values. It is just through this, indeed, that we have a certain right to call the economic process an organic one, an organic process in which spirit then intervenes. It is of the essence of a living organism that something is continually being formed and again unformed. In any organism there must be continual*

> *production and consumption, and this must be so in the economic organism too. There must be a constant producing and a using-up of what is produced.* RE 56

The value of a product increases as the product moves through the production/distribution process. However, at the moment when the producer and/or distributor meets the consumer, a value-creating tension arises because of the value eliminating nature of consumption. Thus, the value-creating process of production reaches a peak and is reversed by the consumer. This tension at the moment of encounter between producer and consumer is itself a value-creating factor. The original value creation is a force in movement, whereas value-creating tension is an arresting force. Rudolf Steiner indicates that the difference between the two is like the difference between kinetic and potential energies in physics.

> *At this point we begin to see in a different light, and from a different point of view, the value-creating forces that we have been considering. Before this point, we have shown only how values arise as the process of production takes its course. At this point, every time a value approaches its moment of devaluation, the whole movement that we have been witnessing thus far will change. So far, we have been observing a progressive, forward movement. Values thus arise through the application of labor to nature; values arise through the application of the spirit to labor; and values arise through the application of the spirit to capital. All of this is a forward movement.*
>
> *In fact, we have been observing the value-creating movement in the economic process. As the devaluing factor of consumption enters into the process at every point, there will be something else as well. There will be a development of values that arises between production and consumption themselves. When a value enters the process of consumption, however, it no longer moves forward. It does not attain a higher degree of value, it no longer moves; for something now stands over against it. This is consumption – with*

its development of need. Here the value enters into a very different sphere from the one we have so far been studying. We have been considering the value in its progressive, forward movement. Now we must imagine its moving up to a certain point and being stopped there. Every time a value is stopped, there arises not a further value-creating movement, but a value-creating tension.

This is the second element in the economic process. In the economic process we have not only value-creating movements but also value-creating tensions. We can observe such value-creating tensions most conspicuously and simply where a consumer stands face-to-face with a producer or merchant, and in the very next moment the creation of value comes to an end, passing over into devaluation. Here there arises a tension – a tension that is maintained in equilibrium by the human need on the other side. Here the value-creating process is stopped. Human need or consumption confronts it, and there arises the tension between production and consumption.

This tension is also most decidedly a value-creating factor – albeit one that is comparable to a force that is restrained, held in equilibrium, rather than to a force that is working itself out. There is here a true analogy with the contrast in physics between kinetic and potential energies – between kinetic energies and those energies of position where an equilibrium is brought about. If you do not take into account these energies of tension, these potential energies, in the economic process, you will be driven to the strangest misconceptions. *RE 56-57*

By taking value-creating tensions into consideration, we can understand how rarity or scarcity affects product values.

Developing the ideas indicated here, one gains an intelligent conception of every economic relationship; otherwise, one is led into the greatest confusion. If, for example, you limit yourself to considering the movements of economic energies, you will never understand why the diamond in the king of England's crown has such an immense value. Here you are at once obliged to have recourse to the idea of economic tension-value. Many economists take into account the rarity of particular products of nature; but we can never understand rarity as a value-creating factor if we regard the movement in the economic process as the only creator of values. We must also learn to understand how there arises here and there – most of all through consumption, but through other relationships as well – what I would call the creation of value by tensions, situations, equilibria. *RE 57*

Values and Spiritual-Cultural Work

Thus far we have only considered the valuation of material goods in the economic process. How do we relate an economic value with cultural work such as education and art? Steiner gives an example of a self-contained village economy and asks on what basis is the work of the teacher or parson valued.

Think of a simple village economy – a self-contained one, if you will. There have actually been such economies, self-contained to some extent at least. It will consist, to begin with, of the things produced; we can imagine even the market and the town from this picture. This economy will consist of the farmers, the workers on the land, the workers in the different trades (those who clothe the people, for instance, and a few others) but no special proletarians. Such a thing will not yet exist, nor need we, in our present line of thought, turn our attention in that direction. Whatever is relevant to the proletariat will appear in due course. But our village economy will also include the schoolmaster and the parson, or two schoolmasters and two parsons. They will have to live on what the others give them, if it is a purely village economy. Whatever develops there of the free spiritual-cultural life will in the main have to develop among the teachers and the parsons; or possibly a parish clerk will be added. Now we must ask ourselves how a proper valuation comes about in this simple economic circuit. *RE 159-160*

Teachers, as a case in point, typically do comparatively little physical work. As far as the economy is concerned, in the case of the teacher, value is not created by work. What matters economically is the effectiveness of the instruction given by the teacher, rather than the energy exerted.

> *Of course one must designate education as an economic value in the highest degree, but it is a question, when one begins to imagine the concept of work in the economic process, whether one can then still retain anything of this concept if one calls education work. Of course work is already done in that those who teach speak, walk around and wear themselves out. Some kind of work is performed. But that is not what flows into the economic process. Their organizing activity, which is not even related to what they do as work, is what flows into that. Consequently the work of education is such a different one. A fidget can do a lot of work with fidgeting. Another can also do a lot of work by thrashing. But the one who gives instruction with a certain quiet rhythm will also do work. But this is not what enters into the economic process, rather it is that individual's free intellectual activity.* RE 236

> *We also already have work that is relatively liberating. On the one hand we have work that is actually tied to the object. This becomes ever freer from the object. In free intellectual activity it is entirely detached from the object. And what such a person "works" is irrelevant. The "work" of teachers is not what actually counts in the economic process. Their authority, their education, everything else is economically relevant, only not what they do as work.* RE 237

Cultural work has value to the extent that it meets a perceived need in the community. This dynamic is parallel to the one in which human needs play a role in the establishment of values of material goods.

> *What is the requisite condition for these spiritual-cultural workers to be able to live in the village at all? It is that the people send their children to school and that*

> *they have religious needs. Spiritual-cultural needs, therefore, are the fundamental premise. Failing such needs, even these few spiritual-cultural workers could not be there.* RE 160

In order to determine the economic value of any type of spiritual product or activity, we must consider what other members of a society must do in order for cultural work to take place. If some people engage in spiritual, artistic, or educational work, then other people must produce additional goods in order for everyone to have sufficient physical sustenance. In essence, cultural workers are to some degree spared the requirement of engaging in physical work. Thus, the correct valuation of cultural work in economic terms is related to the amount of physical work the cultural workers are spared while others make up the difference.

If there were no need for artists, educators, and others working in the cultural domain, then those people would contribute to the life of the community by doing physical work. In order to do their cultural work, these people must be spared the physical labor they would otherwise have to do. Therefore the economic value of their work is equivalent to the value of the physical labor from which they are spared. Inherent in this notion is the need for others in the community to produce additional goods to make up the difference for the work spared by the cultural workers.

> *And we shall have to ask ourselves how will these spiritual-cultural workers economically imbue their products with value – their sermons, for example (even these must be conceived in an economic sense), and their school lessons. How will these things be valued in the whole of economic circulation?*
>
> *This is a fundamental question. We shall gain an answer to this question only if we begin by imagining quite vividly what the others must be doing. They must be doing physical work. Through bodily labor they call forth economic values. If there were no need for sermons and school lessons, the parsons and teachers would have to do physical work. Everyone would be working with their hands and the spiritual-cultural life would drop out of the picture.*

We would no longer be concerned with the economic valuation of spiritual-cultural products. Thus we arrive at the required valuation precisely by observing that parsons and teachers are spared physical labor. If they are to do their spiritual-cultural work, which is desired, they must be relieved from the physical work . . . Therefore the valuation on their side will depend on the amount of physical labor of which they are relieved. This is the measure for the valuation of their work. One person contributes physical labor; another is spared physical labor, and this person's spiritual-cultural achievement has a value corresponding to the amount of physical labor that he or she is spared by virtue of it. Take these two economic aspects and think the process through economically, and you will see that even a sermon must have an economic value; and moreover think of how it acquires this economic value. It acquires it inasmuch as labor is spared, whereas on the other side labor has to be applied. RE 160-161

Take [a] young undergraduate who [has to write his] thesis . . . He sits there a whole year long, and possibly he produces a very creditable piece of work. But, my dear friends, what does this mean? It means that he is clothed and fed for a whole year while he is engaged in this task. What he eats and drinks, the clothes he wears withal, must be the product of so many other peoples' work. HBFJSQ Lecture 2

If it takes a person ten years to create a work of art that is meeting a need, then the value of the work is equal to the values of everything the artist would need to support him- or herself (food, clothing, shelter, etc.) for the next ten years while creating another work.

The same principle runs through the entire spiritual-cultural life. What does it signify, in the economic sense, if a man paints a picture – painting it, shall we say, for ten whole years? It signifies that the picture acquires a value for him inasmuch as it will enable him once more to spend ten years painting another picture. He can do so only if he can spare himself physical labor for a period of ten years. Therefore, the picture will have to become worth as much as the other

> *products made by physical labor during ten years.... In all cases of spiritual-cultural production, if you try to find the concept of value you will arrive at this other concept – the concept of labor that is saved or spared . . .*
>
> *What gives value to the product is in truth the labor that it will save me. On the one side of the economic process the actual doing of work, the bringing of labor to the product, is the value-creating factor; the product absorbs labor – attracts it. On the other side the product rays out labor, begets labor; the value is the original thing that calls the labor into being.*
>
> *We now have, therefore, a means of comparison – namely, labor on the one side and labor on the other side – and we are therefore in a position to relate them, for we may say: if the value in the one case equals "nature times labor," in the other we must call it "spirit minus labor."*
>
> $$V = N \times L$$
> $$V = S - L$$
>
> *The direction is exactly opposite. Physical labor has meaning only inasmuch as the one who wants to contribute it to the economic process actually does it himself or herself; while what is related to the product on the spiritual-cultural side is the labor that one person does for another. It must therefore be entered as a negative in the economic process.* *RE 161-162*

In the history of economics, some economists have claimed that it is labor which gives products their value, while others have insisted that a thing is valuable to the degree that it saves labor. In reality, both of these positions are true, but the one – labor working on nature – is related to nature, and the other – labor spared in cultural work – is related to spirit. Moreover, in reality the two types of activity are never separated completely. Physical production always involves a certain amount of mental work, which results in greater efficiency or sparing of labor, and cultural 'production' always entails some amount of physical work. The fact that labor appears in both processes, although differently, allows a comparison of economic values of natural and cultural products.

It is a remarkable thing. Study the history of economics, and you will always find that what is said is right, but only in a limited sphere. There are economists who believe that it is labor that gives things value – the school of Adam Smith and the school of Marx, for example. But other schools give another definition, which again is correct in a certain sphere. According to them, a thing becomes capital, that is, a source of value, inasmuch as it saves labor. Both points of view are true. The one is true of all that is in any way related to nature, to the soil, the land; while the other is related to spirit or mind. Between these two there is a third. In effect, neither of the two extremes is ever there in its pure form; they are only there in an approximately absolute sense. After all, even in picking blackberries (which acquires economic value only inasmuch as the workers actually go there and do it) – even here there is some spirit or mind at work. If, of two blackberry pickers, one lacks insight and has extra work by picking where the berries are scarce, while the other finds a place where there are plenty and obtains a better yield for the labor, the blackberries of the former worker are of less value, relatively speaking, because the same quantity of berries only brings in the same amount of money. In effect, then, neither extreme is ever realized absolutely. Even the gathering of blackberries entails spirit or mind at work (although we might not call it so) . . .

As I said just now, we have neither of the two extremes in any absolute sense. For on the other side ($V = S - L$), no matter how much painters use their intelligence, they must still do some physical labor if they wish to create anything of economic value. Even if they exercise clairvoyant power (a thing that one cannot grasp at all in terms of economics), even then they must still do some physical labor. Relying on their genius, it may be that they can afford to be lazy; still, now and then they must take up the brush. Some physical work has to be done even in this case, just as some little effort of thought must go even into the picking of blackberries. (Things that take place in real life cannot be grasped merely quantitatively. They have to be grasped while they are actually happening.

Therefore we can grasp them with our concepts only if we realize that the concepts themselves need to be kept in constant movement).

It is between these two extremes that we can perceive more clearly how in real economic life physical and spiritual-cultural work play into one another, moving back and forth. Just as in some machine there is a regulated backward and forward movement, so in industry physical work from the one side and spiritual-cultural work from the other are passing back and forth. It is in this mutual interplay from two directions that we have, as a third, what plays into the economic process between the other two. We have the case where people have to do physical labor, yet by their spiritual or mental power (using their wits) they are relieved from some of it. This is always actually the case, except that it sometimes approximates more to the formula I wrote above ($V = N \times L$), and sometimes more to the formula I wrote below ($V = S - L$). The latter, in effect, would be fulfilled in its entirety only if there could be among the consumers someone who did nothing but save labor by means of his or her spiritual-cultural faculties; and it could only be someone who was born already fully mature. RE 162-164

Every society needs to find the right balance between physical and cultural work. As a civilization advances, cultural work is valued more highly and sought after by society. The more fruitful cultural work is, the more it is desired, and the more its fruits then play back into economic life. At the same time, as cultural work increases in importance, the value-creating power of physical labor is more and more reduced, though numerically rather than qualitatively, as long as physical laborers have a growing need for what the cultural domain offers. In a healthy society, there is mutual compensation between the two realms of work with regard to value, but there are limits to this compensation process. In a community in which there are too many cultural workers, the labor saving power may be too strong, and the relation of production to consumption swings out of balance.

In this way we can look into the economic process from this aspect of valuation, valuing what comes from nature on the one hand and from spirit on the other. At this point we can say that where positive and negative work into one another, somehow an intermediate condition will emerge. Either the positive or the negative can predominate. Let us assume for a moment that the positive dominates. In the village economy it certainly will do so, for in such a community there will be no widespread interest in spiritual-cultural work, beyond what is absolutely necessary. But the more life grows complicated (or, as we are apt to say sentimentally, the more "civilization advances") the more highly, as may be seen even empirically, spiritual-cultural work is valued. That is to say, the more labor is saved, the more a negative element comes in as against the positive. I beg you to consider well, that by characterizing it in this way we are taking hold of a real process. It is not that physical labor is done on the one side and then negated on the other. That would be no real progress in the economic sense; it would at most be a process of nature. All that is done out of physical labor helps to create values. None of the value is destroyed. What counteracts the saving of labor from the other side, counteracts it only in a numerical sense. In a purely numerical sense, it affects the value of physical labor. For this very reason, we are enabled to express in a real way what actually happens. Physical workers are active; spiritual-cultural workers are active – but the achievement in the one case is work that is positively done, while in the other it is a work that in reality signifies a saving of work. Only by this means is an effective valuation brought about.

The aspects are divested of their particularity and it becomes possible to grasp the process in terms of numbers, inasmuch as it is the same factor that emerges on either side and only the valuation is altered. With the advance of civilization, then, spiritual-cultural work increases in importance, and this implies that bodily work has a less powerful effect on the valuing process. Physical strength is of course applied, and it must be so more and more as we go forward. Even the cultivation of the soil must be made more fruitful as civilization advances. More work must be done, in a positive sense. The point is that the physical labor is divested, to some extent, of its value-creating power. Yet this again can be so only if those who perform the physical labor evince a growing need for what has to be achieved from the spiritual-cultural side. Here, once again, a human factor comes into the economic process. You cannot get around it; indeed, with the advance of spiritual-cultural life, this particular human factor makes itself felt as an objective necessity.

It is quite true that, to begin with, when there are only the parson and the teacher, there is not much spiritual-cultural life in our village. But suppose there are two villages. In one village the parson and the teacher are average people; things will go on as they are. In the other village the parson or the teacher, or both of them, are above average people. They will be able to stimulate all manner of spiritual-cultural interests in the next generation and, in all probability, by the time the next generation arises, some other spiritual-cultural worker is brought into the village. Now there are three of them. In this regard the spiritual-cultural has a very fertile power, which in its turn works back into economic life. What, in the last resort, does the process signify? It signifies that precisely labor, or rather the value-creating power of labor, which in the purely material phase of economic life has an infinitely great value, is more and more reduced in course of time by what comes to meet it from the other side. I cannot exactly say it is "devalued"; it is reduced numerically. In the working together between all that is represented by working the land (the tilling of the soil, and so forth), and what is done from the spiritual-cultural side, we have a kind of mutual compensation. And a certain compensation is the only right thing.

Complex conditions arise again here. It may well turn out that in a given place there are too many spiritual-cultural producers; that is, the counteracting labor-saving power may be too strong. The resultant value is then negative, and the people cannot all live together except by consuming one another. Thus there is a limit somewhere to this compensation process. For every economic realm there is a certain balance, in the very nature of the case, between production from the land on the one side and spiritual-cultural production on the other. *RE 164-166*

Machines and Cultural Productivity

In modern times, the creation and use of machines is one of the fruits of cultural life. Human inventiveness and intelligence created them and is needed to operate them. Thanks to the work of human intelligence working on machinery, there have been great advances in productivity in economic life.

> *By . . . machines, technical science has, to put it in a few words, succeeded in providing commodities for public consumption. To the existence of this machinery is entirely due the fact that from four hundred to five hundred millions of tons of coal were brought to the surface per annum for industrial purposes before the War. Now if one calculates the amount of economic energy and power required by those machines, which are entirely the result of human thought and can only be worked by human thought, the following interesting result is arrived at. If we reckon an eight-hour day, we get the startling result that by these machines, that is, through the human thought incorporated in the machines, through the inventive gift of the mind, as much energy and working force are used as could be produced by seven to eight hundred millions of men!*
>
> *Hence, if you picture to yourself that the earth has a working population of about 1500 million men, it has gained, by the inventive genius of human beings in the recent periods of modern civilization, seven hundred to eight hundred millions more. Therefore, two thousand millions of human beings work, that is to say, while the seven to eight hundred millions do not themselves actually work, but the machines work for them. What works in these machines? The human intellect. It is between these two extremes that we can perceive more clearly how in real economic life physical and spiritual-cultural work play into one another, moving*

back and forth. Just as in some machine there is a regulated backward and forward movement, so in industry physical work from the one side and spiritual-cultural work from the other are passing back and forth. It is in this mutual interplay from two directions that we have, as a third, what plays into the economic process between the other two. We have the case where people have to do physical labor, yet by their spiritual or mental power (using their wits) they are relieved from some of it. This is always actually the case, except that it sometimes approximates more to the formula I wrote above (V = N × L), and sometimes more to the formula I wrote below (V = S – L). The latter, in effect, would be fulfilled in its entirety only if there could be among the consumers someone who did nothing but save labor by means of his or her spiritual-cultural faculties; and it could only be someone who was born already fully mature.

Every society needs to find the right balance between physical and cultural work. As a civilization advances, cultural work is valued more highly and sought after by society. The more fruitful cultural work is, the more it is desired, and the more its fruits then play back into economic life. At the same time, as cultural work increases in importance, the value-creating power of physical labor is more and more reduced, though numerically rather than qualitatively, as long as physical laborers have a growing need for what the cultural domain offers. In a healthy society, there is mutual compensation between the two realms of work with regard to value, but there are limits to this compensation process. In a community in which there are too many cultural workers, the labor saving power may be too strong, and the relation of production to consumption swings out of balance. SF 35-36

SEVEN

Capital

[Putting excess capital into land/nature] can be prevented by leading the excess capital, not into nature, where it would become fixed, but into independent spiritual-cultural undertakings, where it vanishes except for the remnant, which must continue as a kind of seed by which the economic process can be maintained. *RE 87*

Instead of common ownership of the means of production, a circulation of the means of production will come about within the social organism . . . *TSR 89*

SEVEN

Capital

Capital Creation

We will start by referring to the illustration on the value creation cycle. *[See Diagram 1, pg. 147.]* As we have seen, nature is transformed into an economic value by human labor and then placed into circulation. Labor in its turn is organized by intelligence, by means of which additional value is created. Through this process, capital arises in the means of production, inventory, or accumulated cash assets. In a healthy economy, capital receives value to the degree that it is put to productive use for economic purposes.

> *You see, we must be clear not only on this, that nature as such receives an economic value only when it enters into the general economic circulation – when it is taken up by labor – and again, that labor receives an economic value only through the way it is organized or divided; and finally, that capital receives a value only through the fact that it is taken over by the human spirit and thus worked into the economic process.* *RE 146*

The most direct consequence of the division of labor is that it makes economic production more efficient, thereby enabling the first phase of capital creation. We can say, then, that capital is first created by labor permeated by intelligence or spirit. A second consequence of the division of labor, given the increasing complexity and use of machinery, is that the human being becomes increasingly separated from nature.

> *. . . Wherever you look, you will always see that this is so. The point of origin of capital always lies in the division,*

the qualitative division, of labor . . . In one respect or another, human labor is permeated by spirit. It is labor-permeated-by-spirit that arises in the process of the division of labor. Where we see capital arise in the course of the division of labor, we have, in the first place, nothing other than labor penetrated by spirit. The first phase of capital always consists in this. Where human labor hitherto was determined only by nature, it is now organized, divided, and so forth, by spirit.

It is indeed necessary to see capital and its formation very clearly from this point of view. Only from this point of view can we understand the function of capital in the economic process. The forming of capital is always a concomitant of the division – that is to say, the qualitative, organic division – of labor.

In this process, however, something of the direct, immediate connection that the human being has with nature when working upon the earth is always loosened. You see, so long as economic life consists merely in the elaboration of nature, all that we deal with are the products of nature, which, on being transformed by human labor, acquire an economic value. The moment the human spirit organizes labor, however – organizes, that is to say, labor as such . . . an emancipation from nature begins to take place. RE 43-44

. . . We may say then that what in a primitive economic condition is originally all together – what one does in egotism for oneself – . . . is now divided up among the whole community. Such is the division of labor. With capital, the single parts are gathered up again into a total, collected process. The forming of capital is a synthesis. RE 46

The Social Necessity and Benefit of Free Access to Capital

It is to the benefit of the whole of society that people capable of producing things of value have access to the capital they need to take initiative – free of charge. This access is necessary in order for the creative activities of individuals to enter fully into the economic process.

. . . Management based on individual capacities, when properly applied, supplies the social organism with goods that are of interest to all who belong to this organism. Whatever a person's circumstances and position, it is in his or her interest that nothing be lost which flows out of individual, human capacities and leads to the creation of goods that serve human life. But such capacities can only develop when people can unfold them through their own free initiative. Whenever this freedom is hindered, humanity is the poorer; to some extent at least, it is deprived of benefits which would otherwise have been available to it . . . It is capital which is the means of rendering these capacities effective in many different realms of society. It is therefore in the real interest of everyone within the social organism to ensure that all ownership of capital is managed in such a way that an individually gifted person or a group of people with particular capacities can gain access to the level of capital that their own free initiative requires. Everyone, from the creative mind to the laborer, must acknowledge that it is in his or her own objective interests not only for sufficient numbers of capable people or groups to have completely unhampered access to capital, but also for them to be able to use their own free initiative in obtaining it. Only they can judge how, by means of capital, their individual capacities will create goods useful to the social organism. *TSR 74-75*

At our present stage of development, the creative activity of individual capacities cannot usefully enter into the economic process without free access to capital. This free access must be available if production is to be fruitful – not because it is advantageous to an individual or a group of people, but because it can best serve the whole community when based on proper social understanding. *TSR 76-77*

. . . Entrepreneurial activity can only play a healthy role in the social organism if the forces at work in this organism allow individual human capacities to unfold in the best possible way. This can only happen if one sphere of the social organism enables those capable of it to have a free rein in

exercising their initiative and making use of their capacities. At the same time, the value of these capacities must be freely recognized by other people. TSR 65-66

. . . The modern process of production, because of its technical perfection, necessitates the initiative of individuals and therefore requires that individuals shall have capital at their disposal, and that they shall be able to carry on production on their own initiative; these are the results of the recent development of humanity. SF 36

Capital and Property Rights

In a healthy threefold society, the state or rights domain ensures that entrepreneurial individuals have free access to capital. Allocations would be made on an individual basis, according to the needs of society. At the same time, the rights domain would guard against the abuse of the power that comes with responsibility and authority over capital. Whatever is produced by way of free access to capital must in turn become available to the whole community. However, this does not imply that the means of production, or capital, should be owned and controlled by the state. Rather, it should circulate, stewarded by capable people *as long as* they are working productively on behalf of society.

. . . The legal and rights sphere's fundamentally democratic focus, which has to do with what affects all people in the same way, will make sure that ownership rights do not gradually become ownership wrongs. This sphere will not itself dabble in ownership and property, but will ensure that capital and property is made freely available to those able to make fruitful use of it and thus put their unhindered capacities at the service of the whole community. Such a structuring would allow ownership rights, or free access to them, to be allocated in a quite personal, individual way in each instance, as long as this seemed useful. TSR 79

. . . We will actually be incapable of believing that any structure which we consider 'ideal' could possibly turn out

perfect and uncontradictory. It is absolutely right for modern socialism to demand that production serving individual profit should be replaced by production serving general consumption. But those who fully recognize what this demand entails will be unable to share modern socialism's conclusions that the means of production must therefore be transferred to common ownership. They will instead see that whatever is produced through individual activity and capacity must subsequently become available to the whole community in the right way. Modern economics has been directed towards creating income through producing quantities of goods. The task of the future, in contrast, will be to find, through associations of people, the type of production which best corresponds with consumption, and the most appropriate channels from producers to consumers. Legal and rights organizations will ensure that any enterprise only remains connected with a particular person or group of people as long as this connection is justified by their individual capacities. Instead of common ownership of the means of production, a circulation of the means of production will come about within the social organism, so that these continually become available to the people whose individual capacities can render them of greatest possible use to the whole community. TSR 89

Since it is possible for capital to be created only in the context and through the workings of society as a whole, its continued use should remain connected to the needs of society. This social requirement, already recognized with regard to intellectual property or copyright, should also apply to all property. If the free access to and use of capital is abused, then that access and use should be revoked. In a threefold society, the goal is not to eliminate private property, but to provide for its proper and just limitations.

Individual capacities must be allowed free access to the capital base; but at the same time the right of ownership connected with this must be able to be revoked at the moment that it becomes a means for the unjustified exercise of power. This social requirement is actually already taken account of in one particular regulation, but only in regard to a person's

> *so-called 'intellectual estate' or copyright. At a certain period after the death of its creator, this estate becomes the property of the community. Underlying this arrangement is a truly social way of thinking. However intimately a purely intellectual or spiritual 'product' is connected with its original creator's individual gifts, it is nevertheless, at the same time, a product of society, and must return to it in due course. But this actually applies to all property. An individual can only produce goods for the community with the cooperation of this wider community. The right to a property cannot therefore be administered separately from the interests of this community. So it is of no use to look for ways of eliminating ownership of the capital base. What we need instead is to administer this ownership so that it can serve the whole community in the most fruitful way possible.* TSR 78

Capital also can become harmful when those who have access to it use their power to control and corrupt the social structure of the economic domain, or when investors accumulate wealth, but make no contribution to production and increase of values. A healthy social structure will not allow capital assets to be isolated or withdrawn from the management of the means of production. Moreover, it will block the possibility of deriving income through dividends, that is, of earning income without working and contributing to the community.

> *When blue collar and white collar workers meet with each other, they need only consider economic issues because legal matters will be dealt with separately under the state's jurisdiction. The blue collar worker can associate freely with the manager of the business, because only the division, on economic principles, of that which they have earned together will be allowed; there will be no economic compulsion resulting from the greater economic resources of the manager. The associative structuring of the economic body will place the blue collar workers' contractual relationship to the business manager in a totally different light. Up to now, they have been forced to fight against the interests of the business manager, but in their new associative role they will share in the fruits of production . . .*

An individual business cannot be socialized; socialization happens only when the production of economic value that a separate business contributes to the total economic life has no antisocial effect. As a result of such genuine socialization, the capitalist system will lose its harmful tendencies. (In my book, Towards Social Renewal, *I have described how capital must function within a healthy threefold organism.) It should be clear by now that one cannot "do away" with capital, since capital is nothing other than the means of production working for the community. It is not capital itself that is harmful, but rather capital in private hands, especially if this private ownership is able to control the social structure of the economic body. But if society can be structured in the manner previously described, then capital can no longer have any antisocial influence. The beneficial social structure will always prevent the capital assets from being isolated from the management of the means of production. It will also put a stop to the attempts of those who strive only for capital assets, but shirk participation in the economic process. One could readily object that others who do participate would gain nothing, should the earning of nonparticipants be "divided up." The objection has some validity, and yet it disguises the truth, for its validity has no significance for the structuring of the social organism. The harmfulness of the nonworking recipients of dividends is not that to a small degree they diminish the workers' earnings, but that the sheer possibility of people being able to have income without working for it lends an antisocial aspect to the whole economic body. The economic body that blocks the possibility to derive income from dividends differs from the one that cannot block it just as human organisms, too, differ – the one is healthy and impervious in all areas to the invasion of a tumor; the other, through the accumulation of unhealthy elements, is beset by a tumorous growth.* *RSO 10-12*

Administration and Transference of Capital

In an associative economy, accumulations of capital are needed so that capable people have the resources necessary to do their work in the world, for the good of society. However, while free access to capital must be available to individuals, capital ultimately must be understood as a community asset rather than personal property. On this basis, capital must circulate freely among capable persons rather than through purchase and sale or inheritance. Once provided with capital and other means of production, including land, entrepreneurs retain rights of access and use for as long as they are productive. When, for whatever reason, they are no longer productive, they pass the capital on to other capable and productive people. Even capital that is generated by a particular individual must remain in the possession of that person only for as long as she or he uses it in a productive way for the benefit of the community.

When, for whatever reason, entrepreneurs are no longer able to make productive use of the capital in their possession, they must arrange to make it available without charge to a successor capable of putting it to further use for the common good. If an entrepreneur is not capable of personally overseeing such a transfer of capital, then the responsibility will pass to a corporation or group within the cultural domain whose purpose is to administer the transference of capital. That group will act according to principles established in the rights sphere and transfer available capital to a successor or successors who have appropriate capacities, skills, knowledge, and social responsibility. In such fashion, capital can freely circulate.

> *An independent economy will also involve changes in private property laws. Socialist theory demands the abolition of private property and its conversion to public ownership, but to informed individuals, these slogans are just meaningless words. Let me illustrate what they could mean. As you know, we are very proud of our philosophers, but our pride does not prevent sound thinking about intellectual property. We realize that intellectual property is not produced by a socialized economy or a collective, but by creative, actively involved individuals. It simply does not work to separate individuals with their abilities and talents from the process of intellectual production. Nonetheless, our thinking on this subject is socially responsible: at the end of a legally prescribed time-period after the death of the inventor*

or author, intellectual property no longer belongs to the heirs but enters the public domain, where it "belongs" to those who can best make it accessible to the general public. Perhaps because we place no special value on spiritual or intellectual activity, we accept time-limits on copyrights as a matter of course; but we make no attempt to deal with physical private property in the same way. Private property should also remain in the hands of its originator only as long as that person is present and applying his or her individual abilities to its management. When the original owner is no longer present, physical personal property should pass into the public domain: that is, to those with the most ability to administer it for the good of all. *FTSF 59*

. . . those who simply say that capital should be abolished or transformed into common property have no idea how capital works in the economic system, especially under the present conditions of production. They do not know that accumulations of capital are needed in order that, through the control of capital, people may work for the public good. For this reason in my book, Towards Social Renewal, *the administration of capital was made, on the whole, dependent on the spiritual organization in co-operation with the independent political and legal organization. Whereas we now say that capital makes business, the impulse for the threefold order of the social organism requires that, although it should always be possible to accumulate capital, provision must be made for capital to be administered by someone who has developed out of the spiritual life the necessary capacity for business, and that this accumulation of capital may be administered by the person to whom it belongs only as long as he or she is able to administer it him- or herself. When capitalists can no longer put their own capacities into the administration of the capital, they must see – or if they should feel themselves incapable of such a task, a corporation of the spiritual organization must assume the responsibility of seeing – that the management of the business shall pass to a highly capable successor, able to carry it on for the benefit of the community. That is to say, the transference of*

a business concern to any person or group of persons is not dependent on purchase or any other displacement of capital, but is determined by the capacity of individuals themselves. It is a matter of transfer from the capable to the capable, from those who can work in the service of the community to those who can also work in the best way for the common good. The social safety of the future depends on this kind of transfer. It will not be an economic transfer, as is now the case; this transfer will result from the impulses of human beings, received from the independent spiritual-intellectual life and from the independent legal-political life. There will even be corporations within the cultural organization, united with all other departments of the cultural life, on which the administration of capital will devolve. SF 118-119

Capital, including land and other means of production, must be evaluated from the perspective of cost only when it is being built up or created. Thereafter, capital loses its value as a commodity to be bought and sold and can only rightfully be transferred from one person to another facilitated by collaboration of both the legal and cultural spheres. Cultural capacities – insight, experience, and practical knowledge – are employed in deciding who should receive the right to use capital that is being transferred, and the legal or rights sphere ensures that the transfer is done in a legally responsible way.

It is impossible to reach a just determination of price as long as the means of production and land function as they now do within the economic system. The disposal of land, systematized in the laws relating to its ownership, and the disposal of the finished means of production (for example, a factory with its machinery and equipment), should be no matter for the economic organization; they must belong partly to the spiritual and partly to the legal. That is to say, the transference of land from one person or group of persons to another must not be carried out by purchase or through inheritance, but by transference through legal means, on the principles of the spiritual organization. The means of

> *production through which something is manufactured – a process which lies at the basis of the creation of capital – can only be looked at from the viewpoint of its commodity cost while it is being built up. Once it is ready for operation, its creators take over its management because they understand it best. They have charge of it as long as they can personally use their capacities. But the finished means of production is no longer a commodity to be bought and sold; it can only be transferred by one person or group of persons to another person or group of persons by law, or rather, by spiritual decisions confirmed by law. Thus, what at present forms part of economic life, such as the laws relating to the disposal of property, to the sale of land, and to the right of disposal of the means of production, will be placed on the basis of the independent legal organization working in conjunction with the independent spiritual organization.* *SF 120-121*

> *In my* Towards Social Renewal *I have tried to show that a truly social way of thinking will not aim at a transference of capital from the control of private persons (or groups) to the community as a whole; on the contrary, it is essential that the private individual should have means, by the use of capital, of placing his or her abilities, unopposed, at the service of the community. When this individual is no longer willing or able to direct his or her abilities to the use of capital, this use must be transferred to another person of similar abilities. It will not be transferred by state prerogative or by economic power, but by finding out, on strength of the training acquired under the free spiritual life, which person will make the most suitable successor from the social point of view.* *RSO 101*

Through the cooperation of all three spheres in a threefold social organism, economic, political, and cultural, capable individuals who want to produce something for society could have sufficient economic power to do so under terms preventing this power from being abused. Such cooperation among the spheres of social life would assure that transfer of capital occurs according to principles that have nothing to do with economic power.

Principles of social justice cannot successfully be cultivated in the realm of purely economic thought. A feeling for and development of these other principles are possible only when people take an interest in the rights and spiritual/cultural life, and are not occupied with and guided by economic interests alone. Economic life must therefore be supported and directed by impulses that flow from the spiritual/cultural and rights life. Only then, with the three spheres working together, will there be just relations among people in economic life.

> *. . . Presently, the best services can be rendered to the community as a whole only by qualified persons through the control of large sums of capital. However, the nature of economics dictates that such services can only consist of the most efficient production of the goods that the community needs. A certain amount of economic power flows into the hands of the people who produce such goods. It cannot be otherwise, and the threefold social order recognizes this. Accordingly, it aims to bring about a society in which this economic power will still arise, but out of which no social evils can grow. The threefold idea does not propose to hinder the accumulation of large sums of capital in individual hands; it recognizes that to do so would be to lose the possibility of employing socially the abilities of these private individuals in the service of the general public. It proposes, however, that the moment an individual can no longer attend to the management of the means of production within his or her sphere of power, these means of production should be transferred to another capable person. The latter will not be able to obtain these means of production through any economic power he or she may possess, but solely because he or she is the most capable person. In practice, however, this can only be realized when the transfer is directed according to principles that have nothing to do with the means of economic power; such principles become possible only when the people themselves, with their interests, are engaged in spheres of life other than the economic. If people are joined together on a legal foundation which produces interests other than economic ones, these other interests will then be*

able to assert themselves. If the human being is absorbed by economic interests alone, those other interests never develop. If the person who possesses the means of production is to have any feeling whatever that the best and most efficient person in any economic position is one who obtains it by ability and not by economic power, such a feeling must grow in a sphere established apart from the economic. In and of itself, the economic life can call forth a sense for economic power but not, simultaneously, a sense for social justice. Therefore, all attempts to conjure out of economic thought itself a code of social justice were bound to fail. *RSO 104-105*

Thus, instead of handing over the means of production to the community, we transfer it from one capable person to another equally capable, that is, the means of production is circulated within the community. This circulation depends on the freedom of the cultural life by which it is effected and upheld. So that we may say, the main factor in the circuit of economic life is the impulse which is at work in the spiritual and in the equity life. It would be impossible to imagine any unity more complete than that effected in economic life by such measures. But the stream that unites itself with the economic organization flows from the free spiritual and the free political organizations. No longer will society be exposed to the chance that is expressed in supply and demand, or in the other factors in our present economic organization. Reasonable and just relations between one human being and another will enter into this new economic life, so that the spiritual, legal and economic organizations will work together as one, even though they are administered separately. Those responsible will carry over from one sphere into another – since they belong to all three – what each sphere needs.
SF 119-120

The means of production will have a one-time cost or economic value: the cost of creating them. Capital dissolves as soon as the creation of the means of production is completed. The producer has a right of access to any accumulation of capital which results from conducting business, as long as it is used to expand production.

When the producer stops directing production, or when capital accumulates and is not being used to expand production, then such capital is to be transferred to other capable people. Entrepreneurs only benefit personally from the business according to what they believe are the capacities they bring to it, and to what seems justified by those who grant and oversee their use of the capital in question. If capital increases under their directorship, they are entitled to a percentage of it, as established by contract. When a producer is no longer productive, the means of production will be transferred as a free gift.

> *. . . In a healthy social organism, capital goods and other means of production will have a one-time cost at the time of delivery. The producer will then be able to manage them, but only for as long as he or she can contribute to production by managing them. The business will then have to be transferred to another, not by sale nor by inheritance, but rather as a free gift to the one best able to manage it. It will have no sale value, and thus no value in the hands of an heir who does not work. Capital with independent economic power will work in the establishment of the means of production; it will dissolve itself instantly when the creation of the means of production is finished. Now, however, capital consists mostly of such "already established means of production."* RSO 12

> *As long as a person or group of people continues in the productive activity that originally connected them with a capital base, they will continue to have the right of access to the capital accumulation that results from operating profits, if these are used for expanding production. But the moment that such a person or group of people stops directing and managing this production, this capital accumulation should be transferred to another person or group engaged in a similar kind of production, or else a different kind but still one that serves the social organism. Likewise, the capital arising through production that is not used for its expansion should be similarly redirected. The only property personally owned by individuals running the enterprise would be what they draw from the business, which would be in accordance with*

> *what they believe to be commensurate with their individual capacities when they take on the management of production, and which at the same time seems justified by the confidence in them of others who allow them the use of capital. If capital is increased through the activity of such people, they would be entitled to an amount of this increase in proportion to the capital increase – like an interest payment [as determined by contract].* *TSR 80*

One way to prevent accumulation of capital would be to institute time-dated money, which would wear out and lose value over time. It would be impossible to accumulate interest on interest. *[Time-dated money will be explained in Chapter Nine on Money.]*

> *. . . Once a certain period has elapsed, ownership of capital returns to the community in an appropriate form. And to ensure that money not active in production processes is not retained by its owners, circumventing the measures implemented by the economic sphere, new minting can take place from time to time. A further result of organizing things in this way is that interest accruing on capital would continually diminish through the years. Money would wear out just as goods do. But such a governmental measure would be right and proper, making it impossible to simply sit back and gain 'interest from interest.'* *TSR 95*

Similar restrictions would be placed on personal savings. Out of their personal insight and discernment, individuals could bequeath their accrued savings to a person or group who would use that capital in a productive manner, but not for purely unearned personal benefit. When a person fails to make arrangements to pass on his savings in an appropriate way, then the rights administration arranges for this to be done within the cultural sphere. Assets may be passed on within a family only if the person inheriting the assets has the capacities necessary to use the capital in a productive way. Transferring capital to unproductive people has a damaging effect on society as a whole. This is a radical departure from typical inheritance laws currently in effect.

Likewise, assets gained through savings, together with the accrued interest, pass after the death of the person who acquired them, or at a certain point thereafter, to a person or group involved in material or cultural production specified in the individual's will – and to such a person or group only, not to someone uninvolved in production, for whom it would just be a kind of private income. And again, if a person or group cannot be directly chosen, the transfer of access to capital can be delegated to a branch of the cultural, spiritual sphere. Only when individuals fail to make arrangements for passing on capital themselves will the rights administration step in and arrange for this function to be organized within the cultural sphere . . .

. . . regulation of the social organism will allow legitimate personal and family initiatives to be brought into harmony with the needs of the wider community. It is of course easy to see that there might be great temptation to transfer property to one's descendants while one was still alive, and that such descendants might be able to seem productive while nevertheless being far less efficient that others more suited to carry on the production. Yet such temptation would be very greatly diminished within a social organism formed in this way. The rights-state would only need to demand that the property passed from one family member to another must be transferred to a sector of the cultural sphere once a certain period after the original producer's death had elapsed. Or some other means could be devised for ensuring that regulations were not breached. Rights administration will only ensure that such transfer occurs. An organization within the cultural sphere must decide who should be the inheritor. Fulfilling these basic premises will allow understanding to develop for the fact that successors and descendants need to be suitably raised and educated for the social organism, and that simply transferring capital as inheritance to unproductive people is socially damaging. People with real social understanding will have no interest in perpetuating their connection with the capital base via people or groups of people whose individual capacities do not justify this. *TSR 83-85*

Both the cultural and rights spheres would be jointly responsible for the transference of capital to descendants. There could be a time limit placed on inheritances similar to copyright laws.

Transferring capital or savings from a deceased person would be regulated by the cultural sphere according to principles established in the rights sphere. There could be a time limit placed on inheritances similar to copyright laws. If there is a healthy threefold social life, people will know how to distribute capital left behind by a deceased person in a useful and equitable way.

> *Social thinking has to be developed in the community of other human beings. And then the social thinker's task is above all to consider how the social order must be laid out if people are to work together rightly at the task of founding social life on the direct experience of social fellowship. Therefore I never say to people: this is how you should organize private property as a means of production, or public property as a means of production. I am bound to say, rather: Try to work towards a threefold ordering of the social organism; then the operations of capital will be regulated from the spiritual realm, and infused with human rights from the political realm. Then spiritual life and the life of rights will flow together with economic life in an orderly way. And then that will come about which, in accordance with certain concepts of justice, will see to it that whatever someone acquires, beyond his or her own needs as a consumer, shall continually pass over into the spiritual realm. It returns once more to the spiritual realm.*
>
> *At the present time this arrangement applies only to spiritual [intellectual] property, where it shocks nobody. A man cannot preserve his spiritual property for his descendants for more than a certain period – thirty years after his death at most. Then it becomes public property. We have only to take this as a possible model for the return flow of everything that is produced by individual effort, and indeed of everything embraced by the capitalist system – a model for the leading back of all this into the social organism. The question then is simply – how is it all to be divided up?*

> *In such parts as will do justice to the immediate spiritual and individual abilities, and also the former individual abilities, of the human beings concerned: it will be a question for the spiritual realm. People will arrange it like that if they are rightly situated within the social order. That is what this way of thinking assumes.* IASQ 64-65

Personal savings from income that is the result of work done on behalf of society should remain one's personal property until death. Capital savings can be passed on to others for use in the production of something needed by society, but not for private pensions and the like. Beyond a certain amount determined in the rights sphere, capital accumulations owing to the means of production must return to society for the common good, since in reality the whole of society is involved in some way in the production of goods and services. Modern inheritance taxes redistribute savings after death to some extent, but in this case the money goes to the government rather than to cultural or economic life directly.

> *This kind of arrangement [transference of capital to capable people] will work for capital accumulation from a certain level onwards, which is acquired by a person or group through the means of production (which includes estate and land ownership), and which is not part of the original terms agreed to as recompense for the exercising of individual capacities.*
>
> *All such earnings, and the savings arising from the individual's (or group's) own efforts and work will remain the property of the individual who acquired them, or his successors, until his death or some later point in time. Until then, interest arising naturally through awareness of legal obligation, and determined by the rights sphere, will be payable by anyone who is allocated use of such savings for the purpose of creating means of production . . . This distinction is in harmony with an awareness of people's rights, and with the interests of the whole community. The savings someone achieves, and makes available to the production process, serve the common interest. It is this which enables production to be managed through individual human capacities.*

> *Capital increase arising from the means of production – after deduction of legitimate interest – owes its existence to the working of the whole social organism. It should therefore flow back into it again in the way I have described. Rights administration will only determine that transfer of the relevant capital accumulation needs to occur in the way described; it will not be its role to make decisions about which material or cultural production should receive this transfer of capital or savings. That would lead to a tyranny of the state over material or cultural production, whose benefit for the social organism is best developed by individual human capacities. But if individuals do not themselves wish to choose where the capital created through them should go, they should be free to delegate this decision to a branch of the spiritual, cultural sphere.* TSR 82-83

Profit Motive and Capital Increase

In the modern market economy, potential profit is usually the determining factor in whether or not something should be produced. In an associative economy, the associations would establish rational correspondences between production and consumption, replacing the potential for profit as the basis for production. Profit would be the *result* of producing a product efficiently that met a societal need, and would indicate that the economic life was functioning in a healthy way, but it would not be the primary *cause* or reason for producing something.

The profit motive must be eliminated not because of its egotistical nature, but because the evolution of social life in our time requires that the production of goods and services no longer be dependent on chances of the market.

> *In estimating the economic significance of profits, impertinent opinions often intrude. Certainly profit-making is an egotistical aim. However, it is unjustified to use this egotism as an argument for eliminating profit from economic activity. For there must be something in the economy that can serve to indicate whether there is a need for a manufactured*

article. In the modern form of economics, the only indicator of this need is the fact that the article yields profits. An article can be manufactured if it yields profits that, in the economic context, are sufficiently large. An article that yields no profits must not be produced because it will upset the price balance of articles in actual circulation. Profits may represent what they will in ethical terms; in conventional economic terms, they represent an indicator for the need to produce an article.

The further evolution of economics does require the elimination of profits, but for the following reason: because they make the production of articles dependent on accidents of the market, the abolition of which is demanded by the spirit of the age. One clouds one's judgments if one argues against profit because of its egotistical nature. Real life demands that within any field one must mount arguments appropriate to the particular situation. Arguments drawn from another field of life may be perfectly true in themselves, but they cannot guide one's judgment toward the real facts.

What is necessary for economic life is that profits as indicators should be replaced by groups tasked with establishing a rational correspondence between production and consumption that will abolish accidents of the market. The change from profit-indicator to a rational coordination of production and consumption, if correctly understood, will result in the elimination of the motives that have hitherto clouded judgment of this issue by removing them to the legal and cultural spheres. *RSO 96-97*

The ideal is to work towards a social structure in which the criterion of capital increase will no longer be the only power to which production is subjected. In an appropriate social structure, increase of capital should rather serve as an indicator that the economic life, by taking into account all the requirements of our bodily and spiritual nature, is correctly formed and organized. *RSO 40*

Under the influence of the threefold idea, the operation of social life will in a certain sense be reversed. Presently, one must look to the increase of one's capital or wages as a sign that one is playing a satisfactory part in the life of the community. In the threefold social order, the greatest possible efficiency of common work will result because individual faculties will work in harmony with the human relationships founded in the legal sphere, and with production, circulation and consumption regulated by the economic associations. Increase of capital, and a proper adjustment of work and the return upon work, shall appear as a final consequence of these social institutions and their activities. *RSO 48-49*

When cultural life flourishes independently of the rights and economic realms, profit as incentive for work becomes redundant. Social understanding will be developed in a free cultural life, out of which socially motivated incentives will arise to replace the profit motive as the primary incentive to work.

If the social organism is to flourish, those who are able to serve the community through their individual capacities should not be deprived of the possibility of using their own free initiative. Where free access to the means of production is involved in such service, the hindrance of this free initiative would harm the general social interest. The usual view of this, in which the entrepreneur needs the incentive of some prospect of profit connected with ownership of the means of production, is not one that I wish to advance. The way of thinking underlying the ideas for social renewal expressed in this book believes that such incentive can become redundant when spiritual, cultural life emancipates itself from the political and economic realms. An emancipated life of spirit will by its very nature develop social understanding out of itself; and from such understanding quite different kinds of incentive from that of economic gain will arise. But it cannot just be a question of which kinds of impulses arouse people's interest in private ownership of the means of production. What is important is whether free access to such means, or an access determined and regulated by the community, more closely corresponds to the needs and conditions of the social organism. *TSR 76*

Land and Capital

In a healthy economic process, contrary to conventional economic wisdom, capital needs be used up, rather than preserved as personal property. Historically, surplus capital created by the efficient use of the division of labor was used to purchase land. This practice should be discontinued because of the negative effects it has on the whole economic process. *[See point (e) on Diagram 2, below.]* When capital is sunk into land, it does not get used up, but becomes congested and stuck. As we have seen, land itself has no real value, but receives value only through its transformation by labor. When capital is united with nature, that is, when land is purchased, instead of a value-creating tension there is a further value-creating movement, which has a negative effect on the economic process.

The more capital that is stored up through direct land purchases and mortgages, the more of an inflationary effect these practices have on the economy. The financial effect of sinking capital into land is similar to the effect caused by issuing more and more paper currency without any corresponding increase in economic productive capacity. The more capital is united with the land, the more rents

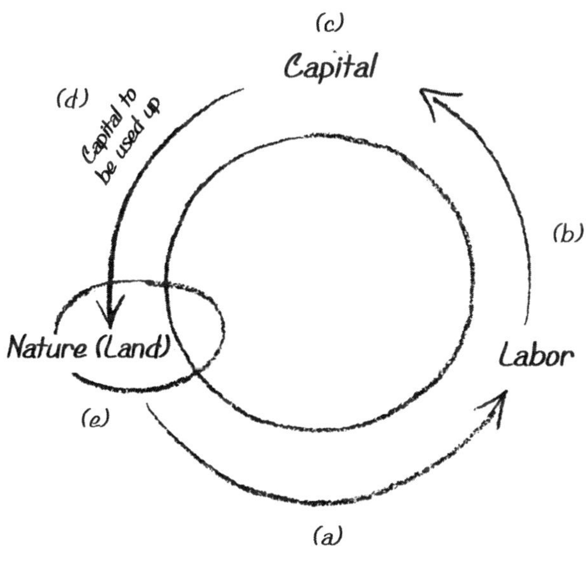

Diagram 2. RE 55

and mortgages, and in turn the prices of goods and services, are artificially driven upwards. Ultimately, the land receives a false value, because it is actually the capital fixed in the land that has value.

> *In the future, the means of production, that is, capital, will circulate freely in the social body just as blood circulates in the healthy human body. Blood must flow throughout the entire body and cannot be allowed to stagnate anywhere. Similarly, capital will not be allowed to accumulate in the form of private property.* FTSF 13

> *The only sensible thing, therefore, will be for the capital at this point* [See point (c) on Diagram 2, pg. 191.] *not to preserve itself in nature, but rather to vanish into nature. How then can capital vanish into nature? So long as it is at all possible to unite capital with nature – that is to say, so long as you can make nature in its original unelaborated condition more and more expensive through the accumulation of capital – so long as this is possible, capital cannot vanish into nature; on the contrary, it penetrates into nature and maintains itself there. In all countries where the law of mortgage makes it possible for capital to unite with nature, therefore, we shall find a congestion of capital in nature, that is, in the land. Instead of the capital being expended at this point* [See point (d) on Diagram 2, pg. 191.] *– instead of its disappearing at this point, instead of a value-creating tension arising – there is a further value-creating movement, which is harmful to the economic process. There is only one way of preventing this. In a healthy economic process we must not and cannot give "real credit" – credit based on the security of land – even to a person working on the land. Only personal credit should be given – that is to say, credit that will enable the person to turn the capital to good account through the land. If we simply unite the land with the capital, the capital will become congested the moment it arrives again at nature. If, on the other hand, we unite the capital with the capacities of spirit of those who administer the land and further the economic process by working upon it, then, you see, the*

capital vanishes. As it reaches nature at this point, it will not become congested; it will not be preserved, but will go right on through nature, back again into labor, and will begin the cycle once more. It is one of the worst possible congestions in the economic process when capital is simply united with nature. Tracing the economic process hypothetically from its initial stages, after labor and capital have evolved from the starting-point of nature, when the capital is enabled to take hold of nature instead of losing itself in nature, we see that economic congestion occurs.

At this point you may, of course, make a serious objection. In the course of this movement, you may say, the capital has come into being. Suppose it now arrives again at nature and there is too much of it. (It would be different if we were able to lead it over into labor – if we were able, let us say, to invent new methods so as to further the processing of raw materials. For in such a case we would be uniting not nature but labor with the capital. If we arrive at this point with our capital and process the raw materials in a more economical way, or open up new sources or the like, then we are leading the capital directly over into labor.) Suppose, however, there is too much capital. The numerous owners of capital will become painfully aware of the fact; they will not be able to start anything with their capital. This is indeed the case if you look into the matter historically. In actual fact, too much capital did arise, and the only way out that it could find was to preserve itself in nature. We thus witnessed in the economic process the so-called rise in the value of land. *RE 59-60*

. . . If I unite capital with nature, the value of nature will of course be enhanced. The more something is mortgaged, the more you will eventually have to pay for it. The value is constantly increased. But is this increase in the value of land a reality? No, it is no reality at all. By its nature, land can never receive a greater value. It can, at most, receive a greater value by being worked upon in a more rational and scientific way; and in that case it is the labor that increases the value. To imagine the land itself, however, the land as such, increased in

> *value is absurd. It is absolute nonsense. If you do improve the quality of the land, you do so only by working upon it. In so far as it is only nature, the land can have no value at all. All you can do is to give it a fictitious value by uniting capital with it. We may say then, that what is called the value of land in the sense of present-day economics is in real truth nothing other than capital fixed in the land. Capital fixed in the land is not a real value but an apparent value – a semblance of a value. That is the point. In the economic process it is high time that we learn to understand the difference between real values and apparent values.* *RE 60-61*

> *In the economic process, the errors and semblances become real and have real consequences. Economically speaking, it makes no essential difference whether, for example, I issue money that has no foundation in reality but represents a mere increase in the amount of paper money, or whether I assign capital value to the land. In both cases I am creating fictitious values. By inflating the currency, I increase the prices of things numerically; but in the reality of the economic process, I effect absolutely nothing except a redistribution, which may do immense harm to individuals. In the same manner, the above described capitalizing of land does harm to those who are involved in the economic process.* *RE 61*

Just as the products of nature are used up when they are transformed by labor, and just as labor transformed by capital is also used up, so too must capital itself be used up until there is only a sufficient amount needed to reinvest in the production of goods and services. This seed capital, however, does not remain congested, but works on in the form of labor, for example, as the more efficient gathering of resources or the transformation of a product.

> *The previous examples have illustrated the essential point in our present context. At this point, [Diagram 2: (e), pg. 191.] nature simply must not be allowed to tend toward a preservation of capital. Capital must be allowed to work on, unhindered, into labor. What is to happen if capital is actually*

there – more of it than we are able to make use of? The only thing to prevent its being there in excess is to see that it is used up along this path [Diagram 2: (d)], so that in the end, only as much of it is left at this point [Diagram 2: (e)] as can enter once more into the work to be done upon the land. Only as much capital is left as is required for this work. The essential and obvious thing is that the capital should be used up, consumed, along this path. Indeed – assuming hypothetically that it could be so – it would be a most appalling thing if nothing were consumed along this whole path. We would have to carry all the products around with us. The process becomes organic only through the fact that things are used up. Just as the products of nature, transformed by human labor, are used up; just as the labor which has been organized by capital is used up. So in its further path, the capital itself simply must be used up – properly used up. This using-up of capital is something that absolutely must be brought about. *RE 62*

. . . Capital must be used up, until we may conceive of what remains as a kind of seed to kindle the economic process anew – once more from the starting point of nature. That alone must remain which may be necessary for a more scientific processing of natural resources – of raw materials, or for an improvement of the land, let us say, by the creation of better manures, and the like. In every such case labor must be applied. It is that amount of capital which can work on as labor that must be withdrawn from consumption. Before this point in the diagram is reached (e), [Diagram 2, pg. 191] the surplus capital, which would otherwise unite with nature in an inorganic way, must be used up. *RE 63*

If we consider the issue of interest rates, we see that the interests and advantages of those involved in the buying and selling of real estate are opposed to those who manufacture products. Low interest rates tend to drive up the price of land and consequently rents and products, whereas low rates tend to reduce production costs and the prices of manufactured products.

> *. . . A state of economic congestion must not be allowed to arise through a fixation of capital in ground rent; as I said, fundamentally speaking, the return for land when it is sold – that is, when land is given a value in the economic process – works in direct opposition to the interests of those engaged in the manufacture of valuable goods. If people wish to manufacture valuable goods with the help of capital, it is to their benefit that the rate of interest should be low. Having less interest to pay, they will be less hampered in their use of the capital they have borrowed. The landowners, on the other hand (I will go fully into these things, as they are of economic significance.), the landowners, or those who have an interest in the land's becoming more expensive, will be able to make it more expensive simply by a reduction in the rate of interest. If they have a low rate of interest to pay, the value of their land will grow; it will become more and more expensive. By contrast, those engaged in the manufacture of valuable commodities will be able to make them for less because of a low rate of interest. Commodities, therefore, which depend mainly on manufacture, become less expensive when the rate of interest is low. Land, on the other hand, which gives a yield without first having to be manufactured, becomes more expensive when the rate of interest is low. You can easily work it out. It is an economic fact.* RE 68-69

Surplus Capital

Only the capital needed for investment in new projects and re-investment in existing ones should remain in the economic process. One important way to ensure that surplus capital is used up is to transfer it to cultural institutions and activities as free gifts. Cultural life depends on such free gifts, and has always done so through the course of history. Accumulated capital is thus transformed into gift capital. What otherwise would have been congested in land or in luxury items disappears into cultural institutions. When capital is used up as a free gift to cultural life, it is the most fruitful thing in the whole economic process, because it functions there as an economic fertilizer.

. . . Capital must not be allowed to become congested. At the place where spiritual-cultural life is most highly evolved in the forming of capital (this "place" is of course spread out throughout the entire economic realm), the excess capital that has been acquired must not be allowed to flow into the land, where it would become dammed up. Provision must be made for the elimination of the excess capital. The capital must not be allowed to become congested in the land. That is to say, at an earlier stage in the process, the congestion must be prevented by a free gift to spiritual-cultural institutions, of the excess that has been acquired. The only exception is that what I described as a "seed" must be allowed to pass on to the land. It is here that the concept of "free gift" confronts us inevitably; there must be free gifts.

Study any of the self-contained economic realms that have arisen in the course of history, and you will see that the free gift is always there. In all essentials, spiritual-cultural life is dependent on what, in the economic sense of the word, are free gifts, pure and simple.

From the simple case in which Charles the Bald, out of what he had available to give away, maintained Scotus Erigena as his court philosopher (whom some have regarded as a rather superfluous piece of furniture!) to the case of Peter's Pence, whereby the Roman Catholics all over the world give their free gifts to the Church in small doses – such gifts are always there. Wherever an economic life, no matter how gigantic it may become, represents an economic domain more or less self-contained, you have the transformation of accumulated capital into gift capital for the maintenance of spiritual-cultural institutions.

In other words, now that we have inevitably come to a closed economic realm, namely that of the entire world, we should reflect upon the fact that one thing is inevitable in a truly economic sense: what would otherwise become dammed up in the land must vanish into spiritual-cultural institutions. I say once more, it must somehow vanish into the spiritual-cultural institutions. It must take effect as a free gift.

For a truly modern economic science, we must seek an answer to the question of how (in the sense of economics) we must buy and sell in such a way that the values, primarily created as food values within the purely material realm, may vanish within the spiritual-cultural domain. That is the great question. I will formulate it once more. What form of payment must we strive for in our economic interactions, so that what is created by the elaboration of nature, where the productive process primarily works for the nutrition of humanity, eventually vanishes in spiritual-cultural institutions? This is the great economic question. *RE 142-143*

. . . [Putting excess capital into land/nature] can be prevented by leading the excess capital, not into nature, where it would become fixed, but into independent spiritual-cultural undertakings, where it vanishes except for the remnant, which must continue as a kind of seed by which the economic process can be maintained. *RE 87*

. . . Assume that the masses of capital, arising in one way or another, are withdrawn from the tendency to become congested on the land and are given to the spiritual-cultural life – it may be in the form of foundations, scholarships, or other such things. These are free gifts. You will begin to see what happens on the one side of your gigantic account book, since it must be such that it comprises the real economic life in its totality . . . In short, from this point of view you can raise a weighty question. What are the most productive transformations of capital in the economic process? What are the most productive of all? Follow out such connections as I have just described; follow especially those portions of available capital that go into foundations, scholarships, and other spiritual-cultural "goods," that in the course of time react to fertilize the whole process of spiritual-cultural production and enterprise of every kind. You will perceive that free gifts are the most fruitful thing of all in the whole economic process. We cannot arrive at a healthy economic process unless, in the first place, it is made possible for people to have something to give; and, in the second place, unless

they have the goodwill to give what they have in a sensible manner. Here, then, we have something that enters into the economic process in a very particular way. RE 107-108

A second important use of surplus capital is to support education and the retraining of workers who either become displaced or simply want to work in a different field.

We must see to it that workers are not restricted to only one skill throughout their lives, but are able to turn their hand to other things . . . you can use up the surplus capital, which would be excessive at this point, to instruct and educate the workers in one thing or another, to be able to transplant them into other callings. You see, therefore, the moment you think in a rational way, the economic process will correct itself. That is the essential thing. RE 65-66

It will be one of the important functions of the economic associations to ensure that sufficient capital will flow into cultural life. The associations will be motivated to do so by the realization that cultural life declines when not enough gift money flows into it.

When one day the associations begin to understand something of the influence of the free spiritual-cultural life on the economic process, we can give them a very good means of regulating the economic circuit. I mentioned this in my book Towards Social Renewal. *The associations will find that when free spiritual-cultural life declines, too little is being given freely; they will grasp the connection. They will see the connection between too little giving and too little free spiritual-cultural work. When there is not enough free spiritual-cultural work, they will realize that too little is being given. When too little is being given, they will notice a decline in free spiritual-cultural work.*

. . . the capital that presses to be invested, the capital that tends to march into mortgages and stay there, must be given an outlet into free spiritual-cultural institutions. That is the practical aspect. Let the associations see to it that the money that tends to get tied up in mortgages finds its way into

independent spiritual-cultural institutions. There you have the connection of the associative life with the general social life. Only when you try to penetrate the realities of economic life does it begin to dawn on you what must be done in the one case or in the other. I do not by any means wish to agitate that this or that must be done; I only wish to point out what is. This is undoubtedly true: what we can never attain by legislative measures – namely, to keep excess capital away from nature – we can attain through the life and system of associations, diverting capital into free spiritual-cultural institutions. I only say that if the one thing happens, the other will happen too. Science, after all, has only to indicate the conditions under which things are connected. *RE 78*

Redefining Ground-Rent and Calculating Subsistence Income

Taking into consideration a basic principle of a threefold social organism that land should no longer be treated as private property, Rudolf Steiner redefines the term ground-rent.*

In contrast to modern usage of the term, Steiner characterizes ground-rent as the economic value of land in a given region in terms of the economic productivity it supports.

He then uses this finite figure of value related to land to determine the subsistence level for each person in a given region through a simple economic formula: dividing the sum total of ground-rent by the number of people inhabiting the area of land in question. The resulting amount or quotient is what every person deserves for their subsistence. No one should receive more unless it is through the agreement of those who are affected by such an allocation.

Ground rent, which can be reckoned according to the productivity of a piece of land in a certain district, yields a certain sum for a State-bounded area. The land takes its

* Editor's note: Typically, the term refers to legal arrangements whereby an individual or individuals own the property or buildings on a piece of land, but someone else owns the actual land or "ground." The above-ground property owner pays the ground owner an annual fee, or ground-rent. These are usually long-term arrangements.

value according to its productivity, that is, in accordance with the way or the degree in which it is put to rational use in relation to the whole economy. It is very difficult today for anyone to gain a clear concept of this simple land value, since in the modern capitalistic economic life interest on capital, or capital in any form, has confused the whole picture of ground-rent, and the true concept of its economic value for the people has been blurred by phantoms in the form of mortgage law and the system of stocks and shares. Strictly speaking, everything has been forced into conceptions that are impossible and false. Naturally a true conception of ground-rent cannot be acquired in the twinkling of an eye. But think of it simply as the economic value of the land in some territory, with regard to its productivity. Now there exists a necessary relation between this ground rent, and what I have referred to as a subsistence minimum. There are many social reformers and social revolutionaries today who dream of the wholesale abolition of ground-rent, who believe, for example, that ground-rent will be done away with by all land being nationalized or communalized. Essentials, however, are never changed by a mere change of form. Whether a whole community owns the land or it is owned by a number of individuals makes no difference to the existence of ground-rent. It is simply obscured and takes on other forms. Ground rent as I have defined it is always there. Take the ground-rent of a certain district and divide it up among the individual inhabitants, then you will get as quotient the only possible subsistence minimum. This is a law as definite and unalterable as a law of physics. It is a primary fact, something fundamental, that in a social organism no one deserves more than is yielded by the ground rent being divided up by the total population. What is earned beyond that arises through coalitions and associations in which conditions are established where one individual can acquire more value than another. But not a whit more can pass into the moveable property of an individual than what I have here indicated. From this minimum, which really exists everywhere even

> *though the real conditions are obscured, arises all economic life in so far as it applies to an individual's moveable property . . .*
>
> *Right thinking, realistic concepts on such matters can be gained – as I showed by the example of the relation of a subsistence minimum to ground-rent* – only when you take your start from the basic principles of the threefold social organism.* SQQC Lecture 2

Land Rent as Capital and the Support of Cultural Life

Accumulated values take on three different forms of capital as they flow through economic life. In conventional terms they are profits, rents, and wages (worker support). Of the three, it is rents that should provide the primary source of support for education and cultural life, including health care. There is no other justification for charging rent on land that is no longer privately owned as is the case in a threefold social organism.

> *The three types of value are profits, rent, and wages. There are no other kinds of value. All economic values that exist fall naturally into these three classes . . .*
>
> *As to rent, the world simply cannot live without it, for from rent the whole spiritual life, education and so on, is maintained. Moreover the sick and aged must also be maintained out of rent . . . We must realize that it is impossible even to begin a discussion if we do not know that the real justification of rent can only consist in it being directed in the channels which I have just mentioned.* HBFJSF Lecture 2

* Editor's note: See Tom Paine, "Agrarian Justice," for a detailed exposition on ground rent and overcoming income inequities. It can readily be found through an internet search.

EIGHT

Credit

In the long run, credit cannot work in a healthy way unless the giver of credit feels himself responsible for all that is brought about thereby. The recipient of credit, through his connection with the whole economic sphere (that is, through the associations), must give grounds to justify his taking this responsibility. For a healthy national economy, it is important not merely that credit should further the spirit of enterprise as such, but that the right methods and institutions should exist to enable the spirit of enterprise to work in a socially useful way. *RSO 49-50*

EIGHT

Credit

Motivation

In modern economic life, when entrepreneurs lack the financial means to apply their capacities productively, a creditor will lend them capital, if confident in their entrepreneurship. The entrepreneur is then able to achieve something that the lender could not. In a capitalist society, the promise of monetary gain is the primary incentive for extending credit. Loan determination is based almost exclusively on potential return on capital. As such, a borrower needs to continually justify his or her acquisition of a loan in financial terms. This complete monetization of confidence and trust in his or her ability and intention to repay a loan often undermines the borrower's dignity. In such exchanges, the merits of the work for which credit is needed become insignificant.

> *... In a community organized purely on a basis of capital and wages, individuals can apply their powers and talents only insofar as they find an equivalent in monetary gain. Consider, moreover, the confidence with which one individual will place his or her forces at the disposal of another in order to enable the latter to accomplish certain work. In a capitalist community, this confidence must be based on a purely capitalist point of view.*
>
> *Work done in confidence of the achievements of others is the social basis of credit. In older civilizations there was a transition from barter to the monetary system; similarly, as a result of the complications of modern life, a transformation has recently occurred from the simpler monetary system to working on a credit basis. In our age, life makes it necessary for people to work with the means that are entrusted to them by others, or by a community, in confidence of their power*

> *to achieve a result. Under capitalism, however, the credit system involves a complete loss of any real and satisfying human relationship to the conditions of one's life and work. Credit is given when there is a prospect of an increase of capital that seems to justify it; one's work is constantly overshadowed by the need to justify it in capitalist terms. These are the motives underlying the giving and taking of credit. And what is the result of all this? Human beings are subjected to the power of a financial sphere remote from life. The moment people become fully conscious of this fact, they feel it to be unworthy of their human dignity.* RSO 45-46

If credit is offered based on economic factors alone, only those initiatives that yield the highest profit will be capitalized. As a consequence, products and services vital to economic and cultural life may be overlooked. A healthy system of credit is possible only when economic values are appropriately related to human needs.

> *Take the case of credit on land. In a healthy society, an individual or a group possessing the necessary abilities may be given credit on land, enabling them to develop it by establishing some kind of production. It must be a development that seems justified on that land in light of all the cultural conditions involved. If credit is given on land from the purely capitalist viewpoint, in the effort to give it a commodity value corresponding to the credit provided, use of the land which would otherwise be the most desirable is possibly prevented.*
>
> *A healthy system of giving credit presupposes a social structure that enables economic values to be estimated by their relation to the satisfaction of people's bodily and spiritual needs. Independent cultural and legal-political spheres will lead to a vital recognition of this relation and make it a guiding force. People's economic dealings will be shaped by it. Production will be considered from the viewpoint of human needs; it will no longer be governed by processes that obscure concrete needs through an abstract scale of capital and wages.* RSO 46-47

In a threefold social organism, economic associations *[See Chapter Five on Associations]*, which bring together producers, distributors, and consumers, will be in a good position to oversee the issuance of credit, because they will have insight into both the wishes of consumers and the needs of producers. In the work of the associations, insights and perspectives from the cultural and rights spheres will play an important role, and the purely capitalist perspective will not hold sway in decisions about the giving and receiving of credit. Moreover, because various associations will work directly with and be responsible to each other, one-sided decisions are minimized, and support of worthy individual initiatives will become more possible. Production will be guided by real needs rather than mere profit. One association's need for credit can be met by other associations.

> *The economic life in a threefold society is built up by the cooperation of associations arising out of the needs of producers and the interests of consumers. These associations will have to decide on the giving and taking of credit. In their mutual dealings, the impulses and perspectives that enter economic life from the cultural and legal spheres will play a decisive part. These associations will not be bound to a purely capitalist point of view. One association will deal directly with another; thus the one-sided interests of one branch of production will be regulated and balanced by those of the other.*
>
> *Responsibility for the giving and taking of credit will thus be left to the associations. This will not impair the scope and activity of individuals with special faculties; on the contrary, only this method will give individual faculties full scope. The individual is responsible to his or her association for achieving the best possible results. The association is responsible to other associations for making good use of these individual abilities. Such a division of responsibility will ensure that the whole activity of production is guided by complementary and mutually corrective points of view. The individual's desire for profit will no longer impose production on the life of the*

community; production will be regulated by the community's needs, which will make themselves felt in a real and objective way. The need one association establishes will be the occasion for the granting of credit by another. *RSO 47*

The division of labor in the production process has contributed to the increased efficiency of economic life, but it has also had the effect of separating people. Consequently, there is a great need to reintroduce a sense of unity and collective responsibility in economic life. This is particularly true in the realm of finance. Through social threefolding, unity can be restored. Both the lender and the recipient of credit experience a sense of social responsibility: the lender for all that is made possible thanks to his loan and the recipient for all that he is able to produce. Economic associations can be instrumental in raising the consciousness of individuals regarding the effects of their actions, including the acts of lending and borrowing.

. . . Modern life has brought about a division of labor in many spheres, for outer methods and institutions demand it. The effects of division of labor must be balanced by vital mutual relations among people in the community. Division of labor separates people; the forces that come to them from the three spheres of social life, once these are made independent, will draw them together again. The division of society has reached its zenith. This is a fact of experience, and it gives our modern social life its stamp. Once we recognize it, we realize the imperative demand of the age: to find and follow the path that leads to reunion.

This inevitable demand of the times is vividly illustrated by such concrete facts of economic life as the continued intensification of the credit system. The stronger the tendency toward a capitalist point of view, the more highly organized the financial system and the more intense the spirit of enterprise becomes, the more the credit system develops.

However, to a healthy way of thinking, the growth of the credit system must drive home the urgent need to permeate it with a vital sense of the economic realities – the production of commodities and people's needs for particular commodities. In the long run, credit cannot work in a healthy way unless the givers of credit feel themselves responsible for all that is brought about thereby. The recipients of credit, through their connection with the whole economic sphere (that is, through the associations), must give grounds to justify their taking this responsibility. For a healthy national economy, it is important not merely that credit should further the spirit of enterprise as such, but that the right methods and institutions should exist to enable the spirit of enterprise to work in a socially useful way.

Theoretically, no one will want to deny that a larger sense of responsibility is necessary in the present-day world of business and economic affairs. To this end, associations must be created that will work to confront individuals with the wider social effects of all their actions. *RSO 49-50*

Capability

In a healthy economy, it is the diversity of human capacities rather than economic activity that creates the flow of capital in the economic process. In the case of credit, Steiner speaks of a 'difference of level' between capital in the hands of the lender who does not know what to do with it, and when the borrower has it and can put it to good use. As with water, this difference of level causes the capital to flow.

In an economic sense, those who receive credit to produce something are both debtors and creators: As debtors they are under an obligation to produce something and return the principal to the lender; as creators, thanks to their receipt of credit, they are liberated to use their capacities to take on an initiative.

So too, in a healthy economy, the amount of credit extended will no longer depend on the financial situation or the risk involved. Rather, it will depend on human capability and will never exceed that which is merited by that capability.

. . . What is it that is brought about through this relationship of lenders and debtors? It is very similar to the "difference of level" we meet with in physics. If you have

water up here, it will flow down there, simply through the difference of level. In like manner, there is a social difference of level between the first position of the capital – the position of the lender who does not know what to do with it – and the second position of the debtor who can make good use of it. This difference works as a difference of level.

But you must pause a moment to consider the active driving force in this difference of level. The active principle is not simply the spirit, which is at work in the whole process. It is the diversity of human talents and dispositions. That is the determining factor in the difference of level. If a lazy-minded person possesses capital, then, in a healthy economic organization, that person will be above, while the clever person will be below. The result is a "drop," or difference of level, and the capital flows downward to the clever person. It is through the difference of level between the talents of individuals that capital is brought into flow. It is not even the positive activity of individuals; it is simply the human qualities of those who are united together in the social organism that produce this "difference of level" and, in so doing, carry forward the economic process. *RE 49*

The one who acquired the money to begin with becomes the lender, the creditor. The other, who receives the money – the individual, the man, we will suppose, who has only spirit – becomes the debtor. You have here a relationship between two human beings. The same relationship will also come about if the lenders are a whole number of people who hand over their extra capital to this individual, so that a higher synthesis is brought about by his intelligence (spirit). That individual is then the debtor, and works on a foundation entirely emancipated from the basis of nature. What he actually receives from the original capitalists themselves is a nonentity in his hands. He will have to give it back again after a time – it does not really belong to him. In effect, it is only from one side that he works economically as a debtor. From the other side he is economically responsible as a creative individual. *RE 47*

> *... there will be a return to a condition which has now almost ceased to exist because of the financial system in which money itself has become an object of economic business, a condition in which the economic life will be re-established on its natural and worthy foundation. It will not be possible in future to carry on business by means of money and for money because economic institutions will have to deal with the respective values of the commodities. That is to say, society will again return to goodness of quality, excellence of workmanship and the capability of the worker. The granting of credit will no longer depend on the condition that money is available or tight, or on the degree of the risk to be taken; it will depend entirely upon the existence of people capable of starting an enterprise or of producing something. Human ability will command credit. Since human capability will condition the amount of credit to be granted, that amount can never be given in excess of human capability. If you merely give money and allow it to be used, the object to which it has been applied may long have ceased to exist, but the money is still the object of transactions. If the money is given for human capability, then, when that human capability comes to an end, the object for which the money is used also ceases to exist.* *SF 47-48*

Mutuality and the Service of Lending

Historically, lending was considered a service in which mutuality played a significant role. Prior to the advent of interest on loans, whenever a lender helped a person in financial need, it was assumed that the favor would be returned if the situation were ever reversed. Similarly mutual aid was assumed in regard to the guarantors of loans. Interest was initially introduced as a substitute for the obligation of returning the favor of a loan. Interest is mutuality transformed into money.

Mutuality also exists throughout the economic process wherever there is division of labor. In the division of labor, people and processes are separated, but then are reunited in the exchanges that happen with money.

. . . You know that there were times when it was considered immoral to take interest on loans; it was considered moral only to lend free of interest. Under these conditions there would be no profit in lending. This is indeed the fact. Originally, lending did not arise from the profit one derives from it – that is to say, from the interest; but it arose from the following presumption. If I lend someone something, this person can do something with it that I cannot do. Take the simplest instance. Suppose that a man is in dire need and that he can alleviate his need if I am in the position to lend him something. Under conditions more primitive than those of today, he would not pay me interest, but the presumption would be that if I, too, am ever in need, he in his turn will help me out. Wherever you trace the matter back in history, you will see that the presupposition of lending is that the other will lend to me in turn when need arises. It even applies to more complicated social conditions, for the same thing happens when someone borrows money from a money-lending firm and needs guarantors. It has always been the experience of money lenders that mutual aid plays a great part even in this service. A comes to a money lender and brings B and C along to stand as security; they enter their names as guarantors. In such a case, money-lending firms always count on the probability that if B ever comes to borrow money, he or she will bring A and C as guarantors; or again, when B has paid the debt, C will arrive one day and will bring A and B as guarantors. In certain circles this is taken as a matter of course. Economists declare that such a law can be assessed just as well as any that can be clothed in a mathematical formula. Of course, these things are to be taken with the well known "grain of salt" that we must always take into account. Our power to do so is part of the mobility of the economic process.

To summarize, therefore, we say that originally, there was no return for the service of lending, except the presumption that the borrower will lend to us again; or if not that, at least will help us in borrowing, as we had helped. Notably, where it is a question of lending and borrowing, human mutuality or "give and take" enters the economic process in a striking way.

If this is true, what is interest? Interest – as has already been stated by some economists – is what I receive if I renounce this "mutuality"; that is to say, if I lend someone something and we agree that this person shall be under no obligation to lend to me. If I renounce this mutual right, the person pays me interest for it. Interest therefore resolves something that takes place between two human beings; it is a compensation for the human mutuality that plays in the economic process.

This is, however, something that we must set in its right place in the whole economic process. In doing so we must of course remember that there is no sense these days in studying economic processes other than those that stand entirely under the sign of the division of labor; for it is these with which we are in fact concerned. When labor is divided and distributed, human beings grow dependent on the principle of mutuality to a far greater extent than is the case when one not only grows one's own cabbages but also makes one's own hats and boots. It is with the division of labor that the dependence on mutuality comes. In the division of labor we have a process working in such a way that the several currents diverge. Yet in the economic process as a whole, we see it come about that all of these different streams tend to unite again, though in a different way, through the exchange that, in the case of a more complicated economic process, takes place with the help of money. Thus at a certain stage the division of labor makes mutuality a necessity. In other words, it involves the same element in human dealings that we find in the case of lending and borrowing. Where much is lent, this principle of mutuality is inherently involved, but in this case it can be redeemed by interest. For interest is mutuality realized. It has been transformed into an abstract form as money. The forces of mutuality are the interest, which has undergone a metamorphosis. And what we see quite plainly here in the payment of interest takes place throughout the economic process. *RE 122-124*

In a threefold society, the enterprise or capital that is amassed through the aid of loan capital is passed on to another capable person after the borrower no longer wishes to continue operations or is no longer capable of doing so. In such cases, capital will be transferred by gift rather than by purchase.

> *. . . selflessness cannot help being inherent in the very circulation of the elements of economic life. This is the case, even in the details. Take, for instance, the case where a man is in a position to receive loan capital on credit, and is thus enabled to establish an enterprise or an institution and to produce something by means of it. He goes on producing so long as his own personal faculties are united with the institution. Afterwards, the thing he has built up will be handed on in the most sensible way to some other individual who has the necessary faculties. It will be transferred as a gift – a gift, not just from one person to another, but one that takes place through the whole course of economic life. We need consider only how such gifts will be enabled in a reasonable way by the threefold social organism. Here the domain of economics borders on the social element in the human being in the most comprehensive meaning of the term. It touches on what needs to be conceived for the social organism as a whole.* RE 128-129

Personal and Real Credit

Lowering interest rates on personal credit has a cheapening effect on the production process and the resultant commodities, whereas lowering interest rates on land exchanges has the tendency to make land prices more expensive.

> *. . . let us consider the question of credit. To place capital into the service of the spirit in the sense that I explained yesterday, the man who produces by means of spirit becomes a debtor. It is only through his having credit that he becomes, or can become, a debtor. At this point in our diagram credit steps in – what may be properly called "personal credit."* [See Diagram 2, point (c), pg. 191.] *A man has credit. The credit can be expressed in numbers. The capital that many others*

advance to him is, so to speak, his personal credit. As you know, this personal credit has a certain consequence, at least if we consider it within our present economic conditions. Its economic effect is connected with the rate of interest.

Assume that the rate of interest is low. If by using spirit to create in the economic process, I become a debtor – that is to say, if I ask for credit – I shall have to pay only a small sum for it. Having less interest to pay, I can produce my goods more cheaply. I shall thus have a cheapening effect on the economic process. We may say, therefore, that personal credit cheapens production when the rate of interest falls. So long as the capital continues to be turned to good account or made valuable by the spirit in the economic process, it is always so. When the rate of interest goes down, those who require credit have more freedom of movement. They can play their part far more intensively in the economic process – more intensively, that is to say, for their fellow human beings. If they lower the cost of their commodities they are playing a fruitful part in the process – at least from the point of view of the consumer.

Let us now take the other side. Assume that credit is given on land – "real credit." When credit is given on land, the situation is essentially different. Assume that the rate of interest is 5%. A person borrowing capital on the security of land must pay 5%. Capitalizing this, you will get the capital corresponding to the particular piece of land – that is to say, you will get the amount which would have to be paid to buy the piece of land outright. Assume now that the rate of interest falls to 4%. More capital can then be "credited into" the land – at least this is what actually happens. We then see everywhere, as a result of a falling rate of interest, land becoming not cheaper but more expensive. When the standard rate of interest goes down, land does not become cheaper but more expensive. "Real credit" makes things more expensive, while "personal credit" makes things cheaper. Real credit makes land more expensive, while personal credit makes commodities cheaper. This is very important in the economic process. It means that when capital returns to nature and simply unites with nature in the form of real credit (in other words, when there is a union of capital with land, that is to say, with nature), then the economic process will tend more and more in the direction of dearness. RE 58-59

Yesterday we brought before our minds the cycle: nature, labor, capital – that is, capital imbued with value by spirit. [See Diagram 2, point (c), pg. 191 and Diagram 3, pg. 257.] *At this point, instead of "capital," I might just as well write "spirit." To begin with we followed out the economic process in this direction, counterclockwise, and we found that at this point, with nature,* [See Diagram 2, point (e), pg. 191.] *congestion must not be allowed to occur, but only so much must be allowed to go through as will act as a kind of seed to carry on the process. A state of economic congestion must not be allowed to arise through a fixation of capital in ground rent; as I said, fundamentally speaking, the return for land when it is sold – that is, when land is given a value in the economic process – works in direct opposition to the interests of those engaged in the manufacture of valuable goods. If people wish to manufacture valuable goods with the help of capital, it is to their benefit that the rate of interest should be low. Having less interest to pay, they will be less hampered in their use of the capital they have borrowed. The landowners, on the other hand (I will go fully into these things, as they are of economic significance), the landowners, or those who have an interest in the land's becoming more expensive, will be able to make it more expensive simply by a reduction in the rate of interest. If they have a low rate of interest to pay, the value of their land will grow; it will become more and more expensive. By contrast, those engaged in the manufacture of valuable commodities will be able to make them for less because of a low rate of interest. Commodities, therefore, which depend mainly on manufacture, become less expensive when the rate of interest is low. Land, on the other hand, which gives a yield without first having to be manufactured, becomes more expensive when the rate of interest is low. You can easily work it out. It is an economic fact.* RE 68-69

The Role of Associations in the Giving and Receiving of Credit

As institutions that facilitate dialogue between the various sectors of economic life, associations are ideally positioned to act as mediators and facilitators in lending or investing and borrowing. Associations can provide the best way for capable people to obtain loan money from people who have the resources to finance their undertakings. Individual initiative will not be hindered by the involvement of associations in the giving and receiving of credit. On the contrary, it will be strengthened.

Associations will not only facilitate initiatives but also will ensure that such enterprises are socially responsible. Credit will be granted by one association in response to a need expressed by another. With the associations serving as intermediaries in the giving and receiving of credit, a great sense of responsibility is fostered and shared. Borrowers are responsible to an association for achieving the desired results from their initiative. In turn, one association is responsible to other associations for making productive use of the borrowers' capacities. This sense of responsibility is necessary on the part of both the giver and the receiver of credit in order for credit to work in a healthy way. *[For a more complete description of how economic associations will facilitate various aspects of economic life, see Chapter Five on Associations.]*

> *In a threefold society economic life is built up by the cooperation of associations arising out of the needs of producers and the interests of consumers. These associations will have to decide on the giving and taking of credit.* *RSO 47*

> *Take the case of those who have money to lend. You would not let them lend it in a senseless way. You would bring them into connection with their association. The association would act as a mediator. The association would provide them with the most sensible way in which to lend – or again, with the most sensible way in which to give.* *RE 154*

> *Responsibility for the giving and taking of credit will thus be left to the associations. This will not impair the scope and activity of individuals with special faculties; on the contrary, only this method will give individual faculties full scope. The individual is responsible to his or her association for achieving*

> *the best possible results. The association is responsible to other associations for making good use of these individual abilities. Such a division of responsibility will ensure that the whole activity of production is guided by complementary and mutually corrective points of view. The individual's desire for profit will no longer impose production on the life of the community; production will be regulated by the community's needs, which will make themselves felt in a real and objective way. The need one association establishes will be the occasion for the granting of credit by another.* *RSO 47*

> *However, to a healthy way of thinking, the growth of the credit system must drive home the urgent need to permeate it with a vital sense of the economic realities – the production of commodities and the people's needs for particular commodities. In the long run, credit cannot work in a healthy way unless those who give credit feel themselves responsible for all that is brought about thereby. The recipients of credit, through their connection with the whole economic sphere (that is, through the associations), must give grounds to justify their taking this responsibility. For a healthy national economy, it is important not merely that credit should further the spirit of enterprise as such, but that the right methods and institutions should exist to enable the spirit of enterprise to work in a socially useful way.* *RSO 49-50*

The Coming Day (Der Kommende Tag) Experiment

The Coming Day was a holding company created during Rudolf Steiner's lifetime, in which businesses and farms came together with cultural endeavors, such as schools and clinics. One of the purposes of the organization was to serve as a structure in which business profits could support the participating cultural entities through gifts and loans, thereby performing some of the essential functions of a bank. It was to be a demonstration model for the ideas of social threefolding. One such idea, practiced by *The Coming Day*, was that surpluses from businesses should flow into cultural activities rather than into investment in land.

According to Steiner, money has played a similarly injurious role in modern economic life to that played by abstract conceptions in the modern life of thought. Both have lifted thinking and experience out of concrete realities, and consequently real needs and activities are no longer of concern in business dealings. The uniting of banking with concrete economic activity within *The Coming Day* was a practical attempt to overcome the injury that has been done by profit-driven capitalism and abstract thought in our times.

> *And then the question was asked: "In what way is it proposed to expand the organization of 'The Coming Day,' so that the Threefold movement may spread?" – Well, here, I must really beg you – especially in the question of an isolated case like this – to bear in mind that the Threefold idea, in its whole character, is something eminently practical; that we are dealing with something that is concrete, and not floating in a blue haze. 'The Coming Day' was founded, because it was recognized that the usual bank-system, as it is today, has gradually in the course of the nineteenth century come to be an injurious element in our economic life. I pointed this out when I was here last time, at another of the study-evenings. I showed that, more or less from the first third of the nineteenth century on, money has played a similar role in the economic life of modern civilization, to that of abstract conceptions in our thinking-process: that it has gradually blotted out all concreteness of aim and effort; that it has spread itself like a cloak over the things that must find their expression in economic energies. And therefore it has become necessary today to found something, which is not merely a bank, but forms a center of concentration for economic forces which are both a bank, and, at the same time, engaged in concrete economic activity: to found, that is, something which combines in itself real, concrete economic activities with the organization of these special branches of economic activity, in the same way as is done by a bank, where economic activities are included, but abstractly, without regard to the conditions of the actual economy. That is to say, a practical attempt is here being made to overcome the injury done by the money-system.*

What is wanted in reality, is to look at practical life, and learn to see where the centers of injury really lie. And one center of injury lies in the fact that the bank-system has taken the economic form that it has today. The bank-system in our economic life today plays the same part as the thoughts in people's life of soul, when they immediately translate everything into abstractions, and trouble themselves no further about the particular, concrete things which one sees and has to do with, but translate everything into lofty abstractions... And so it was possible to make an experiment in a small way, which, let us hope, will grow into something quite big, and in which things could be so arranged, that the money is brought back as it were into the economic activities, and the economic activities carried up into the financial realm; so that money, here, again becomes something which serves to make economic activities more feasible and easier to set in motion. Just as our thoughts are not for the purpose of carrying us aloft into abstract sublimities where we feel happy and comfortable, but of enabling us to set in motion the concrete facts of life; so too, with money, the important thing is to bring it down into actual economic industry, to carry on the different branches of practical economy, and not to sit ourselves down in a bank and 'transact business' in money: for money-transactions in themselves are the most injurious element we have in economic life in the nineteenth and beginning of the twentieth century. Here we have then simply a practical idea, taken up and also practically conceived. And until people recognize that it is a case here of quite practically conceiving ideas down into every particular, they will not succeed in understanding the League for the Threefold Social Order. *OPT 49-50*

NINE

Money

In the social organism there is no such thing as "money as such"; there are only these three kinds of money [loaned money, purchase-money and gift-money]. Moreover, each kind of money becomes what it is only at the moment when it is actually entering into the economic process or passing over from one form of economic process to another. RE 156

NINE

Money

Money as a Measure of Economic Value

The advent of the division of labor necessitated the further development of convenient and efficient ways to track the flow and accumulation of economic values. Money is nothing other than a token that expresses the value that arises in the economic process as a result of the division of labor. In itself, money is abstract; it doesn't matter what is bought with it or what is exchanged for it. Money is important only insofar as it fosters the exchange of products due to its convenience.

> *. . . In the healthy social organism, money will really only be a measure of value; behind every coin or note will stand the actual production of commodities, on whose basis alone people can gain access to money.* *TSR 95*

> *. . . it is essential for something to be there which is related as an abstract element to all the specific elements that are contained in the economic process. What is this something? It is, of course, in the first place, money. Money is nothing but the externally expressed value which is gained in the economic process through the division of labor and transmitted from one person to another.*
>
> *Thus we see that capitalism arises in the process of the division of labor; and in the process of capitalism (at a relatively early stage), the financial system [die Geldwirtschaft]. In relation to all the particular economic processes, money is completely abstract. If you have five francs in your pocket, you can buy a supper, just as well as an*

article of clothing. Regarding the money itself, it is irrelevant what you acquire with it, or what it is exchanged for in the economic process. RE 46

. . . it is not difficult to see that this is what actually happens in the economic process; only it is masked by the fact that money steps in between the objects exchanged. But the money is not the important thing. We would not take the slightest interest in money if it did not foster the exchange of products, making the process not only more convenient but less expensive. We would have no need of money if it were not for the fact that when people bring a product to the market, under the influence of the division of labor, they cannot be bothered to get what they need from wherever it is. They take money for it instead, so that they may supply their needs later on at their own convenience. RE 80

The Illusory Nature of Money as a Commodity

Historically, a commodity was something produced by one person that could be exchanged for something produced by someone else. People had to be productive at a certain level of quality if they wanted to acquire anything in exchange for the products they created. In modern finance, money is often treated as a commodity in itself. This hides its real function as a mediator and facilitator of exchanges.

It is important for the health of the economic process that money does not oscillate between being a commodity to be consumed and being a mediator of exchange. As it circulates, this shifting in the function of money causes constant fluctuations in its value. Money must not be treated as a commodity.

Let us look more closely at these conditions. Let us begin with the old system of natural economy, though it is not so much in evidence in our day. The only factor in the economic process is the commodity produced by the individual. This he or she can exchange for something produced by another. In this natural economic system, according to which one product is exchanged for another, a certain standard of quality must be attained since, if I wish to barter one commodity for another, I must have something that I can exchange for it and that the other accepts as of equal value. This means that people are forced to produce if they want anything. They are forced to exchange something that has a real, an obviously real, value. In place of this exchange of commodities that have a real value in human life, we have introduced finance, and money has become the medium with which one buys and sells, as one buys and sells with real objects in the natural economic system. We need only recall the fact that money, by becoming a real object in economic transactions, deludes people as to its true nature and, by producing this imaginary effect, at the same time tyrannizes them. *SF 38*

As I have already shown in these lectures, everything that enters as a mediator into the process of exchange is money. Suppose I am not content with acquiring as many peas as I can eat myself. Suppose I acquire peas with the object of using them – trading them – in order to obtain some other things that I require . . . whatever we use as money, to be a really useful form of money, must not merely oscillate, like peas, between the function of being consumed and the function of being passed from hand to hand. This change would involve constant fluctuations of value in the process of circulation. We want something that is used for no other purpose than for mediating an exchange; and to this end there must be a certain (albeit only a tacit) agreement among those who use the money. This, then, is an essential point. The money must be used only for an exchange, as a medium; it must not be used for consumption. *RE 146-147*

Money as Power

The possession of money in modern economic life gives a person power, because it is a claim on labor, to be done at one's bidding. Even when money is given away, people have to work for those to whom the money was given. This is so because money in reality is an equivalent for a certain amount of labor done by a certain number of workers that has been given concrete form in the commodity produced.

Suppose someone who has never put forth an effort in behalf of humanity has money. There are such cases. I will consider this extreme instance. Someone who has never put forth an effort in behalf of humanity has money. He buys something for himself with this money. Indeed, he is enabled to fashion for himself an altogether pleasant life by reason of the fact that he possesses this money, which is a claim upon human labor. Fine! This person is not necessarily a bad human being. He may even be a good man; indeed, he may be an industrious person. People frequently simply fail to see into the social structure. They do not possess an interest in their fellow men, that is, in the real social structure. People suppose that they love human beings when they buy something for themselves with their inherited money, for example, or when they even give it away. When it is given away, the only result is that we cause a certain number of persons to work for those to whom the money is given. It is simply a means for acquiring power. The fact that it is a claim upon labor makes it the means for acquiring power. CT 65-66

Money is namely only a 'go-between.' And only because in our day a certain social order exists, an order belonging purely to the State, therefore this $5 note which you have spent in the morning for different items is nothing else than an equivalent for so many days of labor of so many people. A number of people must have completed so many days of work, so much human labor must have flowed into society – must have crystallized itself into merchandise – in order for the apparent worth of the bank note to have any real value, but only at the command of society. The bank note only gives you the power to call into your service so much labor, or to put it another way, to command its worth in work. You can picture it in your mind: There I have a bank note, which assigns to me, according to my social position, the power over so many people. If you now see these workers selling their labor hour by hour, as the equivalent value of that which you have in your purse as the $5 note, then you begin to get a picture of the real facts. SASF 10-11

Money as Rights and Cultural Capacities Realized

Money that circulates carries with it certain rights: one is the right to use it as an economic value in exchange for commodities of comparative value, and another is the right to use it in support of one's spiritual or mental capacities to produce more goods and services.

> *... You cannot really consider the economic process without observing how law plays into it at every point. You cannot think out economic life, nor can you bring to pass whatever it may be that you intend, without considering this interplay of legal rights and economics. The moment you pass from mere barter to trade assisted by money, you see directly how the principle of law plays into economics. How, otherwise, could it be possible in return for a pair of boots to get not a hat, say, but a dollar, or whatever else it may be? I have saved myself the trouble of giving the merchant a hat; I have given him a dollar instead. I have my boots; he has the dollar. How otherwise could this be possible? If the dollar (even if it were a gold sovereign) were recognized by no one to be a real value – a value for which something could be received again in return – if it were not rightly integrated in the whole economic process, the shoemaker might have collected ever so many dollars, but it would be of no avail. The moment money makes its appearance in economic interactions, we see quite palpably the appearance of the element of law. It is extremely important to bear this in mind. We can look at the social organism as a whole only if we pass from purely economic events to events that take place under the influence of the life of rights.* RE 96-97

> *... Thus, the moment we have transformed the commodity into money, that is to say into a lawful right, the right can either be kept (I use the dollar to buy myself something equal in value to the pair of boots); or through my ingenuity I can do something with the money to produce an altogether new value in the economic process.*
>
> *It is here that human faculties come in. Individual faculties, which develop quite freely among people, enter in*

and incorporate themselves in the rights that they acquire with money. In the same way money, which may be regarded – in this sense – as rights realized, incorporates itself outwardly in the commodity. Thus we have now placed into the organic process that we described provisionally when we spoke of nature, elaborated nature, and labor divided and organized by the spirit – we have now placed into this whole process the principle of law or rights and individual faculties. We have found, within the economic process itself, a division that is in truth a threefold order – a Dreigliederung (threefold membering, threefold articulation). It is necessary, however, that we think of this Dreigliederung in the right way. *RE 97-98*

Money as Spirit Realized

Money makes it possible for the human spirit – in the form of intelligence, foresight, creativity, and initiative – to enter into the economic process in the division of labor. When the human spirit takes up money in the form of capital in order to produce something, what was once abstract – money – is transformed into something concrete and specific as goods and services. The formation of capital can be viewed as a synthesis of what was separated through the division of labor.

Capital must be created in the economic process if the spirit is to function at a level beyond that of primitive survival. Someone creates capital and converts it to money capital. This person then lends it to someone else. As such, money represents the values created by the spirit. It is the spirit working in the economy. The money, which was an abstraction in itself, now has concrete value.

. . . Money is the thing absolutely indifferent to the single factors in economic life in so far as they are still influenced by nature. For this very reason money becomes the means of expression, the instrument, the medium for spirit to enter into the economic organism in the division of labor. Without money being created, it is absolutely impossible for spirit to enter in and play its part in the economic organism, which depends on the division of labor. We may say then that what in a primitive economic condition is originally all together

> *– what one does in egotism for oneself – is now divided up among the whole community. Such is the division of labor. With capital, the single parts are gathered up again into a total, collected process. The forming of capital is a synthesis. Those who first emerge as creators of capital, being able to change it into money capital (since money must necessarily appear at this stage), become lenders to others, who possess nothing but their spirit. The latter now receive the money, which is the true and proper representative of economic values created by spirit.*
>
> *We must really consider this thoroughly from the point of view of economics. However evil money may be from a religious or ethical point of view, in the economic sense money is spirit at work in the economic organism. It is so indeed. Once more then, money must be created in the economic process if spirit is to progress at all from the initial point where it applies itself merely to nature. Spirit would remain in an altogether primitive condition if it could do no more than this. To pour again into the economic process what has been achieved by the application of spirit, spirit must be realized in the form of money. Money is the realization of spirit. But the concrete quality comes back into it again. In the first place, money is an abstract thing, for, as we said before, to money it is a matter of indifference whether for the five francs in my pocket I buy an article of clothing or get my hair cut (several times, if you like). The moment money returns to the individual human being, that is, to the individual human spirit, it becomes economically active once more as a concrete and specific fact. The spirit is economically active in the money.* RE 46-47

The overall health of an economy can be expressed as the total commodity values divided by money values, where the numerator, commodity, includes values created by labor transforming nature, and the denominator, money, has to do with values created by the human spirit directing labor. The relation between commodity-value and money-value is an interactive one; it is a relationship of division rather than of subtraction. These values will fluctuate depending on their location and other conditions.

*Money appears at this point [when Labor is organized by the spirit and made into a value] not in its fully abstract nature; it is abstract, to begin with, if I may put it so (abstract, as the substance to which spirit first applies itself), but it grows highly individualized, highly specific, when spirit takes hold of it and uses it for this or that purpose. In doing so, it is spirit as such that determines the value of the money. Here, you see, money begins to gain a concrete and specific value. Whether a person is a fool and throws the money away on something that turns out to be unfruitful, or whether the person applies it in a useful way – this now emerges as a very real value in the economic process. For your denominator, therefore, you will here get something that has to do with money; while your numerator, I need hardly say, will have to do with the fact that you have before you that into which the substance of nature has been transformed. What is a substance of nature, transformed by labor and present in the economic process? It is a commodity. This, then, is the numerator; and for the denominator, corresponding to "labor organized by spirit," you will have money.**

$$\frac{Nl^{v}}{Ls^{v}} = \frac{Commodity}{Money}$$

New values come to light: the commodity value and the money value. In the economic process founded on the division of labor, we must recognize this truth. The quotient of the total commodities present in the economic organism and the money present in the economic organism (taking as "money" not what is counted in the registers, but what is actually taken hold of by spirit in human beings) will represent a real interaction. Money is the divisor. This interaction, which cannot be represented by a subtraction but only by a division, represents the real health of the economic process. To understand what this health consists of, we must learn to understand what is at work in the numerator here and in the denominator. We must understand more and more

* Editor's note: Restated, the equation means: commodity values divided by money values, where *Nl* refers to the commodity values created by nature being transformed by labor; and *Ls* refers to the values created by the human spirit directing labor in an intelligent way.

> *wherein the essential nature of a commodity on the one hand, and of the medium of circulation, the money, on the other hand, consists. The most essential economic question cannot be solved at all unless we proceed in this exact way. We must not forget that whatever appears in economic life will always be fluctuating. The moment the commodity is taken from one place to another, the numerator here will change. I can do nothing other than point out, at every turn, how fluctuating all things are in the economic process.* RE 49-52

Money as Bookkeeping and Medium of Exchange

Transactions involving money are essentially a bookkeeping system that tracks economic values in circulation. Money is a medium of exchange for goods and services. It is an abstract token or symbol of commodities.

> *. . . All money transactions are a matter of bookkeeping. Instead of transferring an entry from the credit to the debit column, you just transfer [pay] the money.* RE 256

> *. . . In the circulation of money we have, in effect, the world's bookkeeping. This is, as everyone can really see for themselves, what should be aimed at. In this way we give back to money the only quality that it can properly have – that of being the external medium of exchange. Look into the depths of economic life, and you will see that money can be nothing else than this. It is the medium of exchange of services or things done. In reality human beings live by the things actually done, not by the tokens thereof.* RE 172

> *. . . By money we detach ourselves from the sound productive process itself. Money is made into an abstraction, so to speak, in the economic process, just as thoughts are in the process of thought. Just as it is impossible to call up by enchantment real ideas and feelings from abstract thought, so it is likewise impossible to bring forth by enchantment something real from money, if that money is not merely*

a symbol for commodities that are produced, if it is not merely a kind of book-keeping, a currency system of book-keeping, in which every piece of money must represent a commodity. SF 49

. . . When some item is transferred or delivered, this simply signifies the entry of an item in another place. In actual practice the transfer is done by passing money and commodities from hand to hand. The principle is fundamentally the same, whether we contrive to record the items in their proper places in an immense bookkeeping system embracing the whole world economy, and so direct things simply by transferring credits; or whether we write out a check and give it to the person concerned, so that the thing is done in external action. RE 172

As far as I can see the actual substance of the money is of no consequence . . . I cannot see the necessity of introducing a currency such as gold. It would be necessary only in the situation where specialized economies were being created. But to the extent that the world economy is actually a reality – it becomes ever more so to the extent that economics emancipates itself – it is possible to make the money out of any substance whatsoever. What does money then become when what I am saying is realized? Nothing but bookkeeping, which is done throughout the whole economic region. RE 256

A New Basis for Determining the Value of Money (Currency)

A bookkeeping system needs a monetary unit of measure. Steiner suggests using the amount of labor necessary to produce an amount of an agricultural product, such as wheat, as the basis for a monetary unit. Once the unit of measure is established, then all other commodities can be measured in terms of their relative value. The total value of all currency is equivalent to the value of goods and services in circulation as a result of the total available means of production.

Thus we are creating a money system based on a real unit of economic value: the amount of work it takes to produce a certain nature product. Since consumption is the basis for assigning value, to a great extent it is possible to derive precise values.

> *If the economic life becomes permeated with a way of thinking such as we have here adopted, the actual measures we take would bring about the result I have stated. It all depends on that. We would find that our currency, representing the day-to-day bookkeeping of world economy, would have to be inscribed, "Wheat producible over a given number of acres." This amount would then be equated to other things. The various products of the soil are the easiest things to compare. You see where it is we must start – our figures must mean something. It simply leads away from reality if money has inscribed on it, "So much gold." It leads towards reality if it has inscribed on it, "This represents so much labor upon x product of nature." We would then have this result. Say there is written on the money "x wheat," all money will be stamped "x of wheat, y of wheat, z of wheat." The real origin of the whole economic life would then be made evident. Our currency would be referred to the usable means of production upon which bodily work is done; that is, the means of production of the given economic region. The only sound basis of currency is the total of the usable means of production.*
>
> *Those who can look into the realities of life with an open mind will see, as they perceive the situation, that this is so. It may be objected that no one value can be precisely equated to another. But to a great extent this can be done. In this method of valuation everything is ultimately valued through consumption; therefore, the values of different kinds of services do not differ so very much from one another. However much of a spiritual-cultural worker I may be, I need so much saved labor every year – as much as I require to maintain myself as a human being. Moreover, by this means it will be evident how and to what extent a spiritual-cultural worker needs something in addition – beyond what a manual laborer needs. When the issue has become as transparent as this it will be acknowledged, because it is transparent.* RE 177-178

The Relation of Money to Value of Cultural and Political-Legal Work

In a healthy social organism, money stands for the potential to acquire products from others, based on the fact that one has also produced goods, or has been relieved of this obligation by others who have produced something on one's behalf. It is possible to assign value to cultural and legal services and products in a system in which the unit of currency is equivalent to the amount of labor it takes to process and deliver a specific nature product to a certain point of development in the economic process. Although the products and services of cultural and legal workers are not considered commodities in their own realms, they are treated as such in the economic arena. In this case, money is a token representing the work these workers were spared because others in the community produce commodities on their behalf. In this way, all money within an economic organism is equal to the value of the total means of production. *[For more details on how cultural activities can be funded, see Chapter Ten, Price Formation, and Chapter Eleven, The Interplay of Spiritual-Cultural and Economic Life.]*

> . . . *Within a healthy social organism, after all, money can represent nothing other than the potential to obtain goods produced by others, from the totality of the economic sphere, by virtue of the fact that one has oneself produced and delivered goods for this sphere. The circulation of money makes an economic sector part of a unified economic organism. Each person produces for every other via the totality of economic life. Within the economic realm we are concerned only with commodity values. In this realm the results and achievements deriving from the cultural and rights realms also assume the character of commodities. The efforts a teacher makes on behalf of her pupils becomes a commodity within the economic realm. A teacher is no more paid for her individual gifts and capacities than a laborer is paid for the strength he puts into his labor. Both can only be paid for anything that can be regarded as commodity, the results of their input of efforts or labor. The parts which free initiative and rights awareness should play in the*

production of a commodity lie outside the economic realm in the same way that the effect of natural conditions is distinct from the actual grain yield in a good or bad harvest. As far as the economic sphere is concerned, the cultural, spiritual sphere and also the state are commodity producers. But what they produce is not a commodity within their own sphere – it only becomes such when it enters economic circulation. Within their own spheres they do not engage in the economic process, but what they have created or produced is commercially managed by the economic organism.
TSR 93-94

Go back to the hypothetical case I gave yesterday – the closed village economy. In such a self-contained village economy you have the manual workers, and I assumed that the only spiritual-cultural workers were the parson and the schoolmaster and possibly the village clerk. It is a very simple economy! Most of the people are doing physical labor, physical work upon the soil; in addition, they have to do enough physical work to provide for the needs (food, clothing, and so forth), of the schoolmaster, parson, and clerk. It will be additional, because the schoolmaster, the parson, and the village clerk do not do their work upon nature themselves. Say that the village economy consists of thirty farmers plus the three – what shall we call them? – "receivers of honoraria." These three supply their spiritual-cultural services. They need the saved labor of the rest. Suppose that each of the thirty farmers gives to these three, or to each one of them, a token, a ticket, on which is written an amount, say ***x****, of wheat – that is, wheat elaborated to a certain point. Another member of the community might give a ticket on which something else was entered, something comparable to wheat for purposes of consumption. These things can be ascertained. The schoolmaster, the parson and the clerk will collect these tickets. Instead of going out into the fields to procure their wheat and rye and beef for themselves, they will hand over their tickets to those concerned, who in their turn will do the necessary labor in addition to their own and will give them the product in exchange. That is a process that cannot help developing of its own accord.*

> *It cannot possibly be otherwise, nor does it make any difference if it occurs to some bright individual to introduce metal coins instead of tickets. Some kind of tokens must be devised, based on the stored-up material labor – labor expended on means of production, labor invested in economic values. And these tickets must be handed over to those who need them, so that they can save themselves the labor.*
>
> *You will see, therefore, that no kind of money can in reality be anything other than an expression of the sum of means of production available in a given region, means of production including in the very first place the land itself, reduced to the form in which it can be most suitably expressed. This will relate the economic process to something that we can at least grasp.* RE 175-176

Impersonal Nature of Modern Banking and Finance

Until recent times, people were directly involved with the things they produced in their entirety, and money was an equivalent for a particular item produced; true economic impulses were also at work in early banking systems. The advent of the division of labor fostered an impersonal relation to both the products produced and to money itself. This abstraction of money made possible the innovation of financial systems, in which money is treated as a commodity and becomes an object of trade and business onto itself. The development of large scale lending and borrowing resulted in the control of the circulation of money being withdrawn from human decision-making, so that it is now a highly impersonal process that follows its own abstract laws. In fact, in a certain sense, human beings themselves are controlled by the money economy.

> *The emancipation of the money-market from the goods-market . . . dates from about the years 1810 to 1815. It was at this period that the earlier, purely economic conditions controlling public life first gave way to a control of public life by the money market. It was the time when the bank-system first really became the dominant factor in economic life. And for economic situations to be created by transactions solely*

in the money-market, on the grand scale that was possible by [the financial panic of 1907], was something which only came about through money having become what I might call an 'actual abstraction' that spreads through our whole economic life and to all other life as well.

We go back in thought to the time when people were themselves involved with the things they produced. Money, in those days, was practically no more than a sort of equivalent for the specific articles produced. People clung to their specific productions; it was in those days by no means a matter of indifference, what one produced; one grew together with one's specific article of output . . . The close association between people and the things they produce is totally disappearing: all that is aimed at now is to bring in a sufficient income to satisfy personal needs. And it comes then to be a question of capital and wages, and how much these will bring in. Just like abstract principles, which can be extended to cover every sort of thing, so this abstract money extends over every conceivable thing. It is after all – in the minds of many people today – a matter of complete indifference, when the object is to earn a certain number of shillings a day, it is a matter of complete indifference whether one does so by manufacturing shoes, or by manufacturing text-books. Money is the actual real abstraction, just as general principles are abstract; and, like them, it can be applied to every sort of thing. And this abstract money, emancipated from the real reality of life, has made the kind of atmosphere possible, in which transactions can then go on such as went on in 1907; and yet these transactions, nevertheless, proceed absolutely and entirely from the will of human beings. *TOBS 11-12.*

. . . With the evolution of the banking system, borrowing and lending develops on an ever larger scale, enters more and more as a prime factor into the economic process. At the same time, precisely in connection with lending, a remarkable phenomenon appears. Through the instrumentality of lending on a large scale, and accompanying the expansion of the banking system, the control of the circulation of money

is withdrawn from the individual. The circulation of money has gradually become a process taking place – I can find no other word to express it – impersonally. Thus, as I said in my first lecture, the time has actually come when money does business on its own account, and human beings fluctuate up and down according to how they are drawn into this whole stream of money economics, money business. They are drawn in far more than they imagine. RE 114-115

. . . Precisely during the last decades of the nineteenth century, the circulation of money became objectified – it became impersonal. This brings me to a peculiar phenomenon of the nineteenth century, particularly of the end of the nineteenth century. In economics, everything depends on an open-minded consideration of life as a whole; we must gain a clear vision – of the whole of life. The phenomenon to which I refer appears, to begin with, in the psychological sphere, but afterward plays a great part in economic life. It is this. Conditions that were brought about in the first place by very real forces afterwards continue rolling on by a kind of social inertia, just as a ball will, when you have given it a certain momentum. These conditions go rolling on and on, even after the original impulses have ceased to be active in them. Down to the first third of the nineteenth century, there were true economic impulses present in the whole system of loan and investment. Then, through the instrumentality of the banking system, these economic impulses began to change into purely financial ones; and in this process the whole thing became not only impersonal but unnatural. Everything was drawn into the stream of money, as it moved itself along. Pure money business, without any natural or personal subject – that is the end toward which, as the nineteenth century drew to a close, everything that had originally been upheld by a personal and natural subject was gravitating. RE 115

The development of the modern financial system has caused people to become increasingly distant from one another socially. In the former natural economy, people depended on each other. They had to work together and make agreements or economic life would collapse.

With a money system, it is not necessary that everyone produces commodities; in fact, money frees people from the economic process because it becomes an economic process in itself. A result of modern financial systems is a growing disconnection between producers and consumers, and workers and investors. It is only by developing economic associations that these gaps can be overcome (as described in the chapter on Associations).

> *. . . When business was carried on in the old natural economic system, the production of commodities was necessary. These were, of course, liable to spoilage, and people had to work, and to continue working, so as to keep up a supply of goods. This is not necessary with money. A man gives over money, lends it, insures himself; that is, money transactions are carried on quite independently of those who produce commodities. Money emancipates people in a certain sense from the actual economic process, just because it becomes itself an economic process. This is extremely significant. [For] in the old natural economy, one individual depended on another. People were forced to work together, to bear with one another. They had to agree on certain arrangements, otherwise the economic life could not go on. Under the financial system the capitalist is, of course, also dependent on those who work, but is quite a stranger to these workers. How close was the tie between consumer and producer in the old natural economy in which actual commodities were dealt with! How remote is the person who transacts business in money from those who work in order that his or her money may yield interest! A deep gulf has opened between one human being and another. They do not get near to each other under the financial system of economy. This is one of the first things to be considered if we wish to understand how the masses of workers (no matter whether they are intellectual or manual workers) can again be brought together with those who also make business possible by lending capital. This, however, can only be done through the principle of association, by which people will again unite with each other as human beings. The principle of association is*

a demand of social life, but a demand such as I have described it, not one resembling those that often figure in socialistic programs. *SF 39-40*

Taxation

To tax income is to tax an abstraction. Money as an expression of economic values is only meaningful when it enters circulation through some type of expenditure. In contrast, income is a temporary removal of money from economic circulation as long as it is in a person's possession. It has no value as such, and receives value only when it is put back into circulation by spending, investing, or being given away. What makes a person wealthy is his or her ability to spend a lot. Therefore, a healthy form of taxation is one in which capital is taxed at the moment it moves into the economic process and becomes productive. In a healthy economic life, taxation on expenditures replaces income tax.

Among all those who today profess to be experts in practical life, there is not a single individual who doubts that an improvement has been made by the transition from all kinds of indirect taxation and other sources of national income to what we call the income tax, especially the graduated income tax. Everyone thinks it is unquestionably right to pay income tax and yet, however paradoxical this may sound to the modern mind, the belief that the imposition of a tax on income is a just measure is only an illusion resulting from the modern financial system of economy . . . Today it must be stated that in a period that is only concerned with turning money into an economic object, incomes cannot escape being an object of taxation.

By imposing taxes, we make ourselves co-responsible with others for the whole financial economic system. Something is taxed that is not a commodity at all, but only a symbol for a commodity. We are dealing with an abstraction from the economic life. Money only becomes a reality when it is spent for something. It then takes its place in the circuit of economic life, whether I spend it on amusement, or for bodily or mental necessities, or whether I bank it to be used in the economic process. Banking my money is a way of spending it. This must, of course, be kept in mind. Money becomes a reality in the economic process at the moment it passes out of my possession into the process of economic life. If people would reflect, they would see that it is of no use for people to have a large income. If they hoard it, it may be theirs, but it is of no use in the economic process. The only thing that benefits a person is the ability to spend a great deal. In public life today, in a life fruitful of results, the ability to spend a great deal is just the sign of a large income. Hence, if a system of taxation is to be created that constitutes a real service of the economic process to the good of the general community, instead of a parasitical growth upon it, capital must be taxed at the moment it is transferred to the economic process. Strange to relate, income tax comes to be transformed into a tax on expenditure, which I beg you not to confound with indirect taxation. Indirect taxation is often the expression of the wishes of rulers of the present day, because the direct taxes and income tax do not ordinarily yield enough. We are not referring to either direct or indirect taxation in speaking of the tax on expenditure; the point in question is that at the moment my capital passes into the economic process and becomes productive, it shall be taxed.

Precisely by this example of taxation, we see how necessary is a change in our method of thinking, and how the belief that a tax on income is first in importance is an accompaniment of that financial system that has appeared in modern civilization since the Renaissance and Reformation. When the economic system is once placed upon its own basis, the only matter to be considered is that capital actually involved in the production of commodities shall supply the means for the manufacture of the products necessary to the community. It will then be a case of a tax on expenditure, but never one on income. *SF 48-50*

Aging Money

All goods and services are sooner or later used up or withdrawn from circulation. Money, however, which is the equivalent of the value of all the goods and services in circulation, does not wear out in so far as its face value does not diminish. Money that remains true to its nature as an equivalent to goods produced should also deteriorate or wear out. In other words, it should expire after a certain period of time.

> *To understand the economic conditions in a closed economic domain, we must see clearly that within the economic domain – in the mutual interplay of production, consumption and commerce (that is, in effect, circulation) – we have on the one hand consumable commodities, some of them relatively lasting, no doubt; while on the other hand we have the thing we call "money." Regarding the form of economy to which these things are subject, it makes an essential difference whether we envision the class of food products for example (consumable products) or of clothing (more durable) or, let us say, of furniture or houses (still more durable). With respect to their use and consumption we have these important differences of durability between different kinds of economic products. As an instance of a very long-lasting economic product, we might point once more to the diamond in the Crown of England, or any other crown. Or, again, we might think of the Sistine Madonna. Such things may be to some extent regarded as a kind of product that will endure; we find them especially among works of art. Now in a social organism subject to division of labor, having therefore an extensive process of circulation, there must be some equivalent of every product. There must be the money value, representing the price. But a very cursory observation of the economic realm will convince you that this equivalent between the commodity value and the money value is fluctuating. A product is worth so much at one place and so much at another. A product can be worth more if it is processed in one way, or less if it is processed in another. Be that as it may, however, in the total economic life you will*

perceive that apart from a few exceptional goods of great durability we always deal with goods that pass away in time. They lose their value, and after a certain amount of time are no longer there.

The one exception, strange to say, in our whole economic life is money. Although it occupies a position of perfect equivalence to the other elements of economic life, money does not wear out. You can get to the root of the matter in this way. If I have $20 worth of potatoes, I must see to it that I get rid of them. I must do something to get rid of them. After a time they are no longer there; they are used up, they are gone. Now if it were in a true relation of equivalence to the goods that are produced, then money, too, would have to wear out, like other goods. That is to say, if the body economic contains money that is incapable of being used up – money that does not wear out – we may well be giving money the advantage over goods, which do wear out. *RE 138-139*

The value of the money in a given exchange is determined by what is received in return for it. Whereas it is obvious when commodities wear out or decay, money does not appear to go through an equivalent process because its face value remains constant. However, the veiled aging of money manifests in price fluctuations, most commonly by way of inflation. This fluctuation is due to the nature of money, not to the products purchased.

In the case of purchase money you have no other foundation on which to estimate its value. No, you have no other need to estimate its value than how much you will get for it. Time makes no essential difference. Whether you buy a pound of meat today or after a certain lapse of time, you must estimate the pound of meat according to its consumption value. Your money may in the meanwhile have acquired a different value in relation to the pound of meat. But for the human being who eats it, the value of the pound of meat cannot, properly speaking, change in course of time. The duration factor, however, is essential. The given pound of meat can only be eaten during a certain period of time. That is to say, it can have a value only for a certain period of time, since it will go bad. This is a very pertinent economic fact. Everything that is a genuine object of use or consumption is subject to decay.

When for the purposes of pure exchange we use money as an equivalent, we must admit that, as opposed to articles that decay, money is an unfair competitor. In normal circumstances, nowadays, money does not seem to decay. I say expressly, it does not seem to decay. Here you can see what an unhealthy element is introduced into economic life when we bring into it relationships that are different from those in reality. By our established institutions money has a fixed numerical value under all conditions. No matter how it may otherwise be placed in relation to social life, money has its face value and is supposed to keep it permanently. But in reality it does not do so. Everything else is honest. Meat after a period, which varies with its quality, begins to smell. Money does not do this, no matter what its quality may be. Money does not openly "smell." Yet, when we see circumstances bring it about that an article grows less or more expensive after a certain time, we are obliged to admit the following. While the article itself, by virtue of its qualities for human life, must retain the same value (for general conditions will ensure its being consumed at the right moment and its replacement with a new one), the same thing is not true of money. Consequently money, as such, as a pure medium of exchange, is an unfair competitor because it does not reveal in any way the fact that it is also really subject to changes. If I have to pay a certain sum of money for a pound of meat today and a different sum of money for a pound of the same meat two weeks later, the difference (the increase, for example) in the money I must pay cannot be because of the pound of meat. It must therefore be because of the money. If the money still bears the same face value, then the money is beginning to tell a lie, for its real value has decreased. If I must give more in exchange for a pound of meat, then the value of the money has decreased. That is quite obvious. In this way, by the act of circulating the money, I bring into the process something that is not really there economically. Economically the facts are otherwise. Economically the situation is that money itself, simply through the economic process, undergoes changes. *RE 147-149*

All money should have an equivalent in the actual production of commodities. After a certain period of time, the ownership of capital should return to the community, particularly, if it is not used in further production. To ensure that money not used in the production of commodities is not held back by the one in possession of it, and that it loses its value when it no longer has living significance, new minting of money should occur from time to time. If money were to wear out by expiring, the possibility of gaining interest on interest would be eliminated, because interest on capital would diminish over time. However, none of this would prevent the accumulation of personal savings from services rendered, which allows a person to make future claims on commodities and services for a certain period of time. The limited life span of money would prevent such savings from becoming a source of financial power.

> *In a healthy social organism, money will really only be a measure of value; behind every coin or note will stand the actual production of commodities, on whose basis alone people can gain access to money. The nature of these circumstances will necessitate arrangements such as I have already formulated, whereby money can lose its value for its owner once it loses the living significance just referred to. Once a certain period has elapsed, ownership of capital returns to the community in an appropriate form. And to ensure that money not active in production processes is not retained by its owners, circumventing the measures implemented by the economic sphere, new minting can take place from time to time. A further result of organizing things in this way is that interest accruing on capital would continually diminish through the years. Money would wear out just as goods do. But such a governmental measure would be right and proper, making it impossible to simply sit back and gain 'interest from interest.' A person who has built up savings, though, has rendered services which allow him or her to claim reciprocal services in the form of commodities at a later date, just as present services or goods can be rightfully exchanged against other present services or goods. But this kind of claim based on past goods or services only holds good up to a*

> *certain point, for it can only be exchanged against reciprocation in the present. It should not become a means of financial power. By implementing such measures, the whole question of currency is placed on a sound footing, for no matter what shape or form money assumes through the influence of other factors, the economic organization will manage currency in such a way that it becomes the rational and healthy medium of its activities.* *TSR 95-96*

Shortcomings in modern economic life are due in part to the fact that the true value of certain elements in the economy is not acknowledged. For example, the economy is disturbed when non-manual workers are not appropriately compensated, when they receive either too much or too little for their work. Aging money allows for appropriate prices to emerge for goods, for the manual work that produces them, and also for cultural work.

One way to allow money to age is to give each bill an expiration date. In effect, this would be similar to the ancient Hebrew custom of forgiving debts during a Jubilee year. The expiration date would not be chosen abstractly, but would be estimated based upon the facts and conditions at the time it was issued, and modified according to realities that unfolded over time. Flexibility with regard to the expiration date is possible when bills are stamped with the date of issue. In this way, the end date can vary.

Although as purchase money its value would remain consistent, the closer money got to the expiration date, the "older" the money would become, and the less value it would have as loan money. It would then convert to gift money, after which point it would eventually be reissued as new money. *[For more on purchase and loan money see pg. 253 in this chapter.]*

The aging of money is not an abstract manipulation. It represents reality. On the contrary, when we use money that was issued thirty years ago as though it still has the same value, then it has a fictitious value.

> *. . . The gradual depreciation of money is not easy to imagine. It would require an extraordinarily bureaucratic system.*

I would emphasize that I do not want to proceed in a programmatic way, that I want only to acknowledge what is – because I recognize that we cannot establish a paradise on earth with economic methods. That would not be possible, but we must try to create the best possible situation. Now one has to ask oneself why we have less than the best possible situation today. It comes about because the various factors of the economy cannot achieve their true value in one place or another, because today it is quite possible that spiritual/cultural workers are by no means paid in the way that is necessary for the whole economy. They are paid either too much or too little; both things do occur. But if they are paid too little they immediately cause prices to change in an unhealthy way because of their low pay. And it is the same if they are paid too much. This needs to be corrected, and it is only a question . . . of what factors would restore commercial balance in economic life. Thus trade will arise in which there are mutually tolerable prices not only for goods but also for cultural as well as the necessary spiritual-intellectual life.

From this it directly follows that money must get old. It is just a matter of how this can be technically carried out. You would be able to bring about a gradual depreciation of money in no other way than by attaching coupons to the paper money that have to be torn off at specific times by a public official. This would result in a very complicated bureaucracy. But it is really never a question of carrying out the depreciation with such external means, but that this valuation is brought about by itself through the actual course of events. This will happen when you more or less simply give money of all kinds a characteristic of change – I mean insofar as it has an end point. Of course this cannot be calculated abstractly, but assuming there is a particular moment, it can to begin with only be approximately determined. Then one needs to make corrections until the situation eventually comes to a possible end point.

Then it would be a matter of again finding out for the world economy what was fundamentally already there as a widespread local economy. Because this is the way the

Jubilee in the Old Testament was celebrated, which is something very similar to the aging of money: the remission of all debts. With the radical remission of all debts, all harmful loans and investments also disappear. You will recall the length of time between Jubilee years, they occurred every fifty years. This Jubilee year, in contrast to what would be necessary today for the world economy, was determined a priori simply by fixing the patriarchal age. For the moment, I do not recall if it is so stated in the Bible, but in any case it was originally the custom to thus fix the human life span. It was correctly calculated that if one takes the whole course of a human life, then everything is contained there: what in youth is there as gift capital, then is there as loan capital, and business capital, that is, commercial or industrial capital. It was assumed that one had a right to consume in youth what one later earns during one's mature years, and then one earns somewhat less towards the end of life. At some time this was looked upon as a kind of borrowing.

Now you see, this was a priori; this would not take place in the world economy in this way. The time periods would be considerably prolonged. But it is also quite clear that when the gradual devaluation of the money begins, this will occur by itself through circulation, because the year it was issued would be printed on the banknote. In actual economic circulation such money will not have a lower purchase value but a lower value for any organizational use. The older it gets, the lower is its use value, so that through the decrease in its use value it can gradually become gift money, and can then be re-issued as young, that is, "new" money again. That must be done only by the association. For products that are as close as possible to nature-products, the work then has its highest value, although the worker is not paid any more than anyone else according to the price formula; but in the economic activity it has the highest value. Only one part goes to the one who is working; the rest goes entirely into the economic process. The possibility to enrich one's own self has thus been taken away from the individual. *RE 251-253*

> *And now let us suppose that we really make up our minds to allow money to grow old. Suppose you have a certain piece of money, no matter what substance it is made of, or what date is inscribed on it. Say it is "1910." And now you take another piece of money with the date "1915." The money marked "1915" begins to exist, as money, economically, in that year. And now suppose that by some reasoned treatment it undergoes the process that is undergone by all other exchangeable products; it loses its value after a certain time. The precise figures I mention are not important; they are merely illustrations. The actual figures required would have to be the subject of infinitely numerous – but perfectly possible – calculations, as we shall presently see. Suppose, therefore, for the sake of example, that the piece of money would have lost its value for economic activity by the year 1940. It would have a definite value only between 1915 and 1940. For that period it would have, as we shall see directly, a determinable value. If money loses its value in the economic process after twenty-five years, a piece of money bearing the date "1910" will have lost its value in the year 1935. Thus I would assign a particular property to the money that I carry around with me; I would assign to it a kind of age. This 1910 money is older; it will die earlier than the 1915 money. Now you may say that is just a scheme. No, what I have just explained to you is the actual reality. That is how the economic process actually wills it. The economic process of its own accord makes the money grow old. The fact that it does not appear to grow old – the fact that we will still buy things with 1910 money in the year 1940 – is only a mask. In doing so we do not really buy with this money; we buy with a fictitious money value.* RE 152

If money is allowed to grow old beginning on its date of issue, its subsequent value will depend on its age. New or young money will be needed for long-term projects, so that it doesn't expire before the project is finished. The desirability for young money for long-term projects gives it greater value than old money has. On the other hand, older money is desirable for short-term projects, because the value of new money is squandered when a project is finished long before the money has expired. Older money receives its cheaper value from being used for initiatives of a more limited nature. As we have seen, aging and corresponding cheapening of the value of money applies to loan money. Purchase money (money used for buying and selling) retains its value.

> *If therefore the money in my purse grows old in this way, if its date of origin has a real meaning (and by "growing old" I mean getting nearer and nearer to its death), then money, like a human being and every other living thing, has a certain value impressed upon it by the fact that it is growing older. The money comes to life and a value is impressed upon it. Why? Suppose you have young money, money of the present year – 1922 money. This 1922 money will be good purchase money, needless to say. But now suppose that I am an entrepreneur and I ask myself how I can supply myself with money for my undertaking. Suppose, according to my calculations, my undertaking must be planned for a period of twenty years. Shall I provide myself with old money or with young money? Then I will think that if I take old money, it will have lost its value in five years, or in two. Therefore it will not do for me to use old money. If, according to my calculations, I must provide for a long period, I must have young money. Thus, under the influence of long-term undertakings, young money receives its particular economic value – a value far greater than that of old money. This economic value really exists – and it is there now. On the other hand, suppose I have to embark on an undertaking that involves calculations covering a period of only three years; in that case I should be a poor economist if I used very young money. The young money, by virtue of its youth, is the most valuable and, accordingly, the most expensive. If I require the money for a shorter period, I shall provide myself with less valuable money. For those who have to apply their spirit – their intelligence – to money, the age of the money can begin to play a part, of which they are quite conscious.*
>
> *Please note that this is not something that does not exist already. It exists, but in a wild, untamed way, which results*

> *in mutual disturbance and unhealthy economic conditions. On the other hand, if you tame money, if you really assign to it a certain age, letting young money – as loan money – be more valuable than old, then you will be impressing the money with its real effective value, the value it possesses through its position in the economic process. This value really inheres in the money only while it is loan money, for even if money is loan money, as purchase money it still retains its former value. You do not need to consider too carefully whether you ought to provide yourself with still other money, for what you as an entrepreneur are going to consume. These things will correct themselves of their own accord.* RE 152-153

There is no one right way to accomplish the aging of money. A variety of measures may be needed. The picture of money growing older or getting used up can be thought of in relation to the picture of a growing and aging human being. We have an idea of how the life of a young human being might unfold, but the reality of how his or her life turns out is likely to be different from what we had thought, either in particulars or more broadly. Money, too, might be used up over time in a number of ways. If the question of money, and of economic life generally, is grasped in a living way, then healthy, appropriate forms will be found that are in harmony with realities.

> *The thought-picture of money growing old or getting used up is a particularly suggestive one. You must relate yourself to such an ideal picture as you would to, let us say, a growing human being. You have a general feeling that a particular person will prove to be very capable in one direction or another. You may have fairly definite ideas of what this person will accomplish. But these ideas could well turn out to have been mistaken. This person may accomplish what is destined in quite other ways. So, too, for the concept of money's being used up in course of time, you may find various ways in which this can be brought about. The way I have tried to present the situation is as one conceived as little as possible along bureaucratic lines; it results naturally from economic life itself.*

Many objections may no doubt be made. Here is a very easy one. How will it be settled that an entrepreneur puts young money and no other into business? After a short time it may no longer be recognizable whether the money was young or not, for business will be going on. In answer to this, you must bear in mind that we do not simply get the money from the sky; we borrow it from someone. Moreover, you can see from my book Towards Social Renewal *that I do not think interest on money should be abolished, provided the money has real value. (On the contrary, I believe that up to a point interest is actually necessary in economic life.) You may wonder how you, as an entrepreneur, can get money from those who might lend it to you if you are going to pay them interest for an extremely short time? They will wish to give you money only on the assumption that they will get interest out of your business for as long a time as possible. Thus, you may find that it is not enough simply to let money grow old in the way described. This may lead you to think out the method in greater detail. For instance, money issued today might be date-stamped, not with the present year but with a future year, in such a way that the value increases up to that year, and after that it decreases.*

In short, a living thing may realize itself in a variety of ways. By the act of grasping it livingly, you give it the possibility to realize itself in the most varied ways, just as living human beings can use their capacities in various ways. This is the essence of a non-dogmatic concept. To make such concepts your own, especially in economics, is to see how well these things enter into real life. Only on this foundation will you be able to make proper use of what is given in the so-called economic science of today out of quite good, but only partial, observations. *RE 169-171*

If a way is found to allow money to age, die, and be reissued, then it no longer will be able to grow and reproduce itself without the creation of new economic values to justify such increase. Although it can be a difficult notion to accept, in a healthy economy it is vital that investments are consumed just like the goods they are used to acquire. Certain exceptions can be made for those personal savings that have been accumulated as a result of an individual's productive work.

> *Long ago, Aristotle said that capital should not produce offspring. At present, however, it is producing offspring that grow big and multiply. We can calculate how many years it takes for a capital investment to double if left to its own devices. Capital, however, should actually serve only as a placeholder for other goods, and all other goods eventually either wear out or become unusable if they are not consumed in a timely manner. Monetary investment must become subject to the fate of all other goods. Our current economy expects capital investment to double over a period of time. In a healthy economy, however, invested funds would vanish over that same time period, simply ceasing to exist. Today people are horrified by the suggestion that their monetary investment will not double in fifteen years but will simply vanish because it is consumed or depreciated along with the goods it used to purchase. Of course certain types of savings could be exempt from this rule.* FTSF 13-14

> *There is something extremely unnatural today in the social order. This consists in the fact that money increases when a person simply possesses it. It is put in a bank and interest is paid on it. This is the most unnatural thing that could possibly exist. It is really utterly nonsensical. The person does nothing whatever. He simply banks the money, which he may not even have acquired by labor but may have inherited, and he receives interest on it. This is utter nonsense. But it will become a matter of necessity, when the provision of the means of existence is separated from labor, that money shall be used when it exists, when it is produced as the equivalent of commodities that exist. It must be used. It must be put into circulation, and the actual effect will be that money does not increase but that it diminishes . . . If you think thus of the transformation of the social order, as this must occur under the influence of this one fundamental principle that I have presented to you, then money will not increase but*

will diminish. After a certain number of years, the bank notes I acquired before the beginning of those years will no longer have any value. *CT 62-63*

Purchase, Loan, and Gift Money

In order to work with money in a healthy way, it is important to understand its fundamental nature. Money does not have a single set of properties. Rather, it changes as it enters and moves through the economic cycle. *[Diagram 3, pg. 257.]* In fact, there are three different kinds of money – purchase, loan, and gift money, depending on when and how it enters the economic process. Purchase money is nothing more than a medium of exchange. Purchase money obtains its value from what it is exchanged for. Loaned money has an essentially different nature. It functions as working capital. The human spirit, working to produce something, gives loan money its value. Ultimately, the value of loan money depends on the way the borrower acts with it. Gift money is all that is used for education in the broadest sense: the development of inner and outer capacities.

Interestingly enough, gift money is actually the opposite of purchase money. Purchase money has value for the person giving it (for a product). Gift money has value only for the person who receives it. Gift money has a negative value with regard to everything that happens in the realm of purchase. Loaned money is the bridge or transition between these two kinds of money. Loaned money should not be held back for purchase money, but must pass over into gift money, where it loses its value.

. . . You see, this circle [see Diagram 3, pg. 257] can be very instructive. We can endow it with all manner of properties, and the challenge will always be how to bring the several economic processes and facts into this circle, which represents for us the cycle of the economic process. Something very important happens when in buying and selling in the market I pay on the spot for what I get. The point is not that I pay for it with money; I might equally well barter it for a corresponding commodity that the other person is willing to accept. The point is that I pay at once. It is this that constitutes "paying" in the proper sense of the word.

... In fact, we cannot do without the concept of "immediate payment." This is the concept that holds good in cases of simple purchase. A thing becomes a commodity on the market, moreover, through the very fact that it is paid for at once. This is generally the case with those commodities that are "nature-transformed-by-labor." For such commodities I pay. Here payment plays the essential part. There must be such payment. I pay at the very moment when I open my wallet and give away my money; and the value is determined in the very moment at which I give away the money or exchange my commodity for another. That is payment. That is one thing that must be in the economic process.

The second factor, which plays a similar part to payment, is the factor to which I drew attention yesterday. It is lending. This, as I said, does not interfere with the concept of payment as such.

Lending, once more, is an altogether different fact, a fact which simply exists. If I have money lent to me, I can apply my spirit to this loaned capital. I become a debtor, but I also become a producer.

In this way, lending plays a real economic part. If I have intellectual/spiritual capacities in some direction, it must be possible for me to obtain loaned capital. No matter where I get it, I must have it. Thus, in addition to payment there must be loan. [Diagram 3, pg. 257.] *Here then we have two very important factors in the economic process: payment and loan.*

By a simple deduction – we must verify it here [Diagram 3] *– by a very simple deduction you can find the third. You will not doubt for a moment what the third factor is. We have had payment and loan. The third factor is gift. Payment, loan, and gift – this is a real trinity of concepts, essential to a healthy economy. There is a prevailing disinclination to include "gift" in the economic process as such; but if there is not an act of giving somewhere, the economic process cannot go on at all. Imagine for a moment what we should make of our children if we gave them nothing. We are constantly giving gifts to our children. If we consider the economic process as a whole – as a process that goes on and on continuously – gift is part of it.*

There is no escaping the fact. It is wrong to regard the transfer of values from hand to hand, representing a process of gifting, as something inadmissible in the economic process as such. Precisely this one of the three is found – with horror by some people – worked out in my book Towards Social Renewal. *There it is shown how values are to be transferred – how means of production, for instance, are to be transferred to one who has the faculties necessary for managing them further by a process that is really identical with giving. Provision must, of course, be made that the giving is not done in a haphazard way. In the economic sense they are nonetheless gifts, and such gifts are absolutely necessary.*

You will find, more and more, this value transfer to be an economic necessity. The trinity of payment, loan, and gift is there in the economic process. Consider the matter thoroughly and you will agree that in every economic process this transfer must be contained. Otherwise, it would be no economic process; it would lead to absurdities at every point. *RE 73-75*

It is necessary above all to understand the essential nature of money. People fail to understand it precisely because it is always there before them without their being able to see what it really is. In the social organism there is no such thing as "money as such"; there are only these three kinds of money [loaned money, purchase money and gift money]. Moreover, each kind of money becomes what it is only at the moment when it is actually entering into the economic process or passing over from one form of economic process to another. In the very process, it is constantly being changed. The point is that we must learn to know money properly before we can pronounce what part it plays when it becomes an expression of the price of something else. *RE 156*

Speaking of money, the first thing we have to deal with is ordinary purchase money – the money we use to buy anything that serves us for consumption. *[See Diagram 3, "Payment" on pg. 257.]* *But we must also consider what we may call loan money. This we have seen in a former lecture.*

Bearing in mind its connection with the whole economic process, is loan money quite the same as purchase money? If you are considering purchase money you will have to ask how purchase money comes into existence among all the other elements of buying and selling. It comes about because those who make use of money, in giving their money, have given something that not only effects an immediate exchange, but have given something that also mediates an exchange. They give something that inserts itself into the exchange. As I have shown already in these lectures, everything that enters as a mediator into the process of exchange is money. Suppose I am not content with acquiring as many peas as I can eat myself. Suppose I acquire peas with the object of using them – trading them – in order to obtain some other things that I require. In that case, simply through this mediating function, I am already transforming what would otherwise be an article of consumption into money . . . whatever we use as money, to be a really useful form of money, must not merely oscillate, like peas, between the function of being consumed and the function of being passed from hand to hand. This change would involve constant fluctuations of value in the process of circulation. We want something that is used for no other purpose than for mediating an exchange; and to this end there must be a certain (albeit only a tacit) agreement among those who use the money. This, then, is an essential point. The money must be used only for an exchange, as a medium; it must not be used for consumption.

Loan money, however, is something essentially different from this purchase money. *RE 146-147*

We must now investigate the occasions upon which money undergoes changes. In addition to exchange money or purchase money we have loan money. Take for instance the loan money that a man obtains in order to begin some enterprise. For him it is not purchase money; for him it becomes working capital. Now you must see that this working capital, this loan money, has an essentially different value – an essentially different property. Loan money is fundamentally different

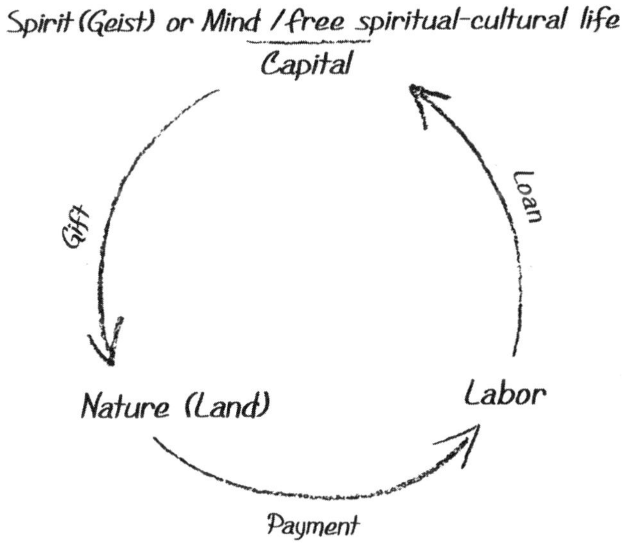

Diagram 3. RE 72

from purchase money. Except for the fact that it still consists of gold, silver, and paper, not many of its original properties are left when purchase money is transferred to the sphere of loan money. It acquires its value in quite a different way. The moment loan money comes into circulation, the human spirit seizes it. Human thinking sets to work, and it is through this entry of human thinking into the process that loan money receives its actual value. When a banknote is lent to a man who is about to undertake some business – at the moment he begins to use it – it would be far more important to write on the note whether the man is a genius or a fool in business. For the value of the loaned money in the whole economic process will henceforth depend upon the way he acts with it.

We must pass from loan money to the third kind of money that I mentioned a few days ago. These days, as a general rule, it is not taken into account, and yet it plays the greatest imaginable part in the economic process. In fact, we must now pass from loaned money to gift money. Gift money, fundamentally speaking, is all that is spent on education. This plays an enormous part in economic life.

> *Gift money, again, is all that is spent on endowments and the like – all that has the effect of preventing the evil damming up of capital in the land by capital investment, which is so ruinous for economic life. At this point we must say that for the person whose livelihood depends on purchase money, gift money simply becomes valueless. It loses its value. Gift money is the opposite of purchase money, as we can see from the simple fact that only one who has received the gift can purchase with it; one who has not received the gift cannot purchase with this particular money!*
>
> *We have therefore three kinds of money, qualitatively different from one another: purchase money, loan money and gift money. To comprehend the relation between these three, we must consider economic systems such as, for instance, the private economies that we assumed hypothetically in the last lecture – economies representing a kind of closed domain. There we shall find that after a certain time all that is loan money passes over into gift money. Nor can it be any different in the case of that closed economic domain that is "World Economy." Loaned money must gradually pass over entirely into gift money. Loan money must not be allowed to be dammed up into purchase money, so as to disturb the latter.*
>
> *Loan money, therefore, passes over into gift money. So it must be in a self-contained economic system. And what does it do in the domain where gift money is working? It loses its value. We may say of the domain of purchase money that the money will here represent a certain value. In the domain of "gift," on the other hand, the money has, with respect to all that obtains in the domain of purchase, a negative value. It lets the purchase value vanish into nothing. Finally, between the two, the transition is brought about through loan money. The loan money itself gradually vanishes into gift money.* *RE 149-150*

All money that is put into the educational system is considered gift money, whether in the form of freely-given gifts directly to schools, or through compulsory taxation. However, giving directly involves consciousness and intelligence, and the results of the gift can be observed. In contrast, tax-based giving becomes disconnected from the intentions of the taxpayer, and what happens to it is not directly observable.

> *. . . All that we put into the educational system is a gift – notably when it is a question of a truly free spiritual-cultural life. When you give directly, your intelligence is in the process. As things are now, you do give, but the gift is absorbed into the general pool of taxation. It vanishes into a vague economic fog, and you do not observe what happens. So the situation runs wild. In the other case, conscious intelligence comes into it.* RE 154

Rather than being allowed to run its own course, money must be guided by economic associations *[as described in Chapter Five, Economic Associations].* Disturbances and irregularities will arise and then must correct themselves with the help of human intelligence active in the associations. Associations will be responsible for ensuring that there are appropriate amounts of purchase, loan, and gift money at a given place and time in order to balance the disturbances and fluctuations in the economic process. To achieve a healthy economy, it is essential that money is not treated in a monolithic way as a commodity or allowed to run wild without human guidance.

In the past, in the system of national economies, when the price of an item became too high, that item would be imported, as a means of correcting the situation. In a world economy, however, these kinds of corrections are no longer possible. Corrections now must be made through the associations based on an awareness of the three kinds of money and the appropriate use of each one.

> *The question to ask is: 'How can existing economic organizations and institutions be integrated in associations?'*
>
> *If such associations can be achieved, commercial experience will enable something to arise that can indeed lead to a genuine social ordering, just as a healthy human organism leads to a healthy life. There will be circulation*

in the economy, circulation of production money, loan money and gift money. There can be no social organism without these three. We may want to rail against gifts and donations, but they are a necessary part. You deceive yourself if you say that a healthy social organism should make gifts unnecessary. Yet you pay tax, and taxes are merely a roundabout way of making donations to schools and other facilities. *RSSB 161-162*

The three kinds of money must be treated in different ways. In the first place, gift money, which is the oldest, must be handed over to an association that will bring the valueless money back again into the whole economic process, by uniting it with labor at the point where the nature process begins. There can be no economic difficulty in this. What then will be the essential difference from the existing practice? It will be that in a self-contained economic system (which, as we saw, is not like a national economy bordering on others, where exports and imports can be carried on) three distinct domains arise, as far as money is concerned: the domain of purchase money, the domain of loan money, and the domain of gift money. When anything occurs that would otherwise have had to be corrected by export and import from another country, it will be corrected by the three domains. If purchase money sets up a disturbance, there will be a corresponding flow between the spheres of purchase money, loan money, or gift money. These things will adjust themselves of their own accord. Irregularities will undoubtedly arise, and having arisen, they must correct themselves. Life cannot go on without irregularities coming in. It is an irregularity when the stomach is full. Accordingly, digestion has to follow. In the same way, circumstances must continually arise under which, for certain commodities, purchase money is too cheap or expensive – and then the cheap money will flow into the other domain, so that on the other side it becomes more expensive again as purchase money. What would otherwise have been corrected by export and import will now correct itself within the self-contained economy. All that is required is actual human reason; this will be brought into the process through the associations, which will be there observing things with their collective experience and taking the proper corresponding measures. *RE 155*

It does actually take place in the economic process that money undergoes metamorphoses; it acquires different qualities as it becomes loan money or gift money. But we mask this fact if we simply let money be money, and use the number inscribed on it as the unit of measurement, and so forth. We mask it and the reality takes its revenge – a revenge that reveals itself in fluctuations of price, with which (though they are actual enough in the economic process) our reasoning faculty cannot keep pace. We ought to be able to follow them. We ought not to let money merely flow into circulation and give it freedom to do what it likes. For we thereby do something very peculiar in economic life. If we require animals for some kind of labor, the first thing we do is to tame them. Think how long it takes to train a riding horse. Think what would happen if we did not tame our animals, but used them wild, taking no pains to train them. But we let money circulate quite wildly in the economic process. If and when it chooses to do so, so to speak, we let it acquire the value it has as loan money or as gift money. And we do not foresee that, when an industrialist has money, from whatever source, which has been wrongly transformed from loan money into gift money, and he pays his workers with it, the result is quite different from what it would have been if he had paid them, say, out of pure purchase money.

In effect, the more a man is obliged to pay his workers with pure purchase money, the less he will be able to give them – that is to say, the cheaper they will have to deliver their products. On the other hand, the more he is able to pay them with money that has already been transformed (that is, that has already passed into the sphere of loan or gift), the higher the wages that he will be able to give them. That is to say, more can be charged for their products in the market. The point is to grasp the matter with our reason.

You see, as things are today, the function of money has constantly had to be corrected. Take the case, for example, of a national economy bordering on other national economies. By letting money function in this wild unguided way, without bringing any intelligence into the process, a national economy may easily find itself in a disastrous position with regard to the price of some kind of goods, or something else that is required. So long as the national economy is one among others (and no repressive measures are adopted), people will simply import the article in question. Their imports will be increased. Things are constantly being corrected in this way. For a world economy, on the other hand, no such correction is possible. We cannot import things from the Moon. If we could import from, or export to, the Moon and Venus and the rest, the world economy would also be like a mere national economy. This is precisely the great question. What becomes of our science of economics – through the fact that the world is now a single, closed economic domain? *RE 150-152*

Issuing Currency

In a threefold social organism, currency should not be issued by the state. Responsibility for issuing currency ought to be handed over to an independent economic realm. Since money only has relevance within the economic realm, any problems with currency cannot be resolved by legislation. They must be addressed from within economic life.

Anyone who thinks that separating out the three spheres of the social organism only has theoretical value, and that it would come about 'by itself' in a unified state, or in an economic structure that encompasses the state and is based on shared ownership of the means of production, should consider the particular kinds of social structure which would necessarily come about in a threefold social organism. The government, for example, would no longer have to take responsibility for money as the statutory means of payment, but would hand this duty over to the administrative bodies of the economic sphere, and their own, specific measures. Within a healthy social organism, after all, money can represent nothing other than the potential to obtain goods produced by others, from the totality of the economic sphere, by virtue of the fact that one has oneself produced and delivered goods for this sphere. TSR 93-94

. . . Modern governments will never solve the question of currency satisfactorily by passing laws, but only when they renounce their control and hand it over to an autonomous economic organism to deal with. TSR 96

Old currency should be removed from circulation, and new funds should be created by a non-governmental bank. This would take place in the economic process between the dispersion of gift money and its subsequent use as purchase money by the recipient of the gift. The associations must be involved at the transition points to facilitate the flow of money through the economic process, from purchase-money, to loan money, to gift money, and finally to its renewal.

. . . a national bank, a state bank, would be impossible. A banking institute would come about between those who have received gift money and those who through their work, namely, cultivation of the soil, once more create new goods that are in their early stages. This rejuvenation would pass directly over from the state to the economy. And that represents what is necessary for the future. Through the fact that it passes into the economy, this measure to rejuvenate it would combine with other economic measures, but not with the state's rules. And thereby relationships to value would also come about which are quite different from the ones that exist under the present fiscal system. We would then have something that already exists. Things are really hidden only because they do not occur in the right place. We would have converted a fiscal system into an economic one. The possibility for the treasury to function economically would be less than that of an economic association. RE 254-255

. . . If you are thinking in a true economic sense, then, where it is a question of free gifts, you will use old money – money that loses its value as soon as possible after the gift is made; provided that the person who takes the benefit of the gift has just enough time to make purchases with it.

At this point, needless to say, there must be some rejuvenating process in the economic process. Money, in fact, must have a successor. The important thing is, as you will readily perceive, that things must not be allowed to happen arbitrarily through the general chaos that the economic state spreads everywhere. The economic state brings about a hopeless confusion of values by failing to distinguish purchase money, loan money, and gift money, though in reality these three are separated all the time. You will readily see that if you do not wish to leave the process to chance – if you wish to bring reason into it – you simply must interpose the necessary associative bodies at the transition points between purchase money, loan money, gift money, and the renewal of money. Take the case of those who have money to lend. You would not let them lend it in a senseless way. You would bring them into connection with their association. The association would act as a mediator. The association would provide them with the most sensible way in which to lend – or again, with the most sensible way in which to give. When a gift takes place (and every individual is free to give or not to give), the money, if it has a year's value as explained above, will not undergo the same process. But the important thing is to bring about sensibly and in accordance with reason the things that happen in any case in the economic process, but behind a mask. The money, when it has served its purpose, must be collected. And then once more, at the beginning of the process of purchase and sale, it must receive its original value. That is to say, it receives its new year number and passes into the hands of those who are dealing once more with nature-products, products of nature that are just beginning to pass into the sphere of labor. For here it is pure purchase and sale that are going on. This is the associative method of managing things. *RE 154-155*

Inflation

Increasing the amount of currency in circulation without a corresponding increase in production has the effect of inflating the prices of goods, particularly the prices of basic necessities. In addition, treating labor and land as commodities has an inflationary effect on the prices of commodities. These actions create fictitious values and do harm to the economic process. Sound prices can only be achieved through the proper valuation of human activity within a threefold social organism whereby labor is removed from the economic process.

> *There are countless economists in our day who say: "If money, the currency, either coin or paper money, is increased ad lib., it loses its value, and the necessaries of life, especially the most indispensable, go up in price." We observe this and see the folly of simply increasing the currency, for the mere increase, as anyone can see, has only the effect of raising the price of the necessaries of life. The well-known endless screw is still turning!*
>
> *There is another thing that is not understood. As soon as labor is paid for in the same way as commodities or products, it must happen as a matter of course that at that moment labor begins to fight for more and more pay, for higher and higher wages. But the money that labor receives as wages plays the same part in determining prices as the mere increase of the money in circulation. This ought to be understood. You may do as many a minister of finance has done and, instead of increasing production and taking care to improve it, you may simply issue banknotes and increase the currency. Then there will be more money in circulation, but all commodities, especially those indispensable to life, will be dearer. People see this for themselves; therefore they see how foolish it is simply to increase the money in circulation. What they do not see is that all the money that is spent in order to pay labor actually has the effect of raising the price of commodities because sound prices can only be fixed within an independent economic system. Sound prices can only be*

fixed when they develop in accordance with the true valuation of human activity. Therefore the idea of the threefold order of the social organism is to detach labor completely from the economic process. SF 41-42

. . . it makes no essential difference whether, for example, I issue money that has no foundation in reality but represents a mere increase in the amount of paper money, or whether I assign capital value to the land. In both cases I am creating fictitious values. By inflating the currency, I increase the prices of things numerically; but in the reality of the economic process, I effect absolutely nothing except a redistribution, which may do immense harm to individuals. In the same manner, the above described capitalizing of land does harm to those who are involved in the economic process. RE 61

Money as a Means to Exercise Social Responsibility

No one can live on money. Those who think we do are blind to the fact that the sole value of money is that it gives us power to make use of the work of others. In this way, our subsistence and well-being are dependent upon the work of others. Because money has the power to command or activate the labor of others, we must practice social responsibility when we make purchases or work with it in other ways. We must become aware of the social relations that stand behind every purchase. At the same time, in recognition of our dependence on the work of others, we must feel a responsibility to compensate society with our work and productive activity.

A healthy social life is possible only when we take sufficient interest in others by picturing the work that someone has done for us with each transaction. Any talk of loving our fellow human being is merely egotistical self-love in disguise if it stops short of a true recognition, in every economic exchange, of what others do for us and a sense of responsibility to work for them in return.

Consider a concrete example. How many people there are today who have an abstract and confused conception of their own personal lives! If they ask themselves, for example,

"What do I live on? . . ." they would say to themselves, "Why, on my money . . . " Money is not something on which we can live . . . This question is intimately connected with the real interest that one individual has in another. People who think they live on the money they have inherited, for example, or have acquired in any way whatever except by receiving money for work, as is the custom today – those who live in this way and suppose that they can live on money have no interest in their fellow human beings, because no one can live on money . . . My money has no value other than that of giving me the power to make use of the labor of others. Under the social conditions of the present time, we do not begin to have an interest in others until we answer that question in the proper way, until we hold the picture in our minds of a certain number of persons working for a certain number of hours in order that I may live within the social structure. It is of no importance to give ourselves a comfortable feeling by saying, "I love people." We do not love people if we suppose that we are living on our money and do not in the least conceive how people work for us in order to produce even the minimum necessary for our life.

But the thought that a certain number of persons labor in order that we may possess the minimum necessities of life is inseparable from another. It is the thought that we must recompense society, not with money but with work in exchange for the work that has been done for us. We feel an interest in our fellow human beings only when we are led to feel obligated to recompense in some form of labor the amount of labor that has been performed for us. CT 54-56

Of course we cannot immediately take in hand the reform of the national economy, which has been forced into such a helpless condition by what is nowadays taught as political economy. But we can at least ask with respect to national education and other such matters: What must be done so that social life and forms are consciously established in opposition to antisocial forces? What is really required? I said that it would be difficult in our time for people to develop sufficient interest in each other. You do not have sufficient interest *if you think that you can buy yourself something with a $5 note and do not remember the fact that this brings about a social relationship with certain other human beings and their labor-power. You only have an adequate interest when in your picture you are able to substitute for each apparent transaction (such as the exchange of goods for a $5 note) the real transaction which is linked with it.*

Now, I would say that the mere egoistic, soul-stirring talk of loving our fellow human beings and acting upon this love at the first opportunity, that this does not constitute social life. This sort of love is, for the most part, terribly egoistic. Many people are supported by what they have first gained through robbing their fellows in a truly patriarchal fashion, in order to create for themselves an object for their self-love, so that they can then feel nice and warm with the thought, "You are doing this, you are doing that." One does not easily discover that a large part of the so-called love of doing good is masked self-love. Therefore, the main consideration is not merely to think of what lies nearest to hand, thereby enhancing our self-love, but to feel it our duty to look carefully at the many-sided social structures in which we are placed. We must at least lay the foundations for such understanding. Yet few today are disposed to do so. *SASF 11-12*

TEN

Price Formation

A 'true price' results when individuals receive, as counter-value for the product they have made, sufficient recompense to enable them to satisfy the whole of their needs, including of course the needs of their dependants, until they will again have completed a like product. *RE 67*

TEN

Price Formation

Price in the Context of Perpetual Circulation

Typically, price is what buyers are most concerned about in a given transaction. However, price is actually the culmination of the economic process. An untold number of economic forces and social relationships influence and determine prices. Pricing is extremely complicated because the economic value of a product constantly changes as it circulates through the economy, and as more work (additional value) is added to a product or service. Therefore, price formation must be fully understood, and fair or "true" price must be determined in the context of the process of circulation.

> *. . . With the concepts to which we have grown accustomed thus far, we cannot truthfully answer the question, for instance, "what is value?" Or, "what is price?" Whatever has value must be considered as being in perpetual circulation . . .*
>
> *You can never develop concepts of economics in reference to the mere external reality. No, you must always develop them in reference to the economic process as a whole. And within this process each thing is continuously changing. Therefore we must speak of the economic process of circulation before we can arrive at such things as value, price, and so forth.*
>
> *In the economic theories of today, you will observe that they generally begin with definitions of value and price. That is quite wrong. First it is necessary to describe the economic process.* RE 11-12

Think about what counts when buying and selling are considered in the economic process. The thing that people care about is the price of a commodity, the price of the piece of goods in question. In the last resort, all the most important economic considerations really merge in this question of price. All the impulses and forces that are at work in economics finally culminate in price. We shall, therefore, first have to consider the problem of price, but it is by no means a simple problem. You need only consider the simplest case. At a given place, A, we have a certain commodity; at place A it has a certain price. But suppose it is not bought there but is transported to another place, B. Our endeavor will then be to add to the price whatever transport charges had to be paid from A to B. Thus the price changes in the process of circulation. There we have the simplest – if I may put it so, the most trite – instance. Of course, there are far more complex cases. RE 15-16

General definitions of price are of little help. Price is always specific to a particular situation. Therefore, the real conditions at the relevant time and place in the economic process must be considered. It is the underlying conditions that precede and surround a transaction that ultimately culminate as price.

. . . we must observe how the price fluctuates with place and time. Then, perhaps, we can trace some of the conditions through which at a given place a given price actually emerges as it does. But there can be no such thing as a general definition stating how the price of a thing is composed: that is an impossibility. Again and again one is astonished to find price discussed in the commonly found works on economics, as though it were possible to define it. We simply cannot define it, for a price is always concrete and specific. Especially in economic matters, it is impossible to get anywhere near the realities with definitions . . .

. . . Economics must stand firmly on the basis of reality. In economics we can speak only of the conditions existing at a given time and at the actual place to which we are referring.

Those who desire the progress of humanity will come to the conclusion that things can be different. To begin with, however, things must be observed in their immediate reality at the particular moment. From all this you will see how impossible it is to approach such a thing as price – a most important concept in economics – by seeking to grasp it with a sharply defined idea . . .

Yet the problem of price is the most important, and all our efforts must be directed to it. We must observe the economic process, and try, as it were, to catch the point where (at any given place and time) the actual price of a given thing results from all the underlying economic causes. *RE 16-17*

The activity of buying and selling is an exchange of values. When values meet in an exchange, the price emerges. Since value itself fluctuates in the course of circulation, price also fluctuates.

Suppose now we find ourselves at any given point within the economic process. The economic process takes its course in the activities of buying and selling. Buying and selling are essentially an exchange of values. There is, in fact, no other exchange than that of values. Properly speaking, it is wrong to speak of an exchange of goods. The "goods" that play a part in the economic process – whether they appear as modified products of nature or modified labor – are always ***values****. It is always the values that are exchanged. Whenever a process of buying and selling takes place, values are exchanged. Now what is it that emerges in the economic process when value and value, as it were, impinge on one another in the process of exchange? It is price. Wherever price emerges, it is always through the impact of value on value in the economic process. For this reason you cannot think truly about price if you have in mind the exchange of mere goods. If you buy an apple for a penny, you may say that you are exchanging one piece of goods for another – the apple for the penny. But you will make no progress in economic thinking along these lines. The apple has been picked somewhere and then transported, and it may well be that various other things have been done around it. All this is labor that has modified it. What you are dealing with* *is not an apple but a product of nature transformed by human labor, representing an economic value. In economics we must always take our start from values. Similarly, the penny represents not a piece of goods but a value, since after all (or so at any rate we must suppose) the penny is but the sign for the fact that there is present in a person who buys the apple another value that he or she exchanges for it.*

Today I am anxious for you to get a clear insight into the fact that in economics we must not speak of goods but of values as what is elementary. It is wrong to try to consider price in any other way than by envisaging the interplay of values. Value set against value gives you price. If, as we saw, value itself is a fluctuating thing, incapable of definition, may we not say that, when you exchange value for value, price, which arises in the process of exchange, is a fluctuating thing raised to the second power? *RE 24-25*

The social relations of buyers and sellers lie behind price formation. A certain amount of money will have a certain value depending on the particular situation of a buyer or seller. Wage payment, too, is really a transaction of sale and purchase. The work and life circumstance of the person who has produced something should be of great interest to distributors, consumers and other producers alike, and should serve as the basis for making economic decisions. Often the root cause of social unrest around prices, including wage disputes, lies in the nature of the social relationships of the people involved in a given economic process.

Yesterday we formulated a very important question, which came to the fore with the transition from national economy to world economy. With this transition, the question of price begins to acquire a very different significance in economic life from what it had before. But there are other things to consider before we can gain a concept of the factors that really determine price. For the price – the public price, so to speak – that eventually emerges in the market, or in the circulation of goods, is really of far less economic importance than what lies behind the forming of prices and of which price formation and price fluctuation are merely the final results.

Now these factors that precede the forming of price, both on the buying and on the selling side, are connected with the social relationships in the middle of which the buyer and seller stand. It is these relationships that determine whether the buyer will attach a greater or lesser value to a certain sum of money. I mean value not only in the subjective sense. Economically speaking, the subjective is important only to the extent that it is properly grounded in the objective – that is, to the extent that it rests on a true judgment of objective processes. The value of money is very important even in an objective sense. The economic question these days cannot be isolated from the social question. One can reach a valid judgment only by observing the interplay of the two. Thus we must recognize that the social discontent underlying the present social disturbances is connected above all with what precedes the forming of prices and of which the forming of prices is merely the final result. As I have shown already, even in the payment of wages – that is, in that price formation that, under the existing economic system, ultimately finds expression in the rate of wages – we really have an instance of purchase and sale. Everything that leads to wage disputes really depends on social relationships in which both the worker and the entrepreneur are involved, relationships the result of which is the kind of price formation that constitutes the payment of wages. *RE 144-145*

True Price

One of Rudolf Steiner's fundamental economic concepts is called the socially correct or true price. Simply stated, a true price arises when, for a product they create, workers receive sufficient income to support their needs until they can again create a similar product. Determination of true price must also take into account the needs of all the producers' dependents.

This formulation of true price is oriented toward the future rather than the past. This orientation is necessary because economic facts change over time, and it is the only way to make sure that the needs of the producers are met during the time when they are working to complete the next product. When price is determined in this way, the value of a product is compared with the value of other goods – those needed by the producers until the next item is completed.

> *You know, perhaps, that in my book* Towards Social Renewal *I tried to express in a formula how we may arrive at a conception of "true price" (as we will call it to begin with) in the whole economic process. Needless to say, such a formula is only an abstraction. It is the object of these lectures – which, I believe, in spite of the short amount of time, will really form a whole – it is our very object in these lectures to work the whole science of economics, at any rate in outline, into this abstraction.*
>
> *The formula that I gave in my* Towards Social Renewal *was as follows. "A 'true price' results when individuals receive, as counter-value for the product they have made, sufficient recompense to enable them to satisfy all of their needs, including of course the needs of their dependents, until they will again have completed a like product." Abstract as it is, this formula is nonetheless exhaustive. In setting up a formula, it is always necessary that it should contain all the concrete details. I do believe, for the domain of economics, that this formula is no less exhaustive than, say, the Theorem of Pythagoras is for all right-angled triangles. But the point is that just as we have to introduce into the Theorem of Pythagoras the varying proportions of the sides, so shall we have to introduce many, very many more variables into this formula. Economic science is precisely an understanding of how the whole economic process can be included in this formula. Today I intend to start from one essential feature of the formula. It is this: The formula does not point to what is past but to what is going to happen in the future. For I say in it, deliberately, that "the counter-value must satisfy the individual's needs in the future, that is, until he or she will have made a like product again." This is an absolutely essential feature of the formula. If we were to demand a counter-value, literally, for the product that is already finished – if we expected this to be true to the real economic facts –*

it might well happen that we would receive a value that would satisfy our needs, say, for only five- sixths of the time we need to finish the new product. The economic facts alter from the past into the future. Those who imagine that they can draw up any kind of table from the past, will invariably go wrong in economics. Economic or business life essentially consists in setting future processes in motion with the help of what went before. Where past processes are thus used to set future ones in motion, it inevitably happens in some cases that the values are considerably shifted. Indeed, they are constantly shifting. Hence in this formula it is essential to say that "If someone makes a pair of boots, the time taken to make them is not the determining factor in the economic sense. The determining factor is the time required to make the next pair of boots." That is the point, and we must now try to understand its fuller implications within the whole economic process. *RE 67-68*

The socially correct value of a piece of goods can only be determined by comparison with other goods. Its value must equal the value of all other goods needed by the producers to fulfill their own requirements until the time when they can again produce a similar piece of goods. This they must do while considering all those requirements necessary in the interest of other people. (Herein must be included, for instance, the needs of their children and what they must contribute for the support of persons incapable of working, etc.) *RSO 12*

The prerequisites for arriving at a true price are the collaboration of both the three primary spheres of social life – cultural, economic, and political – and of producers, distributors, and consumers *[as explained in Chapter Five on Economic Associations]*. Only through such living collaboration is it possible to ensure that workers receive remuneration adequate to meet their needs.

Only within a social organism managed on the basis of free cooperation between its three spheres will it be possible to achieve a healthy relationship between price and commodity. All working people should receive sufficient remuneration for a commodity they produce to meet all of their needs and those of their dependents until they have again produced another such commodity. A price relationship of this kind cannot be administratively determined, but must result from the living involvement of associations active in the social organism. And it will, when cooperation is based on healthy interaction between the three spheres of organization. This sound price relationship will arise with the same inevitability that a sturdy bridge arises when constructed according to the right mathematical and mechanical laws. It is of course easy to object that society does not follow the sort of constant laws which apply to a bridge. But no one will raise such an objection who is able to understand that the ideas in this book try to describe the living laws underlying society, and not mathematical ones. *TSR 131*

The setting of prices will be under the purview of the associations of producers and consumers who will designate groups tasked with the setting of prices in a holistic manner, so that they are equitable and realistic.

How prices are set is the germinal cell of the economy, so to speak. In a more circumscribed [or "closed domain" as explained in the Economic Science Chapter] economy, which should be based entirely on expert knowledge and competence, how will price-setting be accomplished? It will certainly not be left to chance in the free market, as it has been so far in the national and international economies. In the context of associations between individual branches of industry and consumer cooperatives, individuals with the necessary expertise will set prices in a holistic and rational manner, avoiding the crises provoked by the haphazard effects of supply and demand. In the new [associative] economy, where determining the type and character of labor falls to the sphere of rights, what workers receive in exchange for producing goods will allow them to meet all their needs until the next production cycle is complete. The following example is rough, amateurish, and superficial, but it will

> *have to do for today: If I make a pair of boots, the mutually agreed-upon sale price must allow me to purchase everything I need to meet my needs until I have made another pair. Of course society will have to establish organizations to ensure that the needs of widows, orphans, and the sick and disabled are met, and to provide for education and the like. The setting of equitable and realistic prices, however, which is exclusively the jurisdiction of the socially responsible economy, will depend on the formation of corporate bodies for that purpose, whether elected or appointed by joint producer-consumer associations.* *FTSF 57-58*

To be clear, the setting of prices by economic associations does not replace a self-regulating market economy with a state-run command economy. Rather, the intention is to realize the true relative values of products, with the underlying premise that the value of a product should be equal to the values of all commodities to be consumed by the producer during the time period required to produce that product again.

Demand alone cannot determine whether something can be produced at a price that equals the value of what the producer has consumed while producing it. The concept of supply and demand does not take into account the satisfaction of the needs of the community. In a threefold social organism, the intention is to balance the value of products with the legitimate needs of the workers who make the products.

> *Someone might even say, "After all, these social institutions and methods you have in mind amount to nothing more than a conscious arrangement of the very things that 'supply and demand' will surely regulate automatically." It will be clear to one who looks more closely that this is not the point. The social thoughts that originate in the threefold idea do not aim at replacing the free business dealings governed by supply and demand with a command economy. Their aim is to realize the true relative values of commodities, with the underlying idea that the product of an individual's labor should be of a value equal to all the other commodities consumed in the time spent producing it.*

Under the capitalist system, demand may determine whether someone will undertake the production of a certain commodity. Yet demand alone can never determine whether it will be possible to produce it at a price corresponding to its value in the sense defined above. This can be determined only through methods and institutions whereby society, in all its aspects, will bring about a sensible valuation of the different commodities. Those who doubt that such methods and institutions are worth striving for lack vision; they do not see that, under the exclusive rule of supply and demand, needs whose satisfaction would upgrade the life of the community are being starved. They have no feeling for the necessity of trying to include the satisfaction of such needs among the practical incentives of an organized community. The essential aim of the threefold social order is to create a just balance between human needs and the value of the products of human work. *RSO 50-51*

The typical concepts of supply and demand in modern economic science do not represent a complete picture of economic reality. Careful consideration of the dynamics at work in buying and selling reveals that there are supply and demand factors influencing both buyers and sellers. Buyers not only express a demand but they also need to have a sufficient supply of money with which to make purchases. Similarly, sellers not only have a supply of goods but also bring to a transaction a demand for money. Therefore, the development of a price is influenced by whether the person who needs or demands something is able to supply the money needed for a particular product.

Supply of commodities is demand for money, and supply of money is demand for commodities. These are economic realities, since the economic process (in so far as it consists of trade or barter) cannot take place at all, unless there are both supply and demand in the case of both buyer and seller. For what the buyer has as supply (money), must also first have been generated in the economic process somewhere in the buyer's past, or through a demand, just as the commodity that appears as a supply must also first have been developed or produced.

Our concepts are quite unreal if we imagine that price arises from the interaction of what is ordinarily called supply and demand. In actual fact, price does not develop at all as it is defined by this line of thought. The development of price is undoubtedly influenced by the question of whether the demander can become a supplier of money, or whether perhaps, at a given time in the whole working of the economic process, the person cannot become a supplier of money with respect to a given product. The point is not only that there must be a certain number of commodities available as supply, but also that there must be a certain number of people able to develop a supply of money for these particular commodities. This will show you at once that we cannot simply speak of an interaction of supply and demand.

If we look now not to the concepts (which may always be wrongly formed) but to the real facts – the facts of the market, or even of the pure, marketless exchange of commodities and money – it is unquestionable that prices evolve between supply and demand – only the supply and demand are always there on both sides. This is undoubtedly the case, as a pure matter of fact. *RE 93*

Falsification of Prices

In various ways, prices are often falsified. One simple example is when a manufacturer sells off his inventory well below production costs just to be rid of it. The resulting price of the goods would not represent their true value. The goods are worth as much as the same product sold by someone else, but their price has been reduced and thereby, falsified.

Take the case of a man who is a manufacturer on a small scale, who suddenly inherits a large legacy. Tired of the whole factory business, he decides to sell his stock in trade, and does so at an absurdly low price. That does not mean that the commodities decrease in value; it only means that the

> *true price is not paid. In ways like this, prices are constantly being falsified in the actual economic process. We must not forget this. In the course of commercial dealing, prices may often be falsified. There is, nevertheless, a true price. The commodities sold by the man in the above example are worth just as much as the same commodities produced by someone else.* *RE 81*

The underpayment of workers is another condition that falsifies prices. In an economy in which capitalists are pitted against wage workers, an increase in workers' wages only causes other goods to cost more. In a threefold social organism, the associations will decide which factors will affect prices so that they are equitable. What each person produces can then be of the same value as the value of everything he needs until he makes the next product. As long as people work for a wage rather than to answer a social need, prices will always be falsified.

Other conditions that falsify prices are the commodification of land and the issuance of currency with little or no basis in the realities of economic life – of the production, distribution and consumption of goods and services. In both cases, value is falsely created and inflated.

> *In the future, these new corporate bodies will decide which factors in commerce will determine price structures, that is, the value of goods. This is the only way that each individual's production will be exactly comparable in value to everything he or she needs until the next round of production. Economic activity will become equitable; the prices of certain goods will not be out of proportion to the prices of other types of goods. Today, when wages are still embedded in the economic process and production workers are not the independent partners of the intellectual workers who are their managers, the workers are always forced to fight for higher wages. But if higher wages close one hole, they open another: groceries become more expensive, and so on. This can happen only in an economy polluted with capital and wage relationships. By contrast, in an economy in which*

associations or cooperatives determine the value of goods on a rational basis rather than on the basis of supply and demand (which are subject to chance,) every individual will be afforded a humanly worthy existence. Such an economy is truly what the working class is demanding. FTSF 14-15

. . . Those who to this day are still mere wage earners – earners of a living for themselves – how are they to be placed in the whole economic process, no longer as such earners but as people who work out of social necessity? Must this really be done? Assuredly it must. If this is not done, we shall never obtain true prices but always false ones. RE 37

. . . Economically speaking, it makes no essential difference whether, for example, I issue money that has no foundation in reality but represents a mere increase in the amount of paper money, or whether I assign capital value to the land. In both cases I am creating fictitious values. By inflating the currency, I increase the prices of things numerically; but in the reality of the economic process, I effect absolutely nothing except a redistribution, which may do immense harm to individuals. In the same manner. . . capitalizing of land does harm to those who are involved in the economic process. RE 61

Falsification of price also happens when the products of cultural workers are either undervalued or overvalued. Consistent with the importance that Steiner places on a free and vibrant cultural life for the whole of society, he insists that prices reflect the values produced by cultural life as well as goods produced by the economy.

I would emphasize that I do not want to proceed in a programmatic way, that I want only to acknowledge what is – because I recognize that we cannot establish a paradise on earth with economic methods. That would not be possible, but we must try to create the best possible situation. Now one has to ask oneself why we have less than the best possible situation today. It comes about because the various economic factors cannot achieve their true value in one place or another, because today it is quite possible that spiritual/cultural workers are by no means paid in the way that is necessary for the whole economy. They are paid either too much or too little; both things do occur. But if they are paid too little they immediately cause prices to change in an unhealthy way because of their low pay. And it is the same if they are paid too much. This needs to be corrected, and it is only a question. . . of what factors would restore commercial balance in economic life. *RE 251*

Price Fluctuation

As the division of labor expands and new needs arise, there is greater differentiation of products, which leads to increased challenges with price formation. One of the most disturbing and disruptive situations in economic life occurs when the price of a certain product changes radically in relation to other products. The gradual rise or fall of prices as a whole is usually not as upsetting to the economic process.

. . . the further the division of labor extends, and new needs arise in the process, the more does the differentiation of products increase, and the more do difficulties connected with price formation accumulate. The more varied the products are, the more difficult it becomes to bring about their reciprocal valuation – and the valuation can only be reciprocal. This may be seen from the following comparison. There is a reciprocal valuation even in the case of products only slightly differentiated from one another – say, for instance, wheat, rye, and other agricultural products. Follow this process over a long period of time and you will find that the relationship of reciprocal valuation between wheat, rye, and other cereals remains fairly stable. If wheat goes up, the other grains go up; if wheat goes down, the other grains go down with it. This is because there is comparatively little differentiation between these products. As soon as the differentiation becomes greater, this constancy no longer exists.

It may well happen, through various events in the social organism, that some product that someone has been

> *accustomed to exchange for another suddenly shoots up in price, while the other may go down at the same time. Think what shifts are thus brought about in economic relationships. Altogether, the things that happen in the economic sphere depend far more on prices rising and falling relative to one another than on any other circumstance. It is by the relative rise and fall in prices that the difficulties of life itself are introduced into the economic sphere. As to whether the products as a whole rise or fall – if they all would rise or fall uniformly, this would concern us very little. What interests people is that the different products rise or fall to a different extent. This fact is emerging in a very tragic way just now, under the present economic conditions. Products rise and fall in varying measure. Money values, especially, are rising and falling, but in the money values we simply have stored what were once real values. By this rising and falling, an entire mingling and confusion is now being brought about in society.* *RE 86-87*

Associations and Price Regulation

Following the principle of association, the supply of commodities will be regulated in response to real human needs. One key way to ensure that production corresponds to human need is through the distribution of labor. If the price of a product becomes too high, there is clearly a greater need for it. More workers can be assigned in order to increase production and meet the new demand. If prices become too low, workers can be withdrawn and assigned to another activity. Prices will no longer be dictated by the chances of the market or by the state, but instead by human reason and insight. By keeping production apace with demand for products, prices can be kept in relative balance. Ultimately, price really has to do with the distribution of workers. The manipulation of the amount of currency in circulation in order to adjust prices does not create a real solution to prices that are too high or too low.

The stability of prices, or lack of stability, reflects the overall health of the economy. When there are disturbing price fluctuations, it is up to the associations to discover what needs to happen in the overall economic life to restore balance.

[For the purpose of determining prices], and following the principle of association, it will be possible to produce a supply of commodities corresponding to the needs that have been investigated. That is, arrangements must exist with persons who can study the wants of consumers. Statistics can only give the present state of affairs. They can never be authoritative about the future. The needs for the time being must be studied, and, in accordance with these, measures must be taken to produce what is needed. When a product shows a tendency to become too dear, that is a sign that there are too few workers engaged on it. Negotiations must then be carried on with other branches of production to transfer workers from one branch to another where the need lies, in order that more of the lacking products may be supplied. If a commodity tends to become too cheap, that is to say, to earn too little profit, arrangements must be made to employ fewer workers on that particular product. This means that in the future the satisfaction of the needs of the community will depend on the way in which people are employed in industry. The price of a product is conditional on the number of persons engaged in its production. But, through these arrangements, the price will really correspond to the value attached to the commodity in question by the community in accordance with its requirements.

So we see that human reason will take the place of chance, that as the result of the arrangements that will come into existence the price will express the agreements arrived at, the contracts entered into. Thus we shall see a revolution of the market accomplished by the substitution of reason for the chances of the market now prevailing. *SF 46-47*

... For instance, if at any point a certain kind of commodity becomes too cheap or too expensive, those concerned must be able truly to observe the fact. The mere fact in itself is not the point. When, through experiences that can grow only out of the concerted counsels of the associations, they are able to say, as a result of such experiences, "Five units of money for so and so much salt are too little or too much – the price is

too low or too high," then and then only will they be in a position to take the necessary steps.

If the price of a commodity becomes too low, so that those who produce it can no longer receive sufficient remuneration for their excessively cheap services and their excessively cheap products, it will be necessary to assign fewer workers to this particular commodity. Workers will therefore have to be diverted to another kind of work. If, on the other hand, a commodity becomes too expensive, workers will have to be led over into this branch of production. In this way, the associations will always be concerned with a proper employment of people in several areas of economic life. We must be clear on this. A real rise in the price of a given economic article indicates the necessity for an increase in the number of those who are working on this article, while an undue fall of price calls for measures to divert workers from this field of labor to another. In reality we can speak of prices only in relation to the distribution of people among the several branches of labor in the given social organism.

The view that sometimes prevails today, in which people always have the tendency to work with concepts rather than realities, is illustrated by some advocates of "free money" [Freigeldleute]. To them it appears quite simple. If prices anywhere are too high, so that too much money has to be spent in purchasing a certain article, these advocates wish to ensure that the amount of money becomes less; then the commodities will be cheaper, and vice versa. If you think about it thoroughly, however, you will find that this signifies nothing for the economic process. In reality, it is as if by some mischievous device you were to cause the column of mercury to rise when the thermometer indicates that the room is too cold. You are only trying to cure the symptoms. By giving the money a different value you create nothing real.

You create something real if you regulate the labor – that is to say, the number of people engaged in a certain kind of work. The price depends on the number of workers engaged in a given field of work. To try to regulate these things bureaucratically, through the state, would be the worst form of tyranny. To regulate through free "associations" that arise within the social sphere, where everyone can see what is going on – either as members, or because their representative sits on the association, or they are told what is going on, or they see for themselves and realize what is required – that is what we must aim for. *RE 64-65*

We have already seen that the most important question in economics is that of price. The point will now be to observe prices in the sense that I have indicated. The rise or fall, or stability, of prices – the fact that the prices of certain products are too high or too low (for one can have a feeling of these things) – indicates whether or not the economic organism is in good order. It must be for the associations to discover, from the barometer of prices, what is to be done in economic life as a whole. *RE 91*

Fundamentals of Pricing

It is important to identify fundamental factors in the determination of prices, and not just depend on the role of intermediate issues. The seller's need for money is an intermediate issue, and in and of itself should not be the cause of changes in price. Similarly, the cost of production should not be taken as an absolute basis for setting price. Rather, a healthy price should be identified, and then consideration should be given for how to reduce production costs in order to attain a healthy price. Finally, economic concepts should not be formed around an assumption of a competitive relation between buyer and seller. Excessive competition is a fundamental error of today's economic life. True price can occur when a dynamic of cooperation is instead assumed and realized.

. . . You will be told that the conditions determining price levels are the following, so far as the sellers are concerned: their relative need for money, the value of the money, the costs of production that they have to meet, and the competition among buyers. But if you analyze these concepts you will always find that, though you can think about them rightly

enough, you cannot enter with them into the realities of economic life. You would first have to ask yourself if it is an economically healthy state of affairs if prices rise and fall, when it happens that a particular entrepreneur is in need of money at a particular time. Thereby, in accordance with the private need for money, should prices rise or fall in a particular direction? Can the utility value [Gebrauchswert] of money, if we may call it so, work in a healthy way at all? Both prices and utility value can work in a healthy and in an unhealthy way. Or again, speaking of costs of production, it can be desirable for the attainment of a healthy price not to think how the price will come out if costs of production are looked upon as something absolute, but on the contrary, to think how the costs of production for a given article might have to be reduced so that it has a healthy price when it comes into the market. In other words, you need to have concepts that really begin at the beginning. You cannot let a living human being begin life at the age of twenty-five; nor should you let your concepts, which are to enter into real life, begin at any arbitrary point. You should not let your economic concepts begin, for example, with the competition of buyers or sellers. May it not be, under certain conditions, the fundamental error of our economic life that an excessive competition exists between sellers or between buyers? These are matters of principle that must be taken very much in earnest. *RE 171*

ELEVEN

The Interplay of Spiritual-Cultural and Economic Life

In every generation, in the children whom we teach at school, something is given to us, something is sent down from the spiritual world. We take hold of this in education – this is something spiritual – and incorporate it into economic life and thereby ward off its destruction. For economic life, if it runs its own course, destroys itself. *NS 67*

ELEVEN

The Interplay of Spiritual-Cultural and Economic Life

Constructive Forces of Spiritual-Cultural Life

Economic life will decline and ultimately self-destruct without the support of a free cultural life and the guidance of an independent political life. To bring about true social renewal, we need the constructive forces that arise out of creativity and moral values, the fruits of a free cultural life (all that arises from education in the broadest sense). When the free life of the spirit is allowed to work into economic life, this practical sphere of the social organism is fructified. The human being must direct economic life and bring to it what it needs. When economic life is allowed to evolve within itself, without direction from the human spirit, destructive forces will continue to dominate.

It is particularly important to keep this in mind when considering the education of children. Each generation of children brings with it renewing forces for economic life through their ideas, capacities, and creativity. A healthy education removes hindrances to the unfolding of these forces.

> *People of today invent all sorts of social economic systems but are not aware, because they lack the sensitivity of feeling for it, that every economic system like this that they think up leads to destruction; leads definitely to destruction if it is not constantly renewed by an independent, developing spiritual life which ever and ever again works as a constructive element in relation to the destruction, the excretion, of economic life. The working together of the spiritual element of the social*

organism with the economic element is described in this sense in my Towards Social Renewal *. . .*

This is the inner meaning of the threefolding of the social organism; namely that, in a properly thought out threefold social organism, one should be under no illusion that the economic thinking of the present is a destructive element which must, therefore, be continually counterbalanced by the constructive element of the spiritual realm of the social organism. *NS 66-67*

Therefore the greatest social need is to arouse far and wide a clear perception that the only basis upon which humanity can evolve in a healthy way is the cultivation of a new spiritual life. The fruits of this cultivation will be borne in the structuring of the economy. If economic life tries of itself to evolve a new form, it will only propagate – and intensify – its old evils. As long as economic life is expected to make of us what we may become, new evils will be added to the old. Not until humanity comes to understand that human beings – out of their own spirit – must give to the economic life what it needs, will they be able to pursue as a conscious aim what they are demanding unconsciously. *RSO 122*

Spiritual life can only develop on its own free and independent basis. But when allowed to develop in this way, and granted an equal right to subsist side by side with the two other departments of the social organism, it will no longer be an abstract formation, like the spiritual life that has actually been developing for centuries apart from the realities of life. It will develop an impetus to play a direct part in the active, real life of the legal-political and the economic organizations . . . As soon as the human spirit is free to play its part in economic life, it will at once prove its capacity in the practice of life within the economic circuit. All that is needed is to allow its power to enter actively into the practical realm. Then it will play its part. This true view of reality is a necessity. The human spirit must not be hermetically sealed up in abstractions; it must be allowed to influence life. Then at every moment it will fructify the economic sphere, which otherwise must remain sterile, or must be dependent on mere chance for its fructification. *SF 113-114*

It will only be possible to establish an economic order of the community, when the economic organization can be inspired by the independent spiritual life. It will thus not be possible to bring about a sound future unless what is thought in the free life of the spirit is reflected back from economic life. That free spiritual life will not prove itself unpractical, but, on the contrary, prove itself very practical. *SF 125*

In every generation, in the children whom we teach at school, something is given to us, something is sent down from the spiritual world. We take hold of this in education – this is something spiritual – and incorporate it into economic life and thereby ward off its destruction. For economic life, if it runs its own course, destroys itself. This is how we must look at things. *NS 67*

Capacities and Capital

An independent cultural life is necessary so that human beings can freely develop their capacities to the greatest extent possible, and then use these capacities to fructify economic life as entrepreneurs or skilled labor. The extent to which freely-developed human capacities are at work in the various sectors of social life determines the degree to which capital can be used for the benefit of society. In the economic sphere, the availability of capital can enable human capacities to generate creative entrepreneurial activity.

Capable people who want to produce goods or services for society must have free access to capital, and they must be able to obtain it out of their own free initiative. At the same time, the value of people's capacities must be recognized by others. *[How this can be done is discussed in Chapter Seven on Capital.]*

. . . Imagine a free spiritual-cultural life in the social organism – really freed – so that individual faculties are always able to develop fully. Then free spiritual-cultural life will be able to exert an extremely fertilizing influence

on the half-free spiritual-cultural life – that is, on the spiritual-cultural life that enters into the processes of material production [entrepreneurial activity]. Considered in this light, free spiritual-cultural life takes on a decidedly economic aspect. RE 77

. . . Entrepreneurial activity can only play a healthy role in the social organism if the forces at work in this organism allow individual human capacities to unfold in the best possible way. This can only happen if one sphere of the social organism enables those capable of it to have a free rein in exercising their initiative and making use of their capacities. At the same time, the value of these capacities must be freely recognized by other people. TSR 65-66

What can be achieved for the social organism with the support of capital is, by its very nature, dependent on the way in which individual human capacities participate in this organism. It is only through a free cultural and intellectual life that the right impulse for developing such capacities can come about. TSR 69

. . . Whenever this freedom [of initiative] is hindered, humanity is the poorer; to some extent at least, it is deprived of benefits which would otherwise have been available to it. It is capital which is the means of rendering these capacities effective in many different realms of society. It is therefore in the real interest of everyone within the social organism to ensure that all ownership of capital is managed in such a way that an individually gifted person or a group of people with particular capacities can gain access to the level of capital that their own free initiative requires. Everyone, from the creative mind to the laborer, must acknowledge that it is in his or her own objective interests not only for sufficient numbers of capable people or groups to have completely unhampered access to capital, but also for them to be able to use their own free initiative in obtaining it. Only they can judge how, by means of capital, their individual capacities will create goods useful to the social organism. TSR 74-75

Financial Support of Cultural Life

It is through competition that financial support can flow in a healthy way to support those who want to work in a cultural capacity: teachers, artists, researchers, counselors, and so on. Competition presents itself as a useful and necessary element wherein the remuneration of cultural workers is dependent on whether they garner sufficient appreciation and support in their communities. Through competition, cultural life is supported in a way that is consistent with the ideal of cultural freedom, in that such support flows from the free recognition of individuals in society. Consequently, the fate of a cultural undertaking is dependent on whether or not the community wants the type and quality of services or products that cultural workers offer. This reality holds true in the case of more specialized cultural workers such as entrepreneurs, economists, and politicians. The political state itself will be supported by taxation legislation.

> *. . . everything needed to sustain the cultural, spiritual sphere of life will accrue to it from payments made by individuals participating in the social organism, through their free appreciation and understanding. This spiritual, cultural sphere will have a sound basis in the individual initiatives of those capable of such work, which will arise in free competition.* *TSR 91*

> *Technical ideas flow into economic life from the life of the mind and spirit. They are part of the spiritual sphere even if they come directly from people working in politics or economics. The sphere of spirit also includes all organizational ideas and forces which sustain economic and political life. Recompense for this sustaining contribution (of the cultural sphere) to both social realms will either come about via the free agreement of those who need this contribution, or will be regulated by rights formulated in the political sphere.** *TSR 59-60*

* Editor's note: The right of a child to an education and the regulation of who should receive funding as well as how much they should receive is an example of the latter.

A primary task of economic associations would be to assure that there is sufficient support for cultural life.

> *. . . When one day the associations begin to understand something of the influence of the free spiritual-cultural life on the economic process, we can give them a very good means of regulating the economic circuit. I mentioned this in my book* Towards Social Renewal. *The associations will find that when free spiritual-cultural life declines, too little is being given freely; they will grasp the connection. They will see the connection between too little giving and too little free spiritual-cultural work. When there is not enough free spiritual-cultural work, they will realize that too little is being given. When too little is being given, they will notice a decline in free spiritual-cultural work.* *RE 78*

Freedom and Funding in Education

Of the three forms of money – purchase, loan, and gift money – it is gift money that is meant to provide the primary support of cultural activity, especially education. This is not limited to free donations but includes any money spent on cultural activities or services such as education. *[For more on the types of money see Chapter Nine, on Money.]*

From an economic perspective, gift money includes taxes that support cultural activities. In this case, however, it is compulsory gift money, which necessarily lacks the directed intelligence and intention of the givers.

> *. . . All that we put into the educational system is a gift – notably when it is a question of a truly free spiritual-cultural life . . . When you give directly, your intelligence is in the process. As things are now, you do give, but the gift is absorbed into the general pool of taxation. It vanishes into a vague economic fog, and you do not observe what happens . . . In the other case, conscious intelligence comes into it.* *RE 154*

> *. . . Gift money, fundamentally speaking, is all that is spent on education. This plays an enormous part in economic life. Gift money, again, is all that is spent on endowments and the like.* *RE 149*

The threefold principle of the separation of education from the state and the economy not only includes administration but also funding. The notion of free schools is a deception, even a social lie, because there are always necessary costs for education. There must be a means to fund an independent educational system.

> *. . . the movement for the threefold social [organism] . . . strives for the complete disassociation of the educational system from government and industry.* *RSO 75*

> *Throughout the land today you hear the cry for schooling free of charge. What does this really imply? But the cry throughout the land should be: How can we get a form of socialism in which everyone is enabled to contribute in the right way towards educational affairs? Free schooling is nothing less than a social lie, for behind this is hidden either the fact that surplus value finds its way into the pockets of a small set of people who then found a school and thus gain mastery over others; or sand is strewn in the eyes of the public so that they should not realize that among the coins they take from their purse there must be some that go to the upkeep of schools. In all that we say, in the very shaping of our sentences, we must conscientiously strive after truth.* *SBPSE 42*

Government-funded education must cease because of the inevitable restrictions and control by the state that are attached to government subsidies. The idea that people cannot afford to fund independent schools misses the fact that tax money, which provides funds for government subsidies, also ultimately comes out of people's pockets.

People often mistakenly believe that they need the protection and control of the state in the educational system and do not trust cultural workers to manage it themselves.

[What] seems dubious to me is that it should be possible to run a school with the aid of state subsidies. For I very much doubt whether the government, if it pays out money for such a school, would not insist on the right to inspect it. Therefore I cannot believe that a free [independent] school could be founded with state subsidies which in themselves imply supervision by inspectors of the education authorities. *SEWE 314-315*

I was answered in the discussion at the end of a lecture by a secondary school teacher, somewhat in this wise: "We Germans will be a poor nation in the future, and here is a man who wants to make the spiritual and intellectual life independent: a poor people cannot pay for that, there will be no money, therefore we shall have to draw on the national exchequer and pay for education out of taxes. What becomes of independence then? How can we refuse the right of the State to inspect, when the State is the source of income?" I could only reply that it seemed strange to me for the teacher to believe that what was drawn from the Treasury as taxes grew there somehow or other, and would not in the future come out of the pocket of the "poor nation." What strikes me most is the lack of thought everywhere. We need to develop a real practical thinking which sees into the facts of life. That will give us practical suggestions which can be carried out. *POT 123-124*

The enfeeblement of thought in the old unified state has brought people so far that they do not even think about what an absurdity it is to want the state to first order, then protect and support what the cultural members of the social organism should manage. Isn't the idea that the teacher "should be protected and supported by the state" so typical. That is the same as saying, "We don't dare to bring about this condition [a threefold social organism with an independent cultural life] which would be so desirable; we want to be forced." But the motivation does not arise. For on the side from which we should expect it, there exists no understanding – obviously, quite justifiably – for what really should happen. *SWS 27*

Even though Steiner was not in favor of tax-based government-funded education, he did recognize that all children have a right to an education, a right which must be upheld by the state. Although the funding of cultural life generally should result from the free appreciation and support of individuals or groups, the right of a child to an education necessitates legal requirements to ensure educational funding. Two possible ways that education could be funded without direct government financing are through higher income for parents than for single people, and through educational subsidies required from the economy.

> *. . . [A threefold social] organism will create rights and laws based on purely human considerations. Children will have the right to receive an education; a working parent will have the right to a higher income than a single person, receiving this 'extra' through arrangements and regulations based on agreements between all three spheres of society. For example, the right to education can be arranged in such a way that economic administration sets the possible amount of educational expenditure in accordance with the general economic situation, while the rights state, after taking advice from the spiritual, cultural sphere, formulates the individual's rights in this respect. Once again, though, a thinking grounded in reality will only indicate the rough direction such things could take. It is possible that quite different arrangements might turn out to be the best in specific cases. But the 'right' thing will only be found through the purposeful cooperation of all three autonomous spheres of the social organism.* *TSR 92*

> *In my book,* Towards Social Renewal, *I speak about the child's right to education and that, in the future, an educational subsidy will be required from the economy . . . In a healthy society, the child has a right to education.* *EFSC 210*

In a threefold social organism, at the same time that educators are cultural workers, they also belong to economic corporations. Educational subsidies would flow directly from the economic life to these corporations. Teachers, like any workers, would receive an income sufficient to meet their needs. Merit pay would not be appropriate for teachers. All teachers deserve a suitable income.

> *[A] basic principle of the Association for the Threefolding of the Social Organism is to work toward an independent school system, making it free of the state so that the state does not even supervise the schools. The activity of the self-administered schools should arise purely from cultural needs, and much can grow from that . . .*
>
> *It is the task of our time to inform public life about such things. In order to do that, everything cultural must be independent.*
>
> *One might then think: If the state, through its coercive powers, no longer pays the teachers what they need, then it would go badly for the teachers. But the teachers will belong to an economic corporation, similar to other economic corporations. Along with being teachers, they will also be members of the third aspect of the threefold social organism (the economic aspect), and will receive salaries from that independent economic system. The threefold social organism will have an independent economic body just as it has an independent legal body that will democratically take care of legal matters. Similarly, it will also have a free spiritual realm. What today goes into the pockets of teachers indirectly through taxes will, in the future, come directly from economic life. Apart from that, a free spiritual life will foster the appropriate atmosphere for schools and teaching.*
>
> *There must be an evaluation of goods and services. A healthy society, however, should not view or value what a teacher actually gives to the coming generation as something to be paid for. What the teacher extends to other human beings is a gift from the spiritual world. A healthy society will understand that teachers are the media through which human capacities or individual human characteristics are brought out of their dark shadows, where they exist as a part of human nature. It is simply conventional narrow-mindedness to believe in paying according to what is actually accomplished in the schools.*

> *The economic portion of the healthy threefolded social organism has to provide the possibility for teachers to live as others do. In our thinking, we need strictly to separate the potential for earning a livelihood and our evaluation of teaching. There can be no democracy without this healthy impulse.* *TSTSO, TR 30-31*

> *. . . Each person produces for every other via the totality of economic life. Within the economic realm we are concerned only with commodity values. In this realm the results and achievements deriving from the cultural and rights realms also assume the character of commodities. The efforts a teacher makes on behalf of his or her pupils becomes a commodity within the economic realm. Teachers are no more paid for their individual gifts and capacities than laborers are paid for the strength they put into their labor. Both can only be paid for anything that can be regarded as commodity, the results of their input of effort or labor. The part which free initiative and rights awareness should play in the production of a commodity lies outside the economic realm in the same way that the effect of natural conditions is distinct from the actual grain yield in a good or bad harvest. As far as the economic sphere is concerned, the cultural, spiritual sphere and also the state are commodity producers. But what they produce is not a commodity within their own sphere – it only becomes such when it enters economic circulation. Within their own spheres they do not engage in the economic process, but what they have created or produced is commercially managed by the economic organism.* *TSR 94*

Value of Spiritual Work for the Economy as a Whole

To see the value of spiritual-cultural work, we must look in a different place than we do to see the value of physical labor. Purely physical labor takes its value in relation to the past and its continuation. The value of spiritual-cultural work can only be appropriately assessed by turning to the future. Cultural work can be instrumental in incalculable ways far into the future in enhancing the productivity of economic activities, thereby creating a positive effect on the whole of economic life.

> *In the economic process we must speak, as I indicated yesterday, of production and consumption. We must observe both the producing and the consuming processes. The contrast between them has played a great part recently in various widely held economic theories, which in due course have been used for purposes of agitation. There has especially been much dispute of the question of whether spiritual-cultural (intellectual) work, as such, is in any way value-creating in the economic sphere . . .*
>
> *. . . "To what extent (if at all) is spiritual-cultural work economically productive?" Now here it is especially important to distinguish between the past and the future. If you consider and reflect statistically on only the past, with respect to the past and to all that is only the unbroken continuation of the past, you will be able to prove that spiritual-cultural work is unproductive. From the past within the material sphere, only purely material work and its effects can be held to be productive in the economic process. It is quite a different matter when you turn your eye to the future. As we have said, to be engaged in economics is to be working from the past into the future.*
>
> *You need think only of this simple instance. Assume that in some village a craftsman falls ill. Under certain given circumstances – let us say, if he falls into the hands of an unskilled doctor – he will have to lie in bed for three weeks, during which time he will be able to do nothing. Then, he will disturb the economic process to no small extent. If he is a shoemaker, for three weeks his boots and shoes will not be brought to market, taking the word "market" in the widest sense. But now suppose he gets a very skillful doctor who makes him well in a week. He can go back to work again in a week. In all seriousness you can now decide the question, "Who made the boots for the difference of the fourteen days, the shoemaker or the doctor?" In reality it was the doctor.*

Now the situation is altogether clear. As soon as you take into account the future from any given moment onward – toward the future – you can no longer call the spiritual/cultural unproductive. In relation to the past, the spiritual/cultural – or rather, those human beings who work in the spiritual-cultural sphere – are consumers only. In relation to the future they are decidedly productive; indeed they are the producers, for they transform the whole process of production and make it substantially different for economic life. You can see this from the example of a tunnel. What happens when tunnels are built nowadays? They could not be built unless differential calculus had been discovered. To this day, therefore, Leibniz is helping to build all tunnels. The way prices work out in this case has really been determined by that exertion of his spiritual-cultural forces. You can never answer these questions in economics if you consider the past in the same way as the future. Life does not move toward the past, nor does it even prolong the past; it goes on into the future.

Hence no economic thought is real that does not reckon with what is done by spiritual-cultural work, if we may call it so; that is to say, fundamentally, what is done by thinking. But spiritual-cultural work is not easy to comprehend. It has its own peculiar properties, which are not at all easy to grasp in economic terms. Spiritual-cultural work begins the moment work itself – that is to say, labor – is organized. The organizing work of thinking begins the very moment labor itself is organized and divided. Thenceforward, it grows more and more independent. Consider the spiritual-cultural work of those who direct some undertaking within the material sphere. You will see that they apply an immense amount of spiritual-cultural work. Nevertheless they are still working with the resources with which the economic process provides them from the past. Even on quite practical grounds, you cannot ignore the fact that the sphere of spiritual-cultural activity (if I may now call it "activity" instead of work or labor) also includes the entirely free kind of activity. When someone invents differential calculus, and even more so when someone paints a picture, there we have a case of entirely free spiritual-cultural activity. Relatively speaking, at least, we can call it free. Whatever materials are derived from the past – the paints and the like – they no longer have the same significance in relation to the eventual products as do the raw materials, for example, purchased for manufacture. *RE 69-72*

Resources

This section provides a list of various resources to aid readers who want to further explore Rudolf Steiner's economic and social ideas. Our list of selections is not meant to be comprehensive, but more of a sampling of ways readers can further their theoretical understanding of Steiner's social perspectives and how his insights can be practically applied.

This includes listings of:

- Publishers of Rudolf Steiner's Social and Economic Writings and Lectures;
- Basic Texts by Rudolf Steiner on the Threefold Social Organism, Associative Economics, and the Fundamental Social Law;
- Writings by Other Authors on the Threefold Social Organism, Associative Economics, and the Fundamental Social Law;
- Organizations and Initiatives Inspired by Rudolf Steiner's Social Ideas;
- Organizations and Initiatives Working to Some Degree in Harmony with Rudolf Steiner's Social Ideas, But Not Intentionally So.

Unless otherwise noted, descriptions are taken from the organizations' or publishers' websites.

A Selection of Publishers of Rudolf Steiner's Social and Economic Writings and Lectures in English

AWSNA Publications (USA)
www.awsnabooks.org/store

Mercury Press of the Fellowship Community (USA)
www.mercurypress.org

New Economy Publications (UK)
www.associative-economics.com/publications

Rudolf Steiner Press (UK)
www.rudolfsteinerpress.com

Steinerbooks (USA)
www.steinerbooks.org

Basic Texts by Rudolf Steiner on the Threefold Social Organism, Associative Economics, and the Fundamental Social Law

Anthroposophy and the Social Question. Chestnut Ridge, NY: Mercury Press, 1982.

Renewal of the Social Organism. Spring Valley, NY: Anthroposophic Press, 1985.

Rethinking Economics. Great Barrington, MA: Steinerbooks, 2013.

The Social Future. New York: Anthroposophic Press, 1972.

Towards Social Renewal. London, England: Rudolf Steiner Press, 1999.

[For more suggestions, see the Bibliography at the end of the book.]

Texts by Other Authors

Bloom, John. *The Genius of Money.* Great Barrington, MA: SteinerBooks, 2009.

Budd, Christopher Houghton. *Metamorphosis of Capitalism.* New Economy Publications, 2003.

Showing that associative economics not only provides deep historical foundations for our understanding of current events, but also the positive and practical means to address the many issues these developments give rise to, this book outlines a path to metamorphose capitalism.

Budd, Christopher Houghton. *Prelude in Economics.* New Economy Publications, 1979.

This book was intended to acquaint the layperson with economics in comprehensible language, but also to reset the cast of mind for economics generally; it covers many of the main ideas and concepts that characterize an associative approach.

Budd, Christopher Houghton. *Of Wheat and Gold.* New Economy Publications, 1988.

This book sets forth an alternative approach to money that combines both wheat and gold as monetary standards to offer unexpected resolutions to the seemingly intractable problems of today's monetary system.

Edwards, Arthur. *Three Kinds of Money: Rudolf Steiner and the Development of Monetary Economics.* Masters thesis submitted at the University of Buckingham School of Economics, 2009.

Available from the author at mail@arthuredwards.net.

For other publications by Christopher Houghton Budd, Arthur Edwards, and other CFAE authors, see the Centre for Associative Economics:
www.cfae.biz/publications

Karp, Robert. *Towards an Associative Economy in the Food & Farming Movement.* Copyright Robert Karp, 2007.
www.thinkoutword.org/Robert%20Karp%20Essay.pdf

Lamb, Gary. *Associative Economics,* Ghent, NY: AWSNA Publications, 2010.
This comprehensive book on Rudolf Steiner's economic ideas guides one to substantially rethink modern economic life.

Lamb, Gary. "Overcoming Self-Interest in Economic Life – Part I" Rudolf Steiner's Indications on the Ownership, Use of Land and Other Means of Production. Threefold Review, 1996.
http://thecenterforsocialresearch.org/resources/

Lamb, Gary. "Overcoming Self-Interest in Economic Life – Part II" *Rudolf Steiner's Indications on Economic Associations. Threefold Review, 1997.*
http://thecenterforsocialresearch.org/resources/

Lamb, Gary. "The Transformation of the Competitive Market and Capitalism: A Necessity of the 21st Century, " Biodynamics, 2008.
http://thecenterforsocialresearch.org/resources/

Lamb, Gary. "The Fundamental Social Law: Theory and Practice." Biodynamics, 2008.
http://thecenterforsocialresearch.org/resources/

Large, Martin. *Common Wealth: For a Free, Equal, Mutual and Sustainable Society.* Stroud, UK: Hawthorne Press, 2010.
Just when 'the market' nearly took over all areas of life, the credit, climate and democratic crunches came along, challenging us to rebuild a society that works well for all. Common Wealth asks, 'How can we build a more free, equal, mutual and sustainable society?'

Perlas, Nicanor. *Shaping Globalization: Civil Society, Cultural Power and Threefolding.* BC, Canada: New Society Publishers, 2003.
Shaping Globalization argues that global civil society is a cultural institution wielding cultural power, and shows how, through the use of this distinct power, it can advance its agenda in the political and economic realms of society without compromising its identity. The book then outlines the strategic implications for civil society both locally and globally, and explains that its key task is to inaugurate "threefolding:" the forging, where appropriate, of strategic partnerships between civil society, government, and business.

Rohen, Johannes. *Functional Threefoldness in the Human Organism and Human Society.* Adonis Press, 2011.
After decades of meditating on the human organism leading up to his major work Functional Morphology, renowned anatomist Johannes Rohen applies his functional approach to the study of social life. The result is a holistic yet highly differentiated view of human society as a dynamic organism.

Schaefer, PhD Christopher. *Vision in Action: Working with Soul & Spirit in Small Organizations.* Great Barrington: Steinerbooks, 1996.
This is a complete guide to carrying out small-scale projects from inception to organization and long-term growth.

Spence, Michael. *After Capitalism.* Hillsdale, NY: Adonis Press, 2014.
The observations offered in this book provide a basic framework for individuals to consciously understand for themselves how human society, and particularly the economy, works.

Wilken, Folkert. *The Liberation of Work.* Boston: Routledge & Kegan Paul Ltd, 1969.
Until his death in 1981 Wilken was a Professor of Economics at the University of Freiburg; he examined Steiner's ideas in a modern light, amplifying them from an economic perspective.

Wilken, Folkert. *The Liberation of Capital.* London: George Allen & Unwin Ltd, 1982.
See description above.

Businesses, Organizations, & Initiatives Directly Inspired by Rudolf Steiner's Social & Economic Ideas

Camphill Communities

Camphill is a worldwide movement that seeks to enhance the lives of people in need of services and support for daily living as well as people committed to service by creating communities where everyone's contributions are valued without regard to their financial assets, or their intellectual or physical capabilities. Camphills create social arrangements designed to nurture the growth and development of individuals and families that separate money from work so that all community members contribute their time and skills according to their capabilities and all community members receive sustenance based on their needs, in an effort to affirm and embody The Fundamental Social Law.

www.camphill.org

The Centre for Associative Economics

The Centre for Associative Economics promotes an associative approach to modern economic life through research, courses, events, publications, and consultancy. CAE is the founder of the (ae) Guarantee Mark. First established in 1998, the (ae) Guarantee Mark is designed to encourage economic undertakings based on an associative approach to economic life. With its 4 Steps and 4 Criteria, it highlights the main characteristics of an associative approach to business.

www.associative-economics.com
www.cfae.biz/guarantee-mark

The Centre for Social Poetry

A place for the poetry of the human being and the world – from page poetry, to poetic social processes, to a poetic re-imagining of the entire social organism (including economics, politics and culture, as well as how these three spheres interact).

www.socialpoetry.net

The Center for Social Research

Hawthorne Valley's Center for Social Research (CSR) is an independent "think and do" tank that combines research and practical initiatives as a means to identify and implement solutions to modern day social problems. Their constellation of projects strongly reflects their mission and goals for promoting social health: supporting freedom and choice in cultural life, equality and democracy in political life, and associative cooperation in economic life. CSR also oversees the Credere Fund micro grants, which support initiatives that foster the development of innovative ways to express and employ empathy in personal, institutional, and community life.

www.thecenterforsocialresearch.org

Chiemgauer Alternative Currency

Like BerkShares (see Alternative Currencies in the next section), the Chiemgauer is backed and exchangeable for federal currency at a discount. Started by a teacher and a small group of students at a Waldorf School, Chiemgauer is intelligently designed to reflect the deterioration process of the goods it represents and promote the healthy circulation of money from purchase, to loan, to gift through a demurrage-fee (negative interest rate) in an effort to embody Steiner's economic indications.

www.chiemgauer.info

Citizens' Alliance for Universal School Choice in New York State (CAUSE NYS)

CAUSE NYS is an education and research initiative dedicated to providing the citizens of New York State with the information they need to make informed decisions about elementary and secondary education reform, including school funding and student assessments. CAUSE NYS sees education tax credits as a way to work in harmony with Steiner's ideas of the right of a child to an education coupled with funding education directly out of the economy (businesses and individuals) instead of by way of government funding.

www.causenys.org

The Fellowship Community

Founded in 1966, The Fellowship Community is a community of all ages, centered around the care of the elderly. Working and learning together in service to others and in caring for the earth is the central motif of the community life. The community works from a desire to serve others altruistically, and in turn the community takes responsibility for each co-worker, and each co-worker takes reponsibility for the community as a whole.

www.fellowshipcommunity.org

Free Columbia

The Free Columbia courses are intensive explorations into art. Currently an eight-month painting course and a four-month puppetry internship are available, as are week-long intensives in the summer and winter. In addition to painting or puppetry, the full time work includes introductions to the philosophy of aesthetics and social questions in relation to art and economics. Free Columbia is based on an understanding of the importance of creating independent and accessible educational and artistic opportunities. There are no set tuitions for any of their courses or other events. Suggested donation amounts based on what it costs to run courses are provided

www.freecolumbia.org

Institute for Social Threefolding

The Institute for Social Threefolding has been in existence since 1998 [and works] to make content available for people interested in pursuing serious study of social threefolding.

www.threefolding.org

Institute for Social Renewal

The Institute for Social Renewal supports independent schools and forward thinking organizations and individuals to develop the capacities of what will be most needed in society and the new economy – creativity, adaptability, critical thinking and the ability to communicate and collaborate. The work of the Institute for Social Renewal is inspired by Rudolf Steiner and by current leading business, educational, and social reformers.

www.socialrenewal.com

L'AUBIER

L'AUBIER is a company that provides the envelope of finances and real estate – including farmland and farm buildings – for L'AUBIER's various activities: restaurant, hotel, shop, cafe-hotel, and administration buildings. Each business is conducted in a spirit of independent and autonomous partnership with the other activities, encouraged by regular meetings based on full transparency and management accountability. Founded in 1984, their foundation aims to promote research in all areas of life and to encourage the realization of ideals based on anthroposophy.

www.aubier.ch/en

MISSION

MISSION stands for Movement of Imaginals for a Sustainable Society through Initiatives, Organizing, and Networking. It is an organization in the Phillipines founded by Nicanor Perlas, a leading author, activist and former presidential candidate working out of social threefolding.

www.imaginalmission.net

RSF Social Finance

RSF is dedicated to transforming the way the world works with money. In partnership with a community of investors and donors, RSF provides capital to non-profit and for-profit social enterprises addressing key issues in the areas of Food & Agriculture, Education & the Arts, and Ecological Stewardship. Founded in 1936 as the Rudolf Steiner Foundation, RSF Social Finance began making loans to Steiner-inspired organizations in 1984. In the late 1990s, RSF's mission expanded to serve a broader range of clients whose intentions and values are compatible with Steiner's insights on associative economics and social renewal.

www.rsfsocialfinance.org

Social Self

Social Self is a project of Adonis Press that addresses social issues in the light of Rudolf Steiner's insights. It works in close collaboration with the Center for Social Research, and operates, like Adonis Press, within the framework of the Hawthorne Valley Association in Ghent, NY.

www.socialself.org

Think OutWord

Think OutWord is a peer-led training in social threefolding for young adults that began in 2008 and is loosely situated in the northeastern United States. Through the training, participants gain deeper insight into contemporary social phenomena and explore different methods by which they can become increasingly engaged in socially transformative work. Think OutWord also works to practice Steiner's economic ideas in the financing of its conferences and other events.

www.thinkoutword.org

Threefold Now!

Editor's Note: Travis Henry offers a compendium of relevant information and resources about threefolding and the possibilities for separating economic, political and cultural affairs, each with their own leadership. Specifically, the website features pioneering, expert research providing threefold maps, flags, and explanations for the countries and nations of the world and responding to the question: What might a free cultural sector look like, wherein the myriad of humanity's cultural nations might again flourish?

www.sites.google.com/site/threefoldnow

Triodos Bank

Triodos Bank, a bank in the Netherlands with branches in Belgium, Germany, United Kingdom and Spain, is associated with the philosophy initiated by Rudolf Steiner. Triodos only lends to and invests in organizations that benefit people and the environment. They connect savers and investors who want to change the world for the better with entrepreneurs and sustainable companies doing just that. They are the only specialist bank to offer integrated lending and investment opportunities for sustainable sectors in a number of European countries.

www.triodos.co.uk

Waldorf Education

With more than 900 Waldorf schools in 83 countries, Waldorf Education is the fastest growing independent educational movement in the world. In 1919, Steiner spoke about the need for social renewal, for a new way of organizing society and its political and cultural life. He developed Waldorf Education based on a profound understanding of human development that addresses the needs of the growing child. Waldorf teachers strive to transform education into an art that educates the whole child – the heart and the hands, as well as the head.

www.waldorfresearchinstitute.org
www.whywaldorfworks.org
www.waldorfanswers.org

Editor's Note: Steiner intended the Waldorf movement to take the lead in advancing independent education that is free from government control and financially accessible to all.

Organizations and Initiatives Working to Some Degree in Harmony with Rudolf Steiner's Ideas

Editors' Note: There may be little or no conscious effort by the following organizations to work from social threefolding ideals as expressed by Rudolf Steiner. In each case we have tried to show some correlation between the initiative's activities and Steiner's perspectives. It may well be the case that there are other aspects of its activities that are contrary to Steiner's perspectives.

B-Corporations

B Corps are certified by the nonprofit B Lab to meet rigorous standards of social and environmental performance, accountability, and transparency. Today, there is a growing community of more than 850 Certified B Corps from 28 countries and 60 industries working together toward 1 unifying goal: to redefine success in business. Delaware became the 19th state (plus D.C.) to enact benefit corporation legislation.

www.bcorporation.net
www.benefitcorp.net

Relevant Aspects: B-Corps take a practical approach to overcoming self-interest and fostering altruism in business practices by considering the needs and well-being of all stakeholders, an important step towards true price, association, and other related ideals.

Business Alliance for Local Living Economies (BALLE)

BALLE is the fastest growing business alliance of values-aligned entrepreneurs, business networks, and local economy funders in North America. Through collaboration, the members identify and spread innovative solutions and business models for creating healthier, sustainable, and prosperous communities. They have a growing network of 30,000 local entrepreneurs spanning 80 communities.

www.balle.org

Relevant Aspects: BALLE's innovative, mission-driven business alliance practices some important aspects of the principle of association by supporting collaboration and mutual aid in the economic sector.

Basic Income Movement

Basic Income is a form of minimum income guarantee that differs from those that now exist in various European countries in three important ways: it is being paid by the government to individuals rather than households; it is paid irrespective of any income from other sources; it is paid without requiring the performance of any work or the willingness to accept a job if offered.

http://dotsub.com/view/26520150-1acc-4fd0-9acd-169d95c9abe1

www.basicincome.org

Relevant Aspects: The Basic Income movement is a controversial – controversial because it is a government program rather than working with the economic principle of true price – attempt to separate work and income and decommodify labor, basic principles of Steiner's Fundamental Social Law.

CloudPay

CloudPay is a new community-building partnership between local merchants and local nonprofits. When you pay at participating merchants using CloudPay, the merchant no longer has to pay Visa, MasterCard, Discover, or American Express transaction fees, so they donate them to your favorite nonprofit instead!

CloudPay enables you to safely and securely link your mobile phone to a checking account or credit card. CloudPay is a CA Benefit Corporation, based in Santa Cruz, CA.

www.cloudpay.org

Relevant Aspects: CloudPay is a new payment platform that enables a consumer to designate a certain portion of every purchase price to go to their favored cultural organization.

Community Land Trusts (CLT)

Editor's Note: A CLT is a model of land stewardship in which a non-profit entity with an elected governing body holds and stewards a piece of land for the purposes of affordable housing, farming, or other productive uses. Occupants of a CLT own the houses or buildings and any improvements that they make to the land. However, they do not own the land itself, but instead have long-term leases on the land, which are renewable and can be passed on to family members. In this way, the land is no longer subject to speculation and the fluctuations of the market but becomes a matter of secure rights, with consideration given to both the needs of the community and the ecology of the region.

www.centerforneweconomics.org/content/community-land-trusts-1
www.cltnetwork.org

Relevant Aspects: The CLT model provides a viable means to decommodify land and integrates an associative form of stewardship and decision-making.

Community Supported Agriculture and Beyond

Editor's Note: Over the last twenty-five years, Community Supported Agriculture has become an example of how to foster collaboration between producers and consumers. It is a locally-based mutually-supportive economic model wherein consumers share the risk and benefits of local food production with farmers by pledging financial support before the season in exchange for a share of the harvest. The idea of associative community supported initiatives has spread beyond agriculture. Community supported artist collectives, bookstores, musicians, theater companies and more, have emerged.

www.wilson.edu/about-wilson-college/fulton/robyn-van-en-center
www.biodynamics.com/content/community-supported-agriculture-introduction-csa

Relevant Aspects: CSA is perhaps the most widely used associative business model wherein producers and consumers can come together to dialogue and collaborate, considering the real needs of the farmers as well as the local community (an important step towards decommodifying labor and embodying true price). Member-owned models are examples of ways to decommodifying land and capital wherein the community stewards the farm and its assets. Several of the first CSAs in the United States were directly influenced by Steiner's associative ideas.

Complementary/Community Currency Movement

Complementary/community and local currencies are usually used as a complement to a national currency.

Some examples of Complementary Currency are:

BerkShares

Individuals in The Berkshires, MA, trade $95 federal dollars for $100 BerkShares at any of the participating banks and then spend them at face value in participating local businesses. Their use aims to strengthen the regional economy, favoring locally owned enterprises, local manufacturing, and local jobs, and reducing the region's dependence on an unpredictable global economy. The program hopes to eventually uncouple from the dollar and instead use a basket of local commodities as the standard of value for the BerkShares.

www.berkshares.org

Relevant Aspects: BerkShares is particularly impressive because of its flexibility and scope, demonstrating that it is possible to begin to imagine Steiner's call for a new basis for money issuance outside the complete control of government or business interests (Steiner indicated that it should be issued by an autonomous economic organization). BerkShares' intentions to create an independent standard of value for the currency also parallels Steiner's indications.

Deli Dollars

www.smallisbeautiful.org/publications/essay_currency.html

Ithaca HOURS

Editor's Note: Ithaca HOURS (Ithaca, NY) are not backed by federal dollars and can't be freely converted to the national currency, so their most striking attribute is their independence from the dollar. They're valued at $10USD each, as that was the average local hourly wage when the program started in 1991, and businesses and residents are encouraged to use one Hour for one hour of work.

www.ithacahours.com

Relevant Aspects: while the Ithaca Dollar is independent of the US backed dollar, one downside is that it ties money directly to labor (wagery) instead of to the products of labor, because businesses and residents are encouraged to use 1 HOUR for one hour of work. Treating labor like a commodity to be bought and sold was a main concern of Steiner's. However, they also make interest-free loans and grants to local non-profits, fostering a healthy circulation of capital and serving in an associative capacity at the transition point of money issuance.

Local Exchange Trading Systems (LETS)

Editor's Note: LETS systems are local accounting systems that monitor and record transactions of goods and services between members using credits in an electronic (web-based) system. Every transaction is recorded in the accounts of the consumer and producer/provider in question, as a debit and credit respectively, so the quantity of available currency is reflective of the economic activity actually taking place, as opposed to depending on the rule and judgment of a centralized administration, e.g. the state.

www.gdrc.org/icm/lets-faq.html

www.transaction.net/money/lets

Relevant Aspects: LETS reflect the idea that money is an accounting system for our economic transactions and shouldn't be issued by the state or based on government currency. Also noteworthy is the associative gesture of a local non-profit working to issue credit and maintain a healthy medium of exchange at the community level.

The Co-Intelligence Institute and Co-Intelligent Economics

Co-intelligent economics is not one thing, nor is it absolute. It is a guiding vision and sensibility. To the extent an economic system helps living beings and living systems meet their deep needs in healthy, sustainable ways – accessing the wisdom and resources of the whole and its parts on behalf of the whole and its parts – it can be said to be co-intelligent.

www.co-intelligence.org/Economics.html

Relevant Aspects: Co-intelligence can be seen as the wisdom arising from collaborating groups of people in an associative sense, taking the time to understand the perspectives of people in the various aspects of the economy. This multisided intelligence enables participants to make informed decisions rather than relying on the uncontrolled supply and demand or the chances of the market.

Fair Trade

Fair Trade is a simple way to make every purchase matter. When you buy a product with the Fair Trade Certified™ label, you know that the farmers and workers who produced it were paid better prices and wages, work in safe conditions, protect the environment, and earn community development funds to empower and improve their communities.

www.fairtradeusa.org www.fairtradefederation.org

www.equalexchange.coop

Relevant Aspects: The Fair Trade movement 1) begins to understand labor as a rights issue rather than an economic one by ensuring safer working conditions and protecting the environment 2) works in the direction of overcoming self-interest and true price by securing fairer prices and compensation for producers, 3) encourages association, by fostering visibility and acknowledgement between producers, distributors and consumers, and 4) facilitates access to capital and the healthy circulation of surplus capital towards community and business development.

The Gund Institute for Ecological Economics

Ecological Economics is concerned with extending and integrating the study and management of nature's household (ecology) and humankind's household (economics). This integration is necessary because conceptual and professional isolation have led to economic and environmental policies which are mutually destructive rather than reinforcing in the long term. Two groups working on ecological economics are The Transdisciplinary Journal of the International Society for Ecological Economics which is transdisciplinary in spirit and methodologically open and The Gund Institute for Ecological Economics which is a transdisciplinary research, teaching, and service organization focused on developing integrative solutions to society's most pressing problems.

www.uvm.edu/giee

Relevant Aspects: Like Steinerian economics, Ecological Economics works to understand economics holistically and inclusively. Among others, The Gund Institute's efforts to create policies and management instruments that balance what is biophysically possible, ecologically sustainable, socially equitable, and efficient resonate with Steiner's articulation of our world economy and the problematic nature of the dominance of one sphere of society over another such as the economy over the rights/political sphere or culture (e.g. the consequences of corporate power and control for human rights, the environment, etc.)

One Percent for the Planet

One Percent for the Planet is a growing global movement of over 1,400 companies that donate 1% of their sales to a network of more than 3,000 non-profit environmental organizations. The organization's mission is to provide an opportunity for businesses to recognize and mitigate the fact that industry and ecology are inherently connected. However, the model also effectively demonstrates an activist approach to providing economic production to support individuals and organizations promoting and educating around environmentalism.

www.onepercentfortheplanet.org

Relevant Aspects: Promotes the healthy circulation (gifting) of surplus capital from the economy to support cultural life as well as developing an associative network of businesses and non-profit organizations.

Mondragón Cooperative

The Mondragón Cooperative in the Basque region of Spain is perhaps the largest and one of the most successful examples of a worker-owned cooperative with 102 cooperatives and over 100,00 worker-owners.

Mondragón's worker-owners have an established pay scale, which dictates that the highest paid employee may not make more than eight times the lowest paid. Mondragón's cooperatives are required to donate 10% of their annual profits to the cultural realm and another 10% to a pool for future entrepreneurship within the Mondragón community.

www.mondragon-corporation.com/ENG.aspx

Relevant Aspects: Mondragón is more than just one worker-owned cooperative, it's an umbrella of cooperatives that consciously and deliberately work together, transparently and to some degree, associatively. For example, when overstaffing arises, instead of firing worker-owners, they can be retrained and moved to another job within the Mondragón cooperatives. Also, the nature of the organizational structure is such that individuals from all different types of work and levels of responsibility sit together on the board of directors, a democratically-elected body, which promotes better dialogue between entrepreneurs, managers, and workers and provides greater opportunities for perceiving the meaning and value of the work and everyone's part in it.

Other worker-owned cooperatives are:

Evergreen Cooperatives
www.evergreencooperatives.com

United States Federation of Worker Cooperatives
www.usworker.coop

Equal Exchange
www.equalexchange.coop/worker-owned

New Economics Foundation (NEF)

NEF is an independent think-and-do tank that inspires and demonstrates real economic well-being and advocates for economics as if people and the planet mattered. See especially the Happy Planet Index and the publication The Great Transition.

www.neweconomics.org.

Relevant Aspects: NEF projects work to reform our financial system to transform the impersonal nature of modern banking and finance and in this way are relevant to various aspects of Steiner's ideas on capital and credit, such as the healthy circulation of capital and a focus on meeting human needs instead of personal gain and profit. Other projects explore alternative currencies and monetary policy, giving practical models and guidance to decommodify money, explore a new basis for money, and work differently with purchases, loans, gifts, and much more.

Red Tomato Distribution

This distribution company's "Dignity Deal" starts in the winter when Red Tomato staff start a pricing conversation with the farmer to establish three numbers: last year's average, this year's ideal price, and the farmers' personal price floor – the lowest price the farmer can accept without losing both money and dignity. With this information, RT staff are able to negotiate prices with customers with the full farm economics in mind.

http://redtomato.org/fairtrade.php

Relevant Aspects: working with various aspects of the principle of association and reimagining price formation such as feedback loops between buyers, customers, and farmers; transparency; shared risk; and farmer participation in negotiations. In this way, buyers, consumers, and farmers participate in establishing food prices.

Schumacher Center for New Economics

The Schumacher Center works to educate the public about an economics that supports both people and the planet. They believe that a fair and sustainable economy is possible and that citizens working for the common interest can build systems to achieve it. They recognize that the environmental and equity crises we now face have their roots in the current economic system. They combine theoretical research with practical application at the local, regional, national, and international levels – deliberately designing transformative systems and communicating clearly the principles that guide them. Programs include the BerkShares local currency program, the Community Land Trust of the Southern Berkshires, and others.

www.centerforneweconomics.org

Relevant Aspects: The Schumacher Center creates and promotes ways to decommodify land, labor and capital, encouraging an ethic of responsibility and mutuality in economic life through primarily localized programs and initiatives.

Socially Responsible Investing (SRI)

Editor's Note: This is a catch-all term for the practice of loan-issuance and investment in socially- and environmentally-conscious businesses. There are more and more organizations and firms that are helping capital to flow to support community, culture, sustainability and business innovation. SRI works consciously to create new structures and relationships with respect to loan money and the issuing of credit, bringing mutuality and the role of association to the forefront.

Some examples of Socially Responsible Investing are:

Local Investing Opportunity Network (LION)
www.lioninvesting.com www.berkcolumbiainvest.org

Investors' Circle
www.investorscircle.net

Slow Money
www.slowmoneyalliance.org

RSF Social Finance *[More details on pg. 311.]*
www.rsfsocialfinance.org

Bibliography

All references are attributed to Rudolf Steiner. The "GA" designation is an abbreviation for the German word *Gesamtausgabe.* It is a reference system for Rudolf Steiner's *complete works* in German and English.

ASQ: *Anthroposophy and the Social Question,* New York: Anthroposophic Press, Inc., 1958. GA 34: Three essays published in 1905-1906.

BSE: *Brotherhood and the Struggle for Existence,* Spring Valley, NY: Mercury Press, 1980. GA 54: Lecture, November 23, 1905.

CCC: *Child's Changing Consciousness,* New York: Anthroposophic Press, 1996. GA 306: Eight lectures, April 15-22, 1923.

CT: *Challenge of the Times,* New York: Anthroposophic Press, 1979. GA 186: Six Lectures, November 28 to December 8, 1918.

EASQ: *Esoteric Aspect of the Social Question,* London: Rudolf Steiner Press, 2001. GA 193: Four lectures, February 4 to March 9, 1919.

EFSC: *Education as a Force for Social Change,* Hudson, NY: Anthroposophic Press, 1997. GA 192, 296, 330/331: Multiple lectures.

FHE: *The Foundations of Human Experience,* Hudson, NY: Anthroposophic Press, 1996. GA 293 and GA 66: One address and fourteen lectures, August 20 to September 5, 1919, and two lectures, March 15 and 17, 1917.

FSDT: *The Fundamental Social Demands of our Times,* Philmont, NY: Rudolf Steiner Library, Unpublished manuscript. GA 186: Five lectures, December 13-21, 1918.

FSL: *Fundamental Social Law,* Philmont, NY: Rudolf Steiner Library, Compilation of Steiner statements related to the Fundamental Social Law. Typescript edited by Gary Lamb, September, 2007.

FTSF: *Freedom of Thought and Societal Forces,* Great Barrington, MA: SteinerBooks, 2008. GA 333: Six lectures, May 26 to December 30, 1919.

HBFJSQ: *A Historical Background for the Formation of Judgment on the Social Question,* Philmont, NY: Unpublished manuscript, Rudolf Steiner Library. GA 185a: Eight lectures, November 9-24, 1918.

IASQ: *Inner Aspect of the Social Question,* London: Anthroposophical Publishing Company, 1950. GA 193: Three lectures, February 4 to March 9, 1919.

INE: *Ideas for a New Europe,* Sussex, England: Rudolf Steiner Press, 1992. GA 196: Seven lectures, December 12 1919 to February 22, 1920.

IT: *Intuitive Thinking as a Spiritual Path,* Hudson, NY: Anthroposophic Press, 1995. GA 4: Book first published in 1894.

NS: *New Spirituality,* Hudson, NY: Anthroposophic Press, 1988. GA 200: Seven lectures, October 17-31, 1920.

OPT: *On Publicizing the Threefold Social Order,* Philmont, NY: Rudolf Steiner Library manuscript. GA 337: Lecture, June 9, 1920.

PEM: *Polarities in Evolution and Mankind,* London and New York: Rudolf Steiner Press and Anthroposophic Press, 1987. GA 197: Eleven lectures, March 5 to November 22, 1920.

POT: *The Problems of Our Time,* New York, NY: Anthroposophic Press, No publishing date given. GA 193: Four lectures, September 12-15, 1919.

RE: *Rethinking Economics: Lectures and Seminars on World Economics,* Great Barrington, MA: SteinerBooks, Anthroposophic Press, 2013. GA 340: Fourteen lectures, July 24 to August 6, 1922 and GA 341: Six seminars, July 31 to August 5, 1922.

RSO: *Renewal of the Social Organism,* Spring Valley, NY: Anthroposophic Press, 1985. GA 24: Collection of essays, 1915-1924.

RSSB: *Rudolf Steiner Speaks to the British,* London, England: Rudolf Steiner Press, 1998. GA 305.2: Four lectures, August 26-29, 1922.

SASF*: Social and Anti-Social Forces in the Human Being,* Spring Valley, NY: Mercury Press, 2002. GA 186: Lecture, December 12, 1918.

SBPSE: *A Social Basis for Primary and Secondary Education,* Garden City, NY: Waldorf Institute, Adelphi University, 1975. GA 192: Three lectures, May-June 1919.

SEWE: *Soul Economy and Waldorf Education,* Spring Valley, NY: Anthroposophic Press, 1986. GA 303: Sixteen lectures, December 23, 1921, to January 7, 1922.

SF: *The Social Future,* New York, NY: Anthroposophic Press, 1972. GA 332: Six Lectures, October 24-30, 1919.

SPS: *Social and Political Science: an Introductory Reader,* Forest Row, England: Rudolf Steiner Press: 2003. GA various.

SQ: *The Social Question,* London: Anthroposophical Society in Great Britain: Supplement to "Anthroposophical Movement," Vol. IX, No. 23, 1932. GA 190: Lecture, March 30, 1919.

SQQC: *The Social Question as a Question of Consciousness,* Philmont, NY: Rudolf Steiner Library, unpublished manuscript. GA 189: Eight lectures, February 15 to March 16, 1919.

SSFSF: *Spiritual Science as a Foundation for Social Forms,* Hudson, NY: Anthroposophic Press, 1986. GA 199: Seventeen lectures and one address, August 6 to September 18, 1920.

SSSQ: *Spiritual Science and the Social Question,* See **FSL** 11-13. Lecture, March 2, 1908. GA unknown.

SWS: *The Spirit of the Waldorf School,* Hudson, NY: Anthroposophical Press, 1995. GA 297: Six lectures, August 24 to November 27, 1919, and one essay, February 1920.

TBEW: *The Tension Between East and West,* London: Hodder and Stoughton, 1963. GA 83: Ten lectures, June 1 to June 11, 1922.

TEL: *Theosophical Esoteric Lesson,* See **FSL** 9-11: GA 266.1: Lesson, March 3, 1906.

TOBS: *The Threefold Order of the Body Social: Study Series II,* Philmont, NY: Rudolf Steiner Library, unpublished manuscript. GA 24: Lecture, September 15, 1920.

TR: *The Threefold Review,* Philmont, NY: The Margaret Fuller Corporation, 1989-2002. Magazine devoted to Rudolf Steiner's social ideas.

TSR: *Towards Social Renewal,* London, England, Rudolf Steiner Press, 1999. GA 23: Book first published in 1919.

TSTSO, TR: "*The Task of Schools and the Threefold Social Organism,*" Philmont, NY: See *The Threefold Review* **(TR)**, Fall 2002. GA 296: Lecture, June 19, 1919.

T-S: *The Time-Sequence and Spiritual Foundation of Threefolding,* Spring Valley, NY: Mercury Press, 1998. GA 190: Two lectures, March 23 and 29, 1919.

WEA 2: *Waldorf Education and Anthroposophy 2,* Hudson, NY: Anthroposophic Press, 1996. GA 218, 304a: Twelve lectures, November 19, 1922 to August 30, 1924.